Compensation Theory and Practice

Marc J. Wallace, Jr.
University of Kentucky

Charles H. Fay
University of Kentucky

Kent Human Resource Management Series

Richard W. Beatty, University of Colorado at Boulder
Series Consulting Editor

Kent Publishing Company   Boston, Massachusetts
A Division of Wadsworth, Inc.

Editor: John B. McHugh
Production Editor: Michael Paladini
Interior Designer: DeNee Reiton Skipper
Cover Designer: Catherine Dorin
Production Coodinator: Linda Siegrist

Kent Publishing Company
A Division of Wadsworth, Inc.

Printed in the United States of America

1 2 3 4 5 6 7 8 9—87 86 85 84 83

Library of Congress Cataloging in Publication Data

Wallace, Marc J., Jr., 1944–
  Compensation theory and practice.
  (Kent human resource management series)
  Includes index.
  1. Compensation management.   I. Fay, Charles H.
II. Title.   III. Series.
HF5549.5.C67W35   1982   658.3'2   82–21206
ISBN 0-534-01399-6

Series Preface

Historically, the personnel/human resources (P/HR) field has received little attention academically as well as within organizations. Organizations have assumed, incorrectly, that P/HR cannot benefit them because of a dearth of technical information and skills. Colleges of business, reflecting this attitude, often hid P/HR in the teaching of management, seldom including the subject as a course requirement.

Thankfully, much of this is changing. First, the passage of Title VII of the 1964 Civil Rights Act generated interest in human resource planning, selection validation, and performance appraisal. Economic decline, the growth of Teaganomics, and the loss of competitiveness in international markets have also focused attention on the contribution that P/HR can make to organizations.

The books in this series address these issues. The first concerns federal regulation in P/HR management in EEO, job health and safety, and employee benefit plans. The second explores the costing of human resources by measuring the financial impact of behavior in organizations. The volume on performance appraisal became required because of the onus that EEO has placed on criterion measures in organizations for test validation and P/HR decision making. The fourth book, on compensation, address the critical issues of internal, external, and individual equity and how compensation systems may be effectively and efficiently administered. Clearly, fifteen years ago these books could not have been written, but with the growth of technical information in P/HR and the significance of P/HR problems within organizations, these important contributions are now possible. What is most exciting is to see the results of recent research in these important areas being disseminated to students and practitioners. This is a major objective of this series, and it gives me great pleasure to see that plan coming to life. The books in this series are designed to be adopted in university level courses in human resource management and personnel administration. Practitioners, too, will find much valuable information in these books.

For the appearance of this important series, I would like to thank Keith Nave, Wayne Barcomb, and Jack McHugh of Kent Publishing Company, and also the many reviewers who have encouraged the development of this series and provided feedback. The authors included in this series represent the best research in this growing field, and I am proud to be associated with them.

Richard W. Beatty

Foreword

The field of compensation is exciting. Part of this excitement stems from the fact that decisions made regarding compensation have a direct bearing on the success or failure of businesses and other organizations. A second factor is that the economy of the 1980s is forcing employers to be more cost conscious than ever before. As labor costs dominate a greater share of the cost of doing business (more than half of this cost for many organizations), people who make compensation decisions will bear the major responsibility for cost control and effectiveness. Third, society has turned its attention to the issue of compensation and, through the legal environment, will hold employers strictly accountable not only for maintaining employment security for employees but also for protecting and promoting equal employment opportunity. Finally, compensation is interesting because it affects each of us personally. Most of us have frequently pondered whether or not we are making as much money as we should be, whether what we are making is fair when compared to what others are being paid, or whether we could improve income through a career change, a job change, or harder-nosed bargaining with the boss.

We have written *Compensation Theory and Practice* out of a sense of this excitement and hope to share our enthusiasm with you. You may be preparing for a career in personnel and human resources and may even have a specific interest in a career as a compensation specialist. Or, you may be preparing for a career in line management. Both the line manager and the compensation specialist must be intimately familiar with compensation theory and practice in order to make effective compensation decisions. In most organizations, the responsibility for compensation planning and administration is shared between line and the compensation (or personnel) staff. The line manager is immediately responsible for administration but relies on the special expertise of the compensation staff officer to design, evaluate, and recommend wage and salary rates and benefit policies. The staff compensation specialist draws on professional expertise in analyzing wage data from external markets, carrying out job evaluation to estimate the internal worth of jobs, and designing merit systems to link pay and performance. The line manager, however, must translate such plans into practice and make them an operational reality that results in bottom-line results for the organization.

How well line managers and compensation specialists manage their relationship will depend in large part on whether they are operating from the same knowledge base. The line manager ignorant of such topics as labor economics, employee behavior, and equity in compensation will probably view the compensation officer as a source of irritation at best, and an obstructionist at worst. The staff compensation officer ignorant of the real world of line production will quickly become tied up in his own little world of compensation theory and will never bother to link his efforts to the broader objectives of the entire organization. The major objective of *Compensation Theory and Practice* is to provide the line and compensation manager with the same knowledge base about compensation.

We believe that effective compensation decisions require a knowledge of both current theory regarding compensation and specific practices. Both theory and practice have changed dramatically in our field during the last ten years. In *Compensation Theory and Practice* we will analyze these developments and explicitly present the links between theory and practice. In some cases we will show how specific practices make sense in the light of theory and research. In other cases we will show how theory and research suggest practical improvements. Finally, we will show how other practices and problems encountered by line managers are calling for additional theory and research.

Acknowledgements

We are indebted to the many researchers and practitioners who have contributed to the body of knowledge in compensation. We especially acknowledge the research of Thomas Mahoney who, more than any other person in our field, has integrated the rather diverse bodies of economic, behavioral, and sociological theory into a richer understanding of compensation phenomena.

Dick Beatty initially provided the spark that kindled our interest in *Compensation Theory and Practice* and, as consulting editor of Kent's Human Resource Management Series, has provided us with encouragement throughout the project. Jack McHugh of Kent has provided critical support and editorial review so necessary to the success of a book of this nature. Keith Nave, formerly of Kent, committed important resources to our project.

Fred Crandall is a close friend and professional colleague of long standing. We have frequently relied on him for judgments regarding how compensation is actually practiced in organizations. His insights have helped us in building the links between theory and practice presented here. We thank him for sharing his views directly with us in Chapter 11. Sandi Jennings, Miami University of Ohio; Tom Mahoney, Vanderbilt University; and Robert Malone, Loyola University of Chicago reviewed earlier drafts of this manuscript. The final product is improved because of their constructive suggestions.

Joyce Livesay has typed this manuscript from first prospectus to final draft. She has frequently edited and found better ways of expressing ideas. We thank her for this help and for graciously accommodating what became precipitous deadlines.

We thank Richard Furst, Dean of the College of Business and Economics, University of Kentucky, for providing the institutional support and climate that encouraged our efforts. Finally, we thank our families for their support and enthusiasm for our work.

M.J.W.
C.H.F.

Contents

Money cannot buy happiness, but it will soothe the nerves.
—French proverb

I

Compensation Theory

1

"But It's Not Fair!"

No other area of managing relationships with employees is more prone to create problems of achieving fairness than compensation administration—setting wage and salary rates, evaluating jobs, and providing monetary and nonmonetary benefits. *Compensation Theory and Practice* is all about such problems and will show you what basic theory and research tells us about dealing with them. Each of the following cases illustrates quite distinct problems that frequently arise in managing compensation. All of them, however, have a common thread: a norm of equity or fairness has been violated in making a compensation decision: some person or group has been treated unfairly.

Case I   The Denver Nurses. Fairness in compensation practice has·become a legal issue in three major lawsuits in recent years: (1) the Denver nurses case,[1] (2) *Gunther v. County of Washington*,[2] and (3) the *International Union of Electrical Workers (IUE) v. Westinghouse*.[3] Each of these cases involved charges that wages being paid to women are not fair when compared to those being paid to men employees.

The Denver nurses case is a good illustration of the problem. In 1978, nurses employed by the City of Denver charged in United States District Court that they were being discriminated against because of their sex. They demonstrated that nurses were paid lower wage rates than such craft workers as parking meter repairers, tree trimmers, and sign painters. They argued that the work being done by nurses was *at least of equal value* (a comparable worth claim that we will discuss more fully) to the work done by parking meter repairers and other craftsmen. Indeed, they argued that the wage differences did not reflect any difference in the *type* of work being performed or the *value* of work being performed, but rather society's tendency to pay women less for their work than men. In essence, the nurses argued that nurses are paid less than craft workers because their occupation is dominated by women and craft occupations are dominated by men.

The nurses based their charge of "Unfair!" on two federal statutes: (1) the Equal Pay Act of 1963, an amendment to the Fair Labor Standards Act (FLSA) of 1938, and (2) Title VII of the Civil Rights Act of 1964.[4] The Equal Pay Act establishes a standard of equal pay for equal work that prohibits employers from paying women less than men when they are performing jobs that are essentially equal in terms of content (skill, responsibility, effort, and working conditions).

The Equal Pay Act sets up a very narrow definition of fairness with respect to men's and women's pay. Should a woman's job differ from a man's on any of the job content dimensions cited in the Equal Pay Act (skill, working conditions, effort, and responsibility), the employer will be in compliance with the law in setting different wage rates for men and women. The Denver nurses attempted to broaden that basis for considering the fairness of male-female wage differences by demanding that, beyond pay parity for jobs of *equal content*, employers should pay equivalent wage rates for jobs of *equal value* or *comparable worth.*

The comparable worth argument employed by the nurses is based on Title VII of the 1964 Civil Rights Act, which prohibits any employment action that discriminates against a person because of sex, race, color, religion, or national origin. In this case, the employment action involves setting wage rates, and the violation occurs because jobs dominated by women are paid less than jobs dominated by men even though they are of equal value or comparable worth.

The court agreed with the nurses that occupations dominated by women could have historically been paid less than occupations dominated by men and that such discrimination could in fact lead to a violation of a comparable worth criterion of fairness. The court still found against the nurses, however, by citing a fairness criterion based on the marketplace rather than comparable worth. In ruling against the nurses the court commented, "This is a case which is pregnant with the possibility of disrupting the entire economic system of the United States of America. . . . I'm not going to restructure the entire economy of the U.S. Some higher court is going to take that step."[5] The court, in effect, ruled that external market structures are legally acceptable criteria for setting wage rates. Thus, the fact that Denver must pay more to attract parking meter repairers than it does to attract nurses is sufficient reason to pay the former more than the latter.

However, the comparable worth doctrine of fairness is far from dead as a result of the Denver nurses ruling. In a second case, the International Union of Electrical Workers (IUE) charged that Westinghouse had historically established classes of jobs for wage-setting purposes that discriminated against women. Specifically, they demonstrated that Westinghouse had historically segregated "women's" jobs from "men's" jobs and set lower pay rates for women's jobs. The court decided that such a practice discriminated against women employees and was unfair. The practice was ordered stopped. In addition, Eleanor Holmes Norton, chair of the Equal Employment Opportunity Commission in 1980 called the comparable worth issue the most difficult one that has arisen under Title VII of the Civil Rights Act. She predicts that resolution of the problem will have as far-reaching effect on our society as desegregation had during the 1950s.[6] As of this writing, the field of compensation administration has yet to develop a measure of job worth that is independent of the marketplace.[7] Until such a definition is developed and accepted, the conflict inherent in the Denver nurses case between market and nonmarket notions of fairness will continue.

Case II *Quality Stamping, Inc.* Quality Stamping is a highly successful manufacturer of machined parts for office business machines.[8] The company is a major subcontractor to the Office Products Division of International Business Machines. The company was founded by Richard M. Jackson, who is currently president and chairman of the board. Mr. Jackson worked as a machinist for IBM for ten years before going out on his own as a subcontractor in the 1960s.

Under Jackson's direction, Quality Stamping grew rapidly and expanded its operations. Through the 1970s, sales grew at an annual rate of 15 percent. Having begun in Mr. Jackson's garage, the company now occupies two large buildings and employs forty people including ten mechanics, twenty stamping machine operators, six miscellaneous employees, and three secretaries.

Quality Stamping had never experienced any incident involving employee discontent with personnel policies that had not been resolved to everyone's apparent satisfaction. The company had never been subject to a union organization attempt, nor had any employees expressed a desire to form a union. The employee turnover rate was extremely low: 5 percent, or two employees per year on the average. Even in these cases, exit interviews showed that, for the most part, the employees left for personal reasons unrelated to company policies.

Quality Stamping never had a formal wage and salary program. Mr. Jackson's policy had always been to survey comparable wage rates in the area and offer competitive wage rates to start. He also maintained a policy of strict confidence with respect to wages paid. He firmly believed that it would be an invasion of employee privacy to disclose such information.

But Mr. Jackson's brother, an officer in the company, recently read an article in the *Harvard Business Review* that ran counter to Jackson's logic regarding wage secrecy. The author of the *Harvard Business Review* article, a nationally noted industrial/organizational psychologist, argued on the basis of behavioral principles that wage rates must be known by all employees if they are going to have any effect on employee behavior and performance. Thus, a policy of secrecy will make it impossible for wage rates to act as an incentive for employees. In a classic case of the Harvard Business Review Syndrome, the adoption of management ideas read about in a prestigious journal with no thought to their applicability in the current setting, Mr. Jackson decided to switch his policy and make every employee's wage rate public.[9]

He started with the twenty stamping machine operators. A call to the accounting department generated a printout (Exhibit 1.1) that listed each employee, his or her number, number of years employed by Quality (tenure), and hourly wage rate. Jackson posted the printout in the employee lounge about five minutes before the morning coffee break.

Within a half hour, Mr. Jackson received a call from the stamping machine supervisor. According to him, Marjorie Smith had taken a look at the printout, walked over to Helen Pirenne and Kate Shapiro, and begun a violent verbal argument with them. By the end of the day, twelve of the twenty employees had walked off the job and were picketing the plant. They refused to come back to their jobs until either Joanna Zacher, Marge Shriner, Helen Pirenne, Sylvia Reese, and Barb Kasher were brought down in pay or others were brought up. In addition, a group (led by Marjorie Smith) had contacted the International Association of Machinists (IAM) local in their city for help and advice in forming a local union.

Case III   *Gulf States Petroleum Corporation.*   Gulf States Petroleum, based in Houston, Texas, is among the nation's largest producers of oil and petroleum products.[10] The company employs a point factor system for job evaluation. Job evaluation is a system for establishing the relative worth of jobs internally to the employer, and the point factor technique (to be explained fully in Chapter 7) represents these value judgments by assigning points to each job. Thus, two jobs that garner 200 points each are considered to be of equal value to the company.

Exhibit 1.1 Quality Stamping's Wage and Salary Printout

Employee	Employee Number	Tenure	Hourly Wage Rate
M. Smith	002	10	$4.45
L. Barth	003	9	4.45
M. Baran	035	5	3.90
M. Boros	037	5	3.80
J. Zacher	040	1/4	4.85
M. Shriner	043	1/4	5.00
E. McConnell	006	10	4.50
D. Edwards	007	10	4.25
R. Kimble	008	8	4.50
D. Grambsch	009	8	4.50
B. Moore	023	6	3.90
D. Dutton	026	6	3.80
S. Reese	038	1/2	4.10
B. Kasher	040	1/2	4.10
H. Pirenne	042	1/8	4.45
K. Shapiro	043	1/8	4.45
M. Lowe	027	6	4.00
H. Breton	029	5	4.00
L. Alquien	033	2	4.40
H. Bernardo	034	2	4.40

The company's compensation planning committee has a job evaluation problem among their professional and technical series of jobs. The company must pay much higher rates for petroleum engineers and petroleum geologists than for the other jobs in this series. New graduates in those fields regularly command an annual salary of $32,000 to start. Competition among employers for these people is extremely keen and the supply of qualified petroleum engineers and geologists is extremely short. The company not meeting or exceeding the $32,000 rate will not be able to attract qualified people.

The problem comes when the job evaluation results for petroleum engineers and geologists are compared with job evaluation results for the other jobs in the professional and technical series (accountant, statistician, systems analyst, and attorney). The data in Exhibit 1.2 displays the job evaluation results for these jobs. Pay grades 16 through 20 include all the jobs in this family. A

Exhibit 1.2 Job Evaluation for Professional and Technical Series, Gulf States Petroleum Corporation

Pay Class	Job Evaluation Points	Job Family				
		Legal	Accounting	Data	Geology	Engineering
20	300–49	Senior Counsel	Senior Accountant	Senior Statistician	Senior Geologist	Senior Engineer
19	250–99	General Counsel	General Accountant	Statistician	Geologist III	Engineer III
18	200–49	Junior Counsel	Accountant	Systems Analyst II	Geologist II	Engineer II
17	150–99	Attorney II	Auditor II	Systems Analyst I	Geologist I	Engineer I
16	100–49	Attorney I	Auditor I	Programmer/ Analyst	Assistant Geologist	Assistant Engineer

job garnering 100 to 149 points in the job evaluation is assigned to pay grade 16, 150 to 199 points to pay grade 17, and so forth. All jobs in a given pay grade have been judged to have equal value to the company, and a single starting wage rate, midpoint, and maximum rate should be set for all jobs in the pay grade. Thus, for example, the jobs of Attorney I, Auditor I, Programmer/Analyst, Assistant Geologist, and Assistant Engineer should all be set at the same hiring rate, midpoint, and maximum wage rate.

The problem is that Gulf States can hire as many Attorney I's, Auditor I's, and Programmer Analysts as it needs for $22,000 per year, but they have to pay $32,000 for Assistant Geologists and Assistant Engineers. How can Gulf States Petroleum resolve this dilemma? There is an internal demand (based on the job evaluation results) to pay each of the jobs in a given pay grade the same. Yet, external market realities force the company to pay petroleum engineers and geologists nearly $10,000 more per year than attorneys and other professional and technical workers.

As you will see again and again in this book, there is no single best solution to dilemmas of the type facing Gulf States Petroleum. The professional compensation planner must consider alternative strategies for dealing with such problems and choose the one that strikes the best compromise among competing objectives. In this situation, many oil and petroleum companies have adopted the solution pictured in Exhibit 1.3. In this case, the company has not attempted to stretch the job evaluation system to conform more closely to external market differentials. Instead they have created two separate job series for compensation purposes: (1) a legal, accounting, and data series, and (2) a geology and engineering series. Job evaluations are carried out separately within each family, and no job evaluation comparisons are made across series. Thus, an attorney, accountant, or programmer/analyst in the first pay grade (100–149 points) is paid a starting salary of $22,000. A petroleum engineer or geologist in the same pay grade (100–149 points) starts at $32,000 per year.

You might take a few minutes to think about Gulf States Petroleum's dilemma and the solution we have just presented. What are the strengths of creating two separate classes of jobs for compensation purposes? What else might the company have tried to do? What problems might this solution create?

Case IV The Insulting Wage Increase. Mark Williams was extremely unhappy with his 1982 wage increase.[11] He had worked the last two years for General Healthtronics, a manufacturer of high tech medical and health electronic devices, as a patent attorney. He had begun with the company on graduation and was a very eager and hard-working attorney. His superiors were not

Exhibit 1.3   One Solution to Gulf States Petroleum's Dilemma

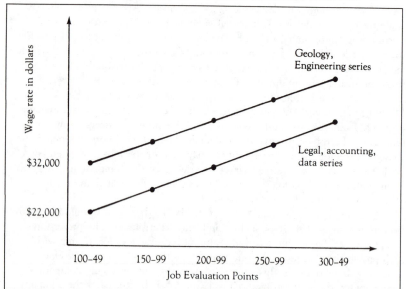

only pleased with his work but had told him he was the best patent attorney working for the company. In fact, he had just returned from a merit review session with his boss, Steve Mackey, who informed him that he would be given the highest wage increase of the fifteen patent attorneys in his division. He would receive a 13 percent increase from $28,000 per year to $31,640, a $3,640 bump.

His new salary sounded pretty good to him until he compared notes with Fred Cadillac, a fellow patent attorney and classmate employed in the same department. Fred was the classic "good ole boy." Never one to work too hard, he came in a few minutes late each day, and was packed and ready to head off for the golf course twenty minutes ahead of quitting time. Extra effort on a particular case was unheard of to Fred, and he had an uncanny skill for riding in on the coattails of others in his group. On cue, at twenty minutes to five, Fred stuck his head into Mark's office and said, "Time to knock off and hit the ball, good buddy! Why don't you join me for a change? I sure as hell can afford to relax a little bit more with the new bread I'll be making next year, thirty-one big ones!"

"How much are you making next year?" asked Mark incredulously. "Actually, I've rounded up a tad," responded Fred, "but I'm slotted in at $30,801.

How much have they signed you up for?" Mark replied that he would be making $31,640. "Well, that makes us just about even, doesn't it!" replied Fred, and left for the golf course. Mark fumed in his office. "All that work and I end up making a little over $800 more than that goof off!" He knew that he and Fred had started with General Healthtronics two years earlier at the same salary of $25,000. He had expected to outpace Fred quickly, however, knowing that they would perform at much different levels. Apparently either the company did not realize this or did not recognize differences in performance when making individual salary adjustments.

After a great deal of thought and agony, Mark approached his supervisor, Steve Mackey. "Steve," he began, "I find this awfully difficult to talk about, but I just can't contain my feelings and I want to have a talk before I leave to find work elsewhere." "What in heaven's name could be so bad?" exclaimed Steve, shaken by the implied threat of losing somebody as valuable as Mark. "The problem is my salary," Mark said. "When you first told me that I would make $31,640 next year, I was really pleased. In fact, I don't even know what I could make on the open market. At any rate, I didn't think anything about it until Fred Cadillac told me he'd be making $30,800 next year. Steve, that's just not fair! You yourself have said in public that Fred is the laziest attorney on board and that he's going to have to shape up in order to make promotion. Also, I did not seek his salary information out; he volunteered it to me and gloated on his way out about how close we are in salary. I guess that's what really burns me!"

"What you're saying, Mark, is that $839 before taxes doesn't accurately reflect the difference between your job performance and Fred's," said Steve. "Darn right!" agreed Mark. "And it's just not fair," he added.

"Mark, I don't have a good answer for you," admitted Steve. "There is no question that you are our best patent attorney and Fred is our worst. Unfortunately, I'm hamstrung by the company's policy of making cost of living adjustments across the board so long as an employee's performance is rated acceptable or above. Here, look at this merit matrix for 1982 adjustments" (Exhibit 1.4). He indicated a sheet of paper on his desk. "This is a policy handed down to me by corporate headquarters. I have no options except to assign a 0 percent for someone rated unacceptable, 11.5 percent for acceptable performance, 12 percent for above average, and 13 percent for outstanding." "Where did they come up with the 11 percent for acceptable?" asked Mark. "The Consumer Price Index moved eleven points last year, so the company established an across-the-board cost of living adjustment of 11 percent," explained Steve.

"Here, let me do a little accounting for you on this sheet of paper (Exhibit 1.5)," added Steve. "Both you and Fred started two years ago at $25,000 per year. In both years you got the highest performance rating, outstanding,

Exhibit 1.4   General Healthtronics 1982 Merit Matrix

	Performance Rating			
	Unacceptable	*Acceptable*	*Above Average*	*Outstanding*
Percent Increase:	0%	11.5%	12%	13%

and Fred got the lowest rating short of unacceptable, acceptable. In 1981 you, and everyone else, were given cost-of-living adjustments of 10 percent, in line with the Consumer Price Index movement for that year. In addition, you received a 2 percent increase on top of that for your outstanding performance. Fred received only a ½ percent increase for performance. We did the same thing again this year. Each of you received an 11 percent cost-of-living adjustment and you received a 2 percent increase on top for performance. Again, Fred received only a ½ percent increase for performance."

"That 2 percent is actually insulting!" complained Mark. "Why should I work overtime on cases, do extra research at the law library, and generally work my butt off for this outfit when all I get for the effort is $422 more than

Exhibit 1.5   Steve Mackey's Calculations

	1981		1982	
Mark	$25,000	1981 Base	$28,000	1982 Base
	2,500	10% COLA	3,080	11% COLA
	500	2% Merit	560	2% Merit
	$28,000	1982 Base	$31,640	1983 Base
Fred	$25,000	1981 Base	$27,625	1982 Base
	2,500	10% COLA	3,038	11% COLA
	125	1/2% Merit	138	1/2% Merit
	$27,625	1982 Base	$30,801	1983 Base

Fred this year on the basis of merit, *before* taxes! It seems to me that I have only two options: adopt Fred's habits or seek work with a company that actually rewards effort and performance! I think you know what my choice will be, Steve," fumed Mark as he stormed out of Steve's office.

You might take a few minutes to think about the problem faced by Steve and Mark. If you were Mark, what would you do? If you were redesigning General Healthtronic's compensation policies, how might you change them in order not to lose employees like Mark?

Compensation Is an Important Issue

Although the specifics varied among the cases we have considered, they all underscore the fact that compensation practice and policy have become hotly debated issues at all levels in our society, ones that will increasingly demand the attention of professionals in personnel and industrial relations.

The Individual

The case of the insulting wage increase illustrates how strongly employees react to pay practices. Authorities in the field of compensation have demonstrated that no factor has a greater effect on emotional reactions of employees than perceptions of fairness and equity.[12] The belief that one is being treated unfairly will have a direct and dramatic effect on employee behavior and performance. The most frequent source of such reactions are mistakes made by management in its compensation practices. Management cannot hope to influence employee behavior and performance toward company objectives unless the compensation system is perceived as fair or equitable by employees.

On the positive side, compensation policies can have a dramatic incentive value in influencing employee behavior. Compensation plays many important roles for employees.[13] First, money is instrumental in achieving a number of valued outcomes for a person: security, safety, housing, and sustenance, as well as living standards, vacations, hobbies. Second, compensation often becomes associated with general levels of anxiety or comfort. Most of us learn to associate a lack of money with events leading to anxiety, and sufficient money with conditions that contribute to feelings of security. Hence, the aphorism at the opening of our book: "Money cannot buy happiness, but it will soothe the nerves." Finally, many employees come to view their level of compensation (relative and absolute) as a symbol of their accomplishment and value to their employer. In sum, compensation is not merely pay for hours worked: it influences employee reactions to their employment in a complex variety of fashions.

The Employer

Effective compensation practices are crucial to the employer, as well. Indeed, as labor costs become an increasingly larger part of the total cost of doing business (labor costs constitute the largest proportion of the budget in labor-intensive operations), an employer's economic survival will depend on how effectively it can improve productivity and control costs in its compensation practices. In the early 1980s, for example, the United States automobile industry provided an example of the need to control labor costs in order to survive. Recent reports show that major auto manufacturers have reverted from a posture of readily granting wage increases demanded in contract negotiations to one of holding the line and even seeking pay cuts in order to stay alive.[14]

Employers, in addition, are more conscious than ever of the fair employment legislation liabilities they may run, particularly with respect to sex discrimination. The three comparable-worth cases cited earlier underscore the need for employers to ensure that they are not unintentionally discriminating against women in their pay practices. The stakes are high in this arena. The cost to Westinghouse in the *IUE* v. *Westinghouse* case was estimated to be several million dollars in damages and penalties.[15]

On the positive side, companies that have met all the conditions necessary for compensation to influence behavior (see our discussions of these conditions in Chapters 4 and 8) report dramatic improvements in their ability to attract qualified employees, to retain valued employees, and to improve work performance and efficiency.[16]

The Society

Compensation practice has become the object of unprecedented attention from a variety of groups and institutions in our society. Advocates of equal employment opportunity for women and minorities are on record as singling out compensation policy as the major target for their efforts and litigation in the 1980s.[17] The U.S. Equal Employment Opportunity Commission as well as the National Organization of Women have both forecast that compensation practices will become subject to at least as much enforcement activity, scrutiny, and litigation as testing and selection were during the 1960s and 1970s.[18]

Even those persons who were not previously concerned with economic and legal ramifications are now looking to compensation issues for ways to improve the performance of organizations. The field of organizational development (OD) provides an interesting case in this regard. People in this field are primarily industrial and organizational psychologists interested in improving the effectiveness of organizations through training and development. Most of the techniques organizational development people have traditionally used have relied heavily on technologies emerging from industrial and organizational psychology. These include group exercises, management by objectives (MBO), brainstorming sessions, sensitivity training, and related methods that focus on changing attitudes and behavior.

We now see the interesting phenomenon of organizational development experts turning their attention to a compensation principle and practice espoused almost eighty years ago by management pioneer F. W. Taylor.[19] Specifically, a recent book titled *Pay and Organizational Development* proposes that pay be used as an organizational development technique.[20] Proponents of the idea have rediscovered Taylor's original proposition that compensation practices can be a powerful tool in creating incentives for employees to change their behavior and performance.[21] Unprecedented attention to pay practices on the individual, employer, and societal levels demands that line and personnel managers look ever more carefully at compensation issues.

Purpose of *Compensation Theory and Practice*

Our purpose in writing *Compensation Theory and Practice* is to provide a thorough introduction to compensation issues and problems challenging compensation managers and the personnel and line managers who depend upon their efforts. We believe that line managers and staff compensation experts must work together closely if compensation practices are to contribute effectively to corporate or organizational objectives.

Our approach in this endeavor will be to integrate the rapidly growing body of compensation theory and empirical research into guidelines for practice. Increasing attention is being paid to compensation problems and issues by researchers in a variety of disciplines: personnel and industrial relations, industrial/organizational psychology, labor economics, and labor and employment law. We will review their work relevant to major compensation problems and draw conclusions for administering actual compensation programs.

A final theme supporting *Compensation Theory and Practice* is the crucial need for strategic planning. Compensation objectives must first be elaborated from a consideration of the broader organizational goals to be served. A mission must be established for the compensation program. Compensation practices such as job evaluation, wage surveys, performance appraisal, cost of living adjustments, and related techniques must be considered on their merits as alternative strategies. In addition, policies must be established and carried out according to the strategic choices that have been made. Finally, the entire process must be audited for goal achievement and appropriate control steps taken. Frequently, under the pressures of day-to-day business, managers lose sight of the planning steps just outlined. Too often such managers consider compensation as "something that happens: everyone has to meet a payroll!" A compensation system that operates in such a fashion, without planning, cannot be expected to contribute to the goal achievement of any organization. Indeed, ignoring the compensation program can actually lead to the death of an organization primarily because labor costs rise out of control.

The Central Notion of Equity

The cases that opened this chapter raise diverse issues and problems. The Denver nurses case involved what is primarily a legal and economic issue concerning definitions of the worth of a job. The Quality Stamping case was primarily a problem involving fairness of individual wage rates for people doing the same job. Those just beginning employment were coming in at wage rates at or above those being paid to people with several years' experience. Gulf States Petroleum had a problem very common among employers today: market dislocations. In this case, market conditions are forcing the wages that must be paid petroleum engineers and geologists out of line with what internal job evaluation would suggest. Finally, the case of the insulting wage increase showed how a mismanaged merit system can actually create disincentives for performance. In this case, the amount of increase given for effective performance was perceived as an insult by the recipient and would probably lead to his quitting the employer.

Each of these cases, however, reflects the critical theme that exists at the center of all compensation theory and practice: equity. You will not become competent in compensation administration until you develop a thorough understanding of this concept.

Equity Defined

Equity is generally defined as anything of value earned through the provision or investment of something of value. An investor, for example, earns equity (ownership) interest in a corporation by providing money (purchasing shares). In compensation, a worker earns equity interest by providing labor on a job.

Fairness is achieved when the return to equity is equivalent to the investment made. For compensation, then, we would define fairness as being achieved when the value of the compensation received is equivalent to the value of the labor performed. Unfairness or inequity occurs when the value of the compensation received does not correspond to the value of the labor performed.

Equity Theory

Research has demonstrated that equity and inequity can create dramatic employee reactions.[22] Indeed, a well-developed body of theory and research has focused on this phenomenon. The belief that one is being treated inequitably (for example, having ten years' experience and being paid less than a newly hired employee as in the Quality Stamping case) directly affects motivation and will, therefore, influence an employee's behavior and performance.

The work of J. Stacy Adams is most frequently cited as the foundation of equity theory.[23] Specifically, he proposes that employees constantly monitor the exchange relationship with their employer. An exchange relationship is one that involves equity: people exchange things of value. In the setting of compensation, the exchange is one of monetary and nonmonetary compensation for labor. According to equity theory, the principle of *distributive justice* is crucial to the employee. Distributive justice occurs when all parties in an exchange relationship have equal outcome/input ratios. That is, the proportionate relation between outcomes and inputs is equal for all persons in the relationship. Thus, distributive justice defines fairness or equity.

The ratios in Exhibit 1.6 make the notion of distributive justice in equity theory more explicit. The theory proposes that employees evaluate their compensation (as well as all other aspects of their employment) by comparing the ratio of their employment outcomes (O_p) to their inputs (I_p) with a similar ratio for a comparison employee or group (O_o/I_o). Outcomes can include many rewards, including monetary and nonmonetary compensation. Inputs can include performance, effort, skills, experience, responsibility, and working conditions. Distributive justice or equity is achieved when the two ratios in Exhibit 1.6 are equal. If an employee or group of employees, however, perceives an inequality between or among these ratios, inequity will be experienced.

You might take several minutes to analyze each of the cases at the

Exhibit 1.6   Ratios Defining Equity

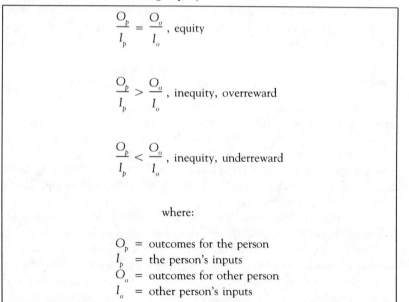

$$\frac{O_p}{I_p} = \frac{O_o}{I_o} \text{ , equity}$$

$$\frac{O_p}{I_p} > \frac{O_o}{I_o} \text{ , inequity, overreward}$$

$$\frac{O_p}{I_p} < \frac{O_o}{I_o} \text{ , inequity, underreward}$$

where:

O_p = outcomes for the person
I_p = the person's inputs
O_o = outcomes for other person
I_o = other person's inputs

outset of this chapter in terms of the equity ratios in Exhibit 1.6. What would these ratios look like for nurses versus parking meter repairers in Denver, for M. Smith versus H. Pirenne at Quality Stamping (see Exhibit 1.1), for petroleum engineers versus attorneys at Gulf States Petroleum, or for Mark Williams versus Fred Cadillac in the case of the insulting wage increase?

A central finding in compensation research is that reactions to equity and inequity are strong and must be considered carefully by compensation managers in making decisions about pay. Indeed, the relative way in which management treats an employee's compensation is at least as important as the absolute level of pay. Perceptions of equity, then, influence the decisions people make about organizations: to accept or reject a job offer, to stay with or leave an organization, and to expend more or less effort on the job. Since these decisions have direct economic consequences for the organization, compensation planners must pay very close attention to equity issues in planning, administering, and auditing compensation practices.

External, Internal, and Individual Equity

Compensation theorists have recognized in recent years that equity is not a simple concept.[24] Indeed, if you tried to create input/outcome ratios in each of the four opening cases to this chapter you would find a variety of factors. Let's consider inputs as an illustration. A petroleum engineer considering the inputs she brings to her work might consider a variety of independent factors. First she might note that a short supply and strong demand for her occupation makes the market tight for her skills, and that she is in a strong position to bid for a higher wage than would be paid for an occupation (for example, elementary schoolteacher) where the market is loose. Economists define the combination (or intersect) of what employers are willing to pay (labor demand) and what employees are willing to accept (labor supply) as an *exchange rate*. The exchange rate or price in the external marketplace for one's occupation is the value that one brings to the job. An employee who compares his or her wage to the wage rate prevailing in the external market for the same occupation is said to be seeking *external equity*.

Instead of looking simply at the external market for one's occupation, an employee may compare the contribution of his or her job to that of another employee's job. Thus, the Denver nurses compared the value of their work as nurses to the city of Denver with the value of the work of Denver parking meter repairers and tree trimmers. They argued that the work of nurses was at least as valuable to the city as the work of the latter jobs. Thus, to pay nurses less violated a norm of *internal equity.*

Finally, employees on the same job frequently count individual effort, performance, and commitment to the employer as a valued input into the ratios in Exhibit 1.6. Thus, in the Quality Stamping case and in the case of the insulting wage increase, the problem centers on individual employee merit (time in grade or tenure and quality of job performance), not on the market rate for jobs or the relative worth of jobs to the employer. This last issue is one of *individual equity.* Let us consider each of these three equity issues in more detail.

External equity.   External equity is a fairness criterion that demands an employer pay a wage rate that corresponds to rates prevailing in external markets for the employee's occupation. Most of us are familiar with the fact that MDs can command higher wages than attorneys, or that business professors can command higher salaries than history professors. These differences have little to do with any differences in the relative worth of these jobs internally to their employers. Rather, they reflect differences in supply and demand across occupational markets. From a purely economic perspective, external equity corresponds to the exchange rates determined by the intersection of the demand for labor (the maximum rates employers are willing to pay) and the supply of labor (the least employees are willing to accept), as in Exhibit 1.7.

Internal equity.   Internal equity is a fairness criterion that demands employers set wage rates for jobs within their companies that correspond to the relative internal value of each job. That is, theoretically, internal equity as a criterion refers to the value of the work performed on a job to the employer. This value may or may not be tied directly to the marketplace. Empirical research, which will be reviewed in later chapters, suggests that internal and external equity can operate quite independently of each other. We know far less about the roots of internal equity than we do of external equity. Some have suggested, for example, that a major factor in internal equity is the economic value that the actual work on a job *produces* for an employer. An alternative conception of internal equity focuses on the value of the labor *itself* that is supplied on a job. The latter basis could include the level of skill a person brings to the job,

Exhibit 1.7   Market Definition of External Equity

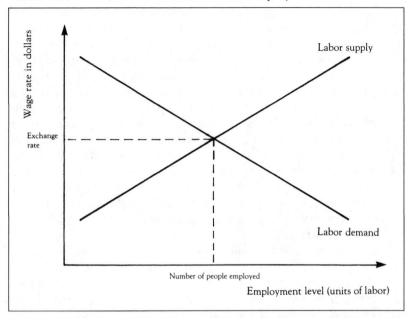

the level of effort a person must expend on the job, and the amount of training that the job requires. Theory in this area is least developed and we will discuss the problems employers face in measuring the internal value of jobs in Chapters 3 (Job Worth) and 7 (Job Evaluation).

Individual equity.   The individual equity criterion demands that employers pay wage rates to individuals (in the simplest case, workers on the same job) according to variation in individual merit. Better workers should receive higher wages on the same job than poorer workers. Factors contributing to merit may include tenure (how long one has been working for an employer) and job performance. In the Quality Stamping case, a tenure criterion was violated when new people were brought in at wage rates the same or higher than those of long-tenured people. In the case of the insulting wage increase, the wage differences between a high performer and low performer did not adequately reflect actual performance differences.

It is extremely important for managers to keep external, internal, and individual equity issues separate in their thinking about compensation objectives.[25] First, they constitute quite distinct objectives in compensation practices. Thus, for example, Denver might achieve an external equity objective by setting nurses' wage rates equal to those prevailing for nurses in the Denver labor market, yet fail to achieve internal equity when these wage rates are compared to those being paid parking meter repairers. Indeed, you will find later in this book that external equity, internal equity, and individual equity involve quite different and confusing sets of characteristics or factors. External equity, for example, deals primarily with external economic phenomena involving interactions of supply and demand. Internal equity, in contrast, deals most frequently with job content factors including level of responsibility, education, skills, effort level, and working conditions required by the job. Such factors are not highly correlated with market conditions in most cases. In many cases, external and internal factors will conflict and managers will face the difficult task of finding a compromise between external market and internal equity demands.

A second reason for considering external, internal, and individual equity as distinct objectives is that management's success or failure in achieving each of them will have quite different behavioral effects on employees. Thus, for example, an employee's job may be priced competitively with the market for that occupation, but he or she may be dissatisfied because that job is not being paid according to its internal worth to the employer. Or, an employee may perceive that his job is being paid equitably according to the external market and internal value criteria, but may still be dissatisfied because he perceives that his wage does not sufficiently reflect differences in merit between himself and another employee.

Finally, plaintiffs in the comparable worth cases discussed at the outset of this chapter are demanding that the issues of internal and external equity be considered separately in making job value judgments and setting wage rates. Their arguments shed doubt that an external equity criterion alone is an adequate measure of job value.[26]

Conclusion: The Order of *Compensation Theory and Practice*

Compensation Theory and Practice is divided into two parts. Part I deals with compensation issues at a theoretical level. In this part we will review and summarize theory and empirical research regarding external equity

(Chapter 2), internal equity (Chapter 3), and achieving individual equity (Chapter 4). Part I will conclude with a consideration of the legal and institutional constraints under which compensation practice operates (Chapter 5).

In Part II we will translate theory into practice by providing guidelines for compensation policy based on the research literature presented in Part I. Chapter 6 will deal primarily with external equity in a review of practice in pricing jobs. In this chapter we will discuss the use of wage surveys and how managers should go about organizing and analyzing external market information.

Chapter 7 is concerned with internal equity, and specifically practices involved with job evaluation. We will present and explain the major techniques of job evaluation and how to design internal structures that satisfy demands for internal and external equity.

Chapter 8 moves directly to the issue of individual equity and will discuss practice in setting wage rates for individual employees. Of specific concern will be the problem of setting individual wage rates that create incentives for desired employee behavior and performance. We will discuss how to deal with seniority, individual merit, incentives, and pay secrecy policies.

In Chapter 9 we discuss the other third of the compensation program: employee benefits. Major types of benefits are discussed. The emphasis in Chapter 9 is on using benefits to complete the compensation package.

Chapter 10 focuses on the need for managers to audit compensation programs for performance on external, internal, and individual equity criteria. Specific topics covered in this chapter include planning, audit and control statistics, budgeting, and communication.

Chapter 11 presents a view of compensation as a profession. You may be considering personnel and industrial relations as a profession and may have a specific interest in the subspecialty of compensation. We will explore our field in this chapter and discuss the major professional bodies, including the American Compensation Association.

Notes

1. *Lemons v. City and County of Denver*, 17 FEP Cases (BNA) 906 (District Court, Colorado, 1978).

2. *Gunther v. County of Washington*, 602 F. 2d 882 (9th Circuit Court, 1979).

3. *International Union of Electrical, Radio, and Machine Workers (IUE) v. Westinghouse Electric Corporation*, 19 FEP Cases 450 (District Court, New Jersey, 1979).

4. Civil Rights Act of 1964, Title VII.

5. *Lemons v. Denver,* op. cit., 1978.

6. Eleanor Holmes Norton quoted by the Bureau of National Affairs, *Fair Employment Practices,* No. 383, November 8, 1979.

7. See, for example, Marc J. Wallace, Jr., Charles H. Fay, and Richard W. Beatty, "Pay Equity and Equal Employment Opportunity: An Analysis of the Legal, Research, and Professional Debate" (Lexington, Ky.: University of Kentucky, College of Business and Economics, 1982), Working Paper in Management.

8. This case was developed by the first author. The names employed bear no resemblance to any person or company.

9. Marc J. Wallace, Jr., N. Fredric Crandall, and Charles H. Fay, *Administering Human Resources* (New York: Random House, 1982), p. 547.

10. This case was developed by the first author. The names employed bear no resemblance to any person or company.

11. This case was developed by the first author. The names bear no resemblance to any person or company.

12. See, for example, Thomas A. Mahoney, *Compensation and Reward Perspectives* (Homewood, Ill.: Richard D. Irwin, 1979).

13. R. L. Opsahl and M. D. Dunnette, "The Role of Financial Compensation In Industrial Motivation," *Psychological Bulletin,* 1966, pp. 94–118.

14. See, for example, "1982 Bargaining Schedule: Labor Seeks Less," *Business Week,* December 21, 1981, pp. 82–87.

15. *IUE v. Westinghouse.*

16. See Edward E. Lawler, III, *Pay and Organization Development* (Reading, Mass.: Addison-Wesley, 1981) Chapter 2 for a full discussion of this issue.

17. Norton, *Fair Employment Practices;* Winn Newman, "Pay Equity Emerges As A Top Labor Issue in the 1980s", *Monthly Labor Review,* April 1982, pp. 49–51.

18. Ibid.

19. F. W. Taylor, *Shop Management* (New York: Harper, 1903); F. W. Taylor, *The Principles of Scientific Management* (New York: Norton, 1911).

20. Edward E. Lawler, III, *Pay and Organization Development* (Reading, Mass.: Addison-Wesley, 1981).

21. We are indebted to Thomas Mahoney for pointing this fact out to us. In addition, see Edwin A. Locke, "The Ideas of Frederick W. Taylor: An Evaluation," *Academy of Management Review,* 1982, pp. 14–24, for a detailed analysis of Taylor's ideas and contributions.

22. See, for example, research reviewed in Mahoney, *Perspectives.*

23. J. Stacy Adams, "Towards An Understanding of Inequity," *Journal of Abnormal and Social Psychology,* 1963, pp. 422–36.

24. Elaine Walster, Ellen Berscheid, and William Walster, "New Directions In Equity Research," *Journal of Personality and Social Psychology,* 1973, pp. 151–76.

25. Marc J. Wallace, Jr. and Charles H. Fay, "Labor Markets, Job Evaluation, and Job Worth: Towards A Model of Managerial Judgments of Job Value" (Lexington, Ky.: University of Kentucky, College of Business and Economics, 1982), Working Paper in Business Administration, No. BA 74.

26. Ruth G. Blumrosen, "Wage Discrimination, Job Segregation, and Women Workers," *Employee Relations Law Journal,* 1980, pp. 77–136.

2

External Equity

$\mathbf{M}$anagers are acutely aware that they are operating in economic environments. No less an authority than Nobel laureate Herbert A. Simon has noted that even if managers do not always make decisions at the margin, they act as if they do.[1] Managers are sensitive to the marketplace for an evident reason: if they ignore markets, their businesses will eventually fail. In the case of compensation, a company that consistently pays wage rates below those prevailing in the external marketplace will find its ability to attract qualified employees, in sufficient numbers and on a timely basis, diminished. Eventually, they will be unable to attract any employees. On the other hand, most employers who consistently pay more for labor than their competitors will lose a competitive edge and may either price their product out of the market or fail to make sufficient profits. Indeed, the United States District Court's decision in the Denver nurses case (cited in Chapter 1) clearly establishes the legitimacy of the marketplace as a criterion of fairness or equity in setting wage rates: the criterion of *external equity*. The purpose of this chapter is to examine that criterion in detail. In the process we will look at forces that determine the demand for labor, the supply of labor, wage rates for labor, and external wage structures. Finally, we will discuss the problems managers face defining labor markets and obtaining accurate wage information from these markets.

Defining External Equity

Practicing managers quickly become sensitive to the fact that wages or salaries different kinds of people can command vary in the extreme. Exhibit 2.1 displays U.S. Department of Labor data for the wages of many common occupations in our economy. Notice that tool and die makers averaged $10.80 per hour in December 1980, more than twice the rate of $5.31 earned by key entry operators. How can we explain such a wide variation? In order to answer this question, we must turn to economics and the subspecialty of labor economics. Labor economists attempt to understand such wage differences as a function of varying supply and demand conditions across labor markets, a topic we will explore in more detail later. At this point, however, we can define external equity as having been achieved when an employer pays wage rates that correspond to those prevailing in external labor markets (for example, those in Exhibit 2.1).

Such a definition may appear deceptively simple at first. Most managers, however, quickly run into some thorny problems when they try to translate the external equity criterion into practice. First, no single wage rate prevails in any single labor market. Exhibit 2.1, for example, shows that hourly earnings for the tool and die makers just cited ranged from $8.80 to $13.60. Janitors' hourly earnings varied from $2.80 to $8.80. Employers face a variety of wage rates and a variety of labor markets. The effective compensation planner recognizes this fact and attends carefully to the task of defining external wage rates and external markets as accurately as possible.

Many Markets

Labor economists have long pointed out that there is no such thing as a single, homogenous market for labor.[2] Rather, employers face a series of rather discontinuous or segmented labor markets (early theorists referred to them as Balkanized).[3] Movement from one labor market to another is quite restricted in most cases. It would be quite difficult, for example, for an attorney to become a physician, or a professor of accounting to become a physicist.

In addition to barriers preventing easy movement from one market to another, supply and demand conditions vary substantially across markets. Economists focus on this fact as the major explanation for wage differences among occupations, and compensation analysts as a matter of practice, must be sensitive to such wage variation.

Of practical concern to the manager is accurately defining labor markets for compensation planning purposes. The work of labor economists on this problem suggests that the following factors are potentially important in defining the limits of a labor market segment:

geography

education and/or technical background required to perform the job

industry

experience required by the job

licensing or certification requirements

union membership

Wallace, Crandall, and Fay have pointed out that quite frequently a combination of these parameters will be used in defining a labor market for a particular job.[4] A company trying to set a wage rate for an electrician, for example, will be looking at a market largely defined first by its geographic proximity to their place of business and second by persons who will be willing to join the union that represents electricians once they are employed as a condition of their employment (for example, the International Union of Electricians). Few electricians would be willing to commute more than twenty miles from their home to work and, in this case, the company has a union security agreement in their labor contract that requires a new electrician to join the union (a union shop agreement).

In constrast, consider the market faced by a research and development firm such as Bell Labs trying to establish market rates for engineering physicists. In this case geography is not much of a determining parameter. The market for such talent is virtually international. Major universities supply such people across the nation, and engineering physicists are far more concerned with job opportunity and prospects than they are with geographic locale. Factors other than geography become crucial, however. The person must hold a Ph.D. in engineering physics (in the extreme case the market may be defined by a small number of universities specializing in this type of training). In addition, the person may need a specific type of postgraduate experience.

As a strategic matter, employers must define the appropriate market

Exhibit 2.1   Area Wage Survey: Hourly Earnings[1] of Office and Plant Workers in Lexington–Fayette, Ky., December 1980

Occupation	Number of workers			Hourly earnings (all workers)[1]		
	All	Men	Women	Mean	Median	Middle range
SECRETARIES[2].........................	420	1	417	$6.72	$6.34	$5.33– $7.93
SECRETARIES, CLASS A..............	16	–	16	7.60	6.84	6.11– 8.21
SECRETARIES, CLASS b..............	89	–	89	6.79	5.76	5.37– 7.96
SECRETARIES, CLASS C..............	161	1	160	7.15	7.75	5.41– 8.45
SECRETARIES, CLASS D..............	91	–	91	6.58	6.70	5.90– 7.33
SECRETARIES, CLASS E..............	61	–	61	5.44	5.07	4.61– 5.81
STENOGRAPHERS......................	64	–	64	6.51	6.92	5.73– 7.18
STENOGRAPHERS, SENIOR............	47	–	47	6.75	7.18	6.17– 7.18
STENOGRAPHERS, GENERAL...........	17	–	17	5.83	5.79	4.83– 6.12
TYPISTS[2].............................	26	6	20	5.51	4.04	3.65– 5.41
TYPISTS, CLASS b..................	23	6	17	5.57	3.93	3.61– 7.75
FILE CLERKS.........................	37	–	37	3.76	3.49	3.35– 4.25
FILE CLERKS, CLASS C..............	37	–	37	3.76	3.49	3.35– 4.25
SWITCHBOARD OPERATORS..............	35	–	33	4.31	3.93	3.28– 5.15
KEY ENTRY OPERATORS[2].............	160	2	158	5.31	4.94	4.60– 5.80
KEY ENTRY OPERATORS, CLASS A.....	62	2	60	6.15	5.82	4.92– 6.83
KEY ENTRY OPERATORS, CLASS B.....	97	–	97	4.79	4.65	4.36– 5.25
COMPUTER OPERATORS[2]..............	131	99	32	7.16	7.44	5.61– 8.65
COMPUTER OPERATORS, CLASS B......	85	61	24	6.54	6.35	5.23– 7.98
DRAFTERS[2]..........................	129	104	23	6.38	6.05	5.18– 7.86
DRAFTERS, CLASS A.................	12	11	1	8.41	–	–
DRAFTERS, CLASS B.................	42	36	6	7.32	7.59	5.99– 8.36
DRAFTERS, CLASS C.................	66	52	12	5.68	5.50	4.63– 6.83
ELECTRONICS TECHNICIANS[2].........	64	59	5	8.95	8.80	8.30– 9.37
ELECTRONICS TECHNICIANS, CLASS b.	12	10	2	10.64	–	–
MAINTENANCE ELECTRICIANS..........	97	97	–	9.63	9.12	8.85– 11.18
MAINTENANCE MECHANICS (MACHINERY)..	264	262	2	9.10	8.86	8.01– 9.61
MAINTENANCE MECHANICS (MOTOR VEHICLES)...........................	80	80	–	8.79	8.00	7.05– 11.18
TOOL AND DIE MAKERS................	193	193	–	10.80	10.60	10.00– 11.84
STATIONARY ENGINEERS..............	7	7	–	8.39	–	–
BOILER TENDERS.....................	17	17	–	8.52	7.07	7.07– 10.18
TRUCKDRIVERS[2][3]...................	508	502	6	8.66	7.46	6.70– 11.97
TRACTOR–TRAILER..................	348	347	1	9.31	8.08	6.85– 11.97
SHIPPING PACKERS..................	36	21	15	5.79	5.54	4.10– 7.82
MATERIAL HANDLING LABORERS........	209	201	8	5.99	5.95	5.67– 6.97
FORKLIFT OPERATORS................	395	386	9	6.90	6.79	6.10– 7.41
GUARDS[2]............................	78	75	3	6.80	7.30	4.90– 8.36
GUARDS, CLASS B..................	76	73	3	6.86	7.60	4.94– 8.36
JANITORS, PORTERS, AND CLEANERS....	523	399	124	4.13	3.50	3.10– 4.85

[1] Excludes premium pay for overtime and for work on weekends, holidays, and late shifts. Incentive payments, such as those resulting from piecework, production bonuses, and commission systems, are included in the wages reported; nonproduction bonuses are excluded. Cost-of-living allowances are considered as part of the workers' regular pay. Hourly earnings reported for salaried workers are derived from regular salaries divided by the corresponding standard hours of work. The wages of learners, apprentices, and handicapped workers are excluded. The mean is computed for each job by totaling the earnings of all workers and dividing by the number of workers. The median designates position — half of the workers receive the same or more and half receive the same or less than the rate shown. The middle range is defined by two rates of pay: a fourth of the workers earn the same or less than the lower of these rates and a fourth earn the same or more than the higher rate.
[2] Includes workers other than those presented separately.
[3] Includes all drivers regardless of size and type of truck operated.

NUMBER OF WORKERS RECEIVING STRAIGHT-TIME HOURLY EARNINGS (IN DOLLARS) OF--

2.80 AND UNDER 3.20	3.20–3.60	3.60–4.00	4.00–4.40	4.40–4.80	4.80–5.20	5.20–5.60	5.60–6.00	6.00–6.40	6.40–6.80	6.80–7.20	7.20–7.60	7.60–8.00	8.00–8.80	8.80–9.60	9.60–10.40	10.40–11.20	11.20–12.00	12.00–12.80	12.80–13.60
-	-	-	12	41	35	40	46	38	24	22	24	38	49	25	16	7	3	-	-
-	-	-	-	-	-	-	1	4	3	1	1	1	2	-	1	-	2	-	-
-	-	-	-	4	10	13	19	15	2	2	-	2	-	3	14	5	-	-	-
-	-	-	1	22	8	13	8	8	2	2	9	23	42	20	1	1	1	-	-
-	-	-	3	4	3	6	9	9	16	15	11	9	5	1	-	-	-	-	-
-	-	-	8	11	14	8	9	2	1	2	3	1	-	1	-	1	-	-	-
-	-	-	5	4	6	-	5	6	6	21	3	3	2	-	3	-	-	-	-
-	-	-	4	3	2	-	2	2	4	21	3	1	2	-	3	-	-	-	-
-	-	-	1	1	4	-	3	4	2	-	-	2	-	-	-	-	-	-	-
-	5	8	2	2	2	1	-	-	-	-	-	-	-	-	6	-	-	-	-
-	5	8	2	1	1	-	-	-	-	-	-	-	-	-	6	-	-	-	-
-	25	2	4	-	6	-	-	-	-	-	-	-	-	-	-	-	-	-	-
-	25	2	4	-	6	-	-	-	-	-	-	-	-	-	-	-	-	-	-
-	15	4	6	-	3	-	1	2	3	-	-	1	-	-	-	-	-	-	-
-	2	8	21	35	29	21	8	10	5	7	2	2	9	-	1	-	-	-	-
-	-	-	2	10	11	6	3	5	4	7	2	2	9	-	1	-	-	-	-
-	2	8	18	25	18	15	5	5	1	-	-	-	-	-	-	-	-	-	-
-	-	-	6	3	11	13	7	10	5	9	8	4	33	15	7	-	-	-	-
-	-	-	6	3	11	11	6	6	3	7	7	4	20	-	1	-	-	-	-
-	-	6	13	6	11	12	14	8	7	9	9	10	13	8	3	-	-	-	-
-	-	-	-	-	-	-	-	2	-	-	-	-	5	3	2	-	-	-	-
-	-	-	-	-	1	3	8	1	4	1	4	7	7	5	1	-	-	-	-
-	-	2	11	6	8	9	5	5	3	8	5	3	1	-	-	-	-	-	-
-	-	-	-	-	-	-	-	1	-	4	3	4	6	31	3	10	2	-	-
-	-	-	-	-	-	-	-	-	-	-	-	-	-	1	-	9	2	-	-
-	-	-	-	-	-	-	-	-	-	-	-	-	19	49	-	8	21	-	-
-	-	-	-	-	-	-	6	-	-	-	-	8	106	63	30	22	26	3	-
-	-	-	-	-	-	-	8	-	-	15	13	-	10	11	-	4	3	16	-
-	-	-	-	-	-	-	-	-	-	-	-	-	3	37	13	59	66	11	4
-	-	-	-	-	-	-	-	-	-	9	-	1	6	-	-	-	-	-	-
-	-	-	-	-	-	-	-	-	-	9	-	-	-	-	8	-	-	-	-
-	10	27	48	4	16	5	-	1	65	76	13	-	9	-	-	-	160	74	-
-	1	6	-	4	1	5	-	1	65	76	13	-	4	-	-	-	98	74	-
8	-	-	6	-	1	7	3	-	-	-	-	5	-	-	6	-	-	-	-
-	3	9	6	11	13	5	64	42	-	12	40	-	-	-	4	-	-	-	-
-	12	-	2	-	4	18	34	111	45	46	53	-	23	3	42	-	2	-	-
-	4	2	-	7	14	2	-	-	6	-	5	2	30	6	-	-	-	-	-
-	4	2	-	5	14	2	-	-	6	-	5	2	30	6	-	-	-	-	-
184	94	49	8	48	42	16	9	24	21	15	9	-	4	-	-	-	-	-	-

Source: Bureau of Labor Statistics, March 1981.

carefully before attempting to get external wage rate information. If they make mistakes in defining the external market, their wage rate estimate will be inappropriate. A compensation planner who defines the market too narrowly may estimate an external wage rate much higher than needed in order to attract adequate labor, driving up costs unnecessarily. On the other hand, too loose a definition of the market's boundaries may result in estimating an external rate below what the company will have to pay in order to attract labor.

An Example

In practice the art of properly defining a labor market can become quite complicated. The Lexington, Kentucky, labor market for assemblers provides a good example of this point. Geographically, Lexington and the Bluegrass district is quite distinct, situated roughly eighty miles south of Cincinnati, Ohio, and eighty miles east of Louisville, Kentucky. In the 1980s there are approximately thirty divisions of major companies with assembly operations in this market, including IBM's Office Products Division, Square D, Trane Corporation, WABCO (Westinghouse Airbrake), an American Can Company Dixie Cup Division, Clark Equipment Company, Whirlpool, Hobart, and Rockwell International. All of these companies are paying roughly the same starting hourly rate for assembly workers except Rockwell International, which is paying almost twice the rate of the others. The reason for this is that the employees at Rockwell's plant, its truck axle division, are represented by the United Automobile Workers (UAW) and have a labor contract that is negotiated at the industry level and specifies the same wage rate for all employees covered, whether in Detroit, Atlanta, or Lexington, Kentucky. Such a contract is an artificial constraint, not representative of economic conditions in the Bluegrass market. It would be irrational for other employers in this market to set their rates in competition with Rockwell's as long as there are enough assemblers seeking work locally.

Wage and Employment Determination: Understanding the Dynamics of Demand and Supply

Managers will find it fruitful to turn to basic economic theory in an effort to understand why wage rates vary across occupations and labor markets. An economic view of labor markets focuses on the interaction of the demand for labor, or how much employers are *willing to pay,* and the supply of labor, or how much workers are *willing to accept,* to answer the following questions:

1. What level will the wage rate be for an occupation?
2. How many people will be employed?
3. How much more will an employer have to pay to attract more employees?
4. How would the number of people a company would employ change if the wage rate were lower? were higher?

Exhibit 2.2 represents a very simple illustration of supply and demand. The vertical axis displays wage rates from $1.00 to $25.00 per hour. The horizontal axis displays the number of employees hired by a company, from 100 to 1,000. Economic theory regarding labor demand and labor supply attempts to explain wage rate levels (the vertical axis) and number of people employed (horizontal axis). The major economic theory addressing the question of wage level and employment is called the *Marginal Revenue Product* (MRP) model.[5] At the level of an entire labor market (for example, the market for electrical engineers) the MRP model is a theory of wages, explaining why electrical engineers command wage rates that are different from those of secretaries, for example. At the level of the single employer, MRP is a theory of employment level, explaining, for example, why IBM will employ fifty electrical engineers at its Lexington, Kentucky, division.

Labor Demand

Exhibit 2.3 displays a single employer's demand for labor (line *D*). This line is called the firm's Marginal Revenue Product (MRP) function and represents the *additional revenue product* (product produced multiplied by the price at which the employer can sell the product) that each additional unit of labor (or new employee added) will generate. For the manager, the MRP function (or curve) represents the highest wage a company is willing to pay for various amounts of labor. In our example, for instance, $10.00 is the highest wage rate the company would be willing to pay for 500 employees. The price this company would be willing to pay gets higher with less employment and lower with additional employment.

Theoretically, the labor demand curve (MRP function) could take

Exhibit 2.2   The Interaction of Labor Demand and Supply

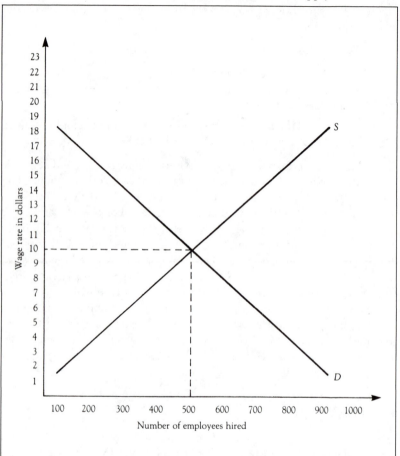

on any form. In our example, it slopes downward from left to right, indicating that as additional employees are hired, the revenue product generated per employee drops. This is a characteristic slope for companies operating at the margin in many different labor markets for the following reasons:

1. A firm's demand for labor is a *derived demand.* It is derived from the market demand for the company's product or service. The slope of the demand for the company's product or service will influence the slope

of the company's demand for labor. Many companies (especially large firms characteristic of our economy) face downward-sloping demands for their products. The lower the price of an automobile, the more cars will be sold. Thus, we would expect the demand for labor in a typical firm to have a downward slope.

2. Technological and physical limitations come into play in the short run. Most employers cannot add physical plant and equipment continuously. They build a building, outfit it with equipment, and hire em-

Exhibit 2.3   The Interaction of Labor Demand and Supply When Supply Is Elastic

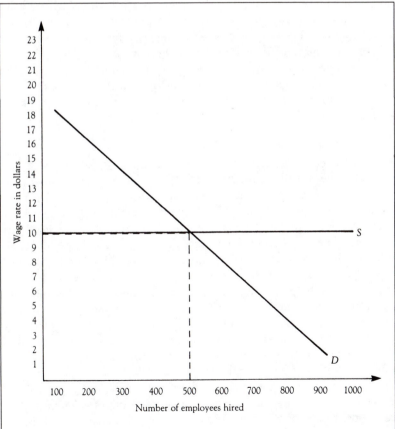

ployees as needed. At some time in the hiring process the employer will reach what economists call a point of *diminishing returns to scale*. That is, as the number of employees hired begins to approach the physical and technological capacities of the work site, each employee will become less efficient. For this reason, as well, we would expect an employer's demand for labor to slope downward from left to right.

Mahoney has pointed out that when companies are not operating at the margin, marginal revenue product cannot be interpreted as determining the employer's level of demand for labor. In these cases it is more realistic to view labor demand as determined by the organization's sales forecasts and plans for production. Still, Mahoney points out that an understanding of the concept of *average net revenue product* (the revenue product produced per unit labor minus all production costs other than labor) is of direct relevance in determining wage rates and differences in wage rates employers are willing to pay the same occupation.[6]

If we were to combine the employer's demand for labor (*D* in Exhibit 2.3) with all other employers' demand for labor in the market, we would obtain the aggregate or total demand for labor in that specific market.

Labor Supply

Economic theory is less well developed and explicit concerning the supply of labor (line *S* in Exhibits 2.2 and 2.3). Technically, labor supply is a function or curve representing the *minimum wage rate* necessary to attract a given number of employees. Classical economic theorists assumed that markets were perfectly competitive (characterized by many small employers and many people seeking employment under conditions of perfect information, mobility, and long-run equilibrium). Under these conditions, we would expect the supply function faced by single employers in the market to be perfectly horizontal (see Exhibit 2.3). This condition would imply that employers could hire as many additional employees as they need at a single wage rate ($10.00 per hour in our example). This is probably true for many small employers in the United States today.

More recent theoretical developments, however, suggest several reasons for expecting large employers to face labor supply functions that slope upward from left to right as illustrated in Exhibit 2.2.[7] We will examine three of these developments here: the work of economist Lloyd Reynolds, the work of economists in the field of human capital theory, and the special case of a labor union.

Lloyd Reynolds

Economist Lloyd Reynolds suggested five conditions under which we could expect an individual employer to face an upward-sloping supply of labor:[8]

1. **Monopsony.** Monopsony is an economic concept describing a market in which one large purchaser dominates the market. Markets dominated by a few large purchasers would approach this condition, as oligopoly approaches monopoly when we think of sellers. In our example, General Motors, Ford, and Chrysler could be considered close to monopsonistic purchasers of labor in the Detroit, Michigan, labor market. Monopsonists find that because of their size they must pay increasingly higher wage rates to attract additional units of labor. Unlike the small competitive employer in classical economic theory, the monopsonist has a significant effect on the entire labor market when expanding or contracting employment.

2. **Employee ignorance of job openings.** It is possible to imagine labor markets in which people have perfect information about all job openings. However, we know that in reality, information is imperfect and often costs resources to obtain. Thus, we might expect an already employed person who is reasonably satisfied with his or her current employment to be unaware of and unaffected by a wage being offered by a competitor for the same job. The only problem with this explanation, as Reynolds points out, is that it proposes that knowledge of a wage rate is a positive function of the level of the rate. Thus, the higher the wage rate, the more people will be aware of and influenced by it. Reynolds (as well as Adam Smith) rejects this logic, but the issue remains unresolved empirically to date.[9]

3. **Variation among workers for monetary and nonmonetary reward combinations.** Compensation experts have pointed out that monetary reward, in the form of a wage rate, is only one element in the total reward structure of interest to a prospective employee. Working conditions, chances for advancement, flexibility of working hours and job assignment, and interpersonal relationships are just a few nonmonetary conditions that may be of equal concern. Reynolds proposes that different employers represent to employees different combinations of monetary and nonmonetary rewards. For example, employees who are unwilling to face commuting hassles even for higher wage rates may prefer to remain in

lower-paying jobs closer to their homes. If we presume that, at any point in time, employed workers have found employment with a satisfactory balance of conditions, then an employer who wants to expand his employment may have to raise wages to compensate new employees for leaving what is for them already a preferred combination of wage and nonwage conditions.

4. **Overcoming risk.** Thomas Mahoney and other compensation theorists have carefully pointed out that a person changes jobs and accepts an offer of employment with a certain amount of personal risk.[10] Consider someone, currently employed by a company as an engineer, who receives an offer of employment from a competitor. She is completely familiar with her current employment situation. She not only knows the rate of her payment but she knows all the positive and negative nonmonetary aspects of her job. She knows what it is like to work for her supervisor and with her coworkers, for example. In contrast, she does not have the same knowledge about the job being offered. All she knows for sure is the wage rate being offered. She has no way to know about things like working conditions, supervision quality, relations with coworkers, and similar conditions until she is actually on the job. Economic theory suggests that the bidding competitor will have to offer an economic premium to make it worth the engineer's while to take on the risk of a job change.

5. **Geographic barriers.** Finally, we know that many occupational markets have geographic constraints. Thus, for example, it is unlikely that the market for assembly workers in Dallas, Texas extends beyond the immediate environs of that community. Unless faced with unemployment (which unfortunately is the case in the early 1980s), a worker in Detroit, Michigan, would be unlikely to seek work in Dallas.

There is an extremely important warning to managers considering the influence of these five conditions on the supply of labor, and it is especially relevant in the 1980s. Reynolds warns that conditions such as monopsony, employee ignorance, preferences for monetary and nonmonetary combinations of conditions, risk, and geographic barriers hold true only as the *market approaches full employment.* When unemployment sets in and deepens, these conditions would not influence labor supply, and employers should find the supply of labor relatively flat and elastic. Thus, in the 1980s, thousands of workers are leaving the upper midwestern centers of Detroit, Cleveland, Dayton, and similar communities, where unemployment rates are the highest since the Great Depression, and moving to Dallas, Houston, Phoenix, and other Sun Belt employment centers, where jobs are more plentiful.

Human Capital Theory

A branch of economic theory developed in the 1960s that proposed that a person offering his services on the market carries value to the extent that he has had to expend money, time, and other personal resources acquiring skills necessary to perform a job. Thus, a physician invests time and money to acquire the skills employed in the practice of medicine, because he expects financial gain. Consider, further, the differences between an occupation that requires a substantial outlay in training cost and time (for example, an attorney) and one that requires only minimal levels of such cost (for example, an assembly-line job). We would expect, on the basis of training cost alone, that it would be more difficult to attract additional attorneys than assembly-line workers. Economist Gary Becker provides the most complete analysis of this reasoning.[11] According to this logic, the costs of training and other preparation restricts entry into the occupation and creates an upward slope to the supply curve faced by individual employers.

Economist Lester Thurow presents an alternative view of labor supply that would also lead one to expect an upward sloping (inelastic) supply of labor to the firm.[12] Thurow proposes that wage competition does not take place in the labor market, logic that runs contrary to the MRP model presented earlier. According to traditional economic theory, workers compete for wages. Thurow finds reason to doubt this; he believes instead that workers compete for *job openings* or opportunities. Indeed, he hypothesizes that a queue (or waiting line) forms for every job opening that comes onto a market. He believes, further, that the workers in the queue represent varying levels of skills and aptitude relevant to the job. Finally, he argues, the employer orders those in the queue according to these qualities and selects the best prospect. The best prospect will be least costly to train and orient and will be the most productive. Each person back in the queue will be more costly to train and will be less productive, even though the same wage is being paid. Thus, the cost of each successive unit in the queue increases, leading to an upward-sloping supply of labor faced by the firm.

The Special Case of a Labor Union

So far in our analysis of labor supply, we have considered only economic factors that would contribute to an upward slope in the supply of labor faced by an employer. Economist Alan Cartter has examined how a labor union can also influence the supply of labor to a firm.[13] Although it is not accurate to consider a union representing a group of employees as a broker of labor (federal law, for example, prohibits agreements by which employers agree to hire only union members in most cases), it is correct to consider the union as the *sole bargaining agent* for a group of employees. The union, then, influences the wage to be paid labor through the process of collective bargaining.

Cartter has analyzed the tradeoffs the union must consider between employment levels and wage rates when entering a labor negotiation. His analysis is presented in Exhibit 2.4. The straight lines in the exhibit (N_1 to N_{12}) represent alternative levels of labor demand on the part of the employer with whom the union is about to bargain. N_6 is the employer's current level of demand, and point P_1 represents the current wage/employment bargain. The kinked lines L_1 to L_{11} are called indifference curves and represent points of indifference in tradeoffs between wage rates and employment levels for the union negotiators. Thus, for example, all wage/employment combinations along L_3 are equally valued by the union. The union, however, would prefer to get an agreement that falls on the indifference curve farthest to the upper right in Exhibit 2.4. Thus, for example, L_2 is valued more highly than L_1, L_3 is more valued than L_2, and so forth.

The analysis in Exhibit 2.4 tells us that the union will seek a wage and employment combination that places it on the highest indifference curve, given the employer's demand curve. Thus, if the employer's demand increases from N_6 to N_8 in Exhibit 2.4, we would expect the union to bargain for a wage/employment combination of P_2 because that would place the union on the highest indifference curve (L_7) possible, given labor demand (N_8). Any other combination of wage rate employment along N_8 would place the union on a lower indifference curve.

The line connecting each of these preferred wage/employment combinations is called a *wage preference path* by Cartter and constitutes the estimate of suppy faced by the firm in collective bargaining. The shape of the wage preference path is kinked at point P in Exhibit 2.4 and

Exhibit 2.4   Union Preferences Between Wages and Employment

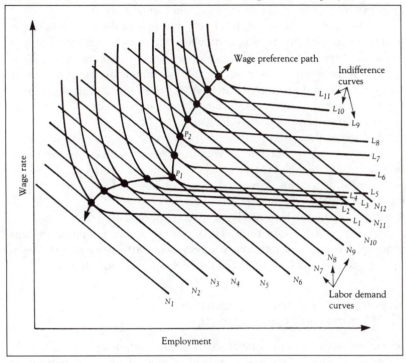

Source: Allan M. Cartter, *Theory of Wages and Employment* (Homewood, Ill.: Richard D. Irwin, Inc., 1959), p. 91. Used by permission.

represents the union's changing interests depending on whether it anticipates an expansion or a decline in labor demand from the present point.

If the union leaders, for example, anticipate an expanding demand for labor, they will pursue increases in wage rates at the expense of employment. Thus, as Cartter points out, the union will emphasize wage issues and play down expansion or even security of employment.[14] If, on the other hand, the union anticipates that labor demand will contract, it will place a priority on maintaining wage rates even at the expense of employment levels. Thus, unions often bargain for seniority as the basis for laying off employees. An exception to this pattern was negotiations between the United Automobile Workers (UAW) and major automobile manufacturers in the early 1980s. In this case, unemployment had become so pervasive that the union was willing to trade wage rates for employment security. In many cases, unions were willing to forego increases in wage rates in order to maintain or increase employment levels.

In summary to this point, it is likely that at least three kinds of factors lead to an upward-sloping supply of labor, which most firms face, at least in the short run: (1) factors creating labor scarcity (monopsony, employee ignorance, preferences for monetary and nonmonetary rewards, risk in changing jobs, and geographic barriers), (2) the varying degrees of human capital represented by people available for employment, and (3) trade union preferences in collective bargaining.

Economic theory tells us that at the level of an entire labor market the supply of labor available at various wage rates takes on an upward slope from left to right (as in Exhibit 2.2) in the short run. There are several reasons for this. First, the supply of labor is limited in the short run at the level of the market. If supply is to increase, more people will have to be attracted into the labor market, from nonwork or from other markets. In many occupations, entry to the market is limited or time consuming because of training requirements, certification, union membership requirements, or the need for geographical movement.

Wage and Employment Determination: The Demand and Supply Interaction

So far we have examined labor demand and supply by themselves. In order to understand how forces in external labor markets influence wage and employment levels, we must examine the interaction of labor demand and supply. Refer back, once more, to Exhibits 2.2 and 2.3. Marginal Revenue Product (MRP) theory predicts that the wage level and employment level in a given labor market will be determined by the *intersection* of the labor demand and supply functions. Thus, at the level of the market, the workers in the occupation whose market is modeled in Exhibit 2.2 make $10.00 per hour because of both demand and supply conditions. Ten dollars is the price that clears the market. It is the price *both* that employers are willing to pay and that employees are willing to accept.

Labor economists refer to the price that clears the labor market as the *exchange rate* of labor; it represents a major basis for considering the value of a job. Indeed, *external equity* is defined as the *exchange rate for labor on a job clearing in the external labor market.*

To answer the question of how much labor will be employed we must consider Exhibits 2.2 and 2.3 at the level of the firm. The MRP model predicts that each firm will continue hiring labor until the last employee hired is equal to its marginal revenue product. At this point, the marginal cost of labor to the employer is exactly equal to the marginal revenue it generates: there is no more profit to be made. If the employer stops hirinig short of this point he is foregoing profit that could be made. If the employer hires beyond this point, he will be incurring losses. Thus, the employer maximizes profit when the MRP of the last employee hired equals its marginal cost.

External Wage Structures

A final task for managers in managing external equity is to become familiar with external wage structures. It is important to recognize (as we pointed out at the beginning of this chapter) that companies face a variety of labor markets in staffing their jobs. Levels of supply and demand vary across these markets and, thus, it is not surprising to find a considerable variation in wage rates across occupations (see, for example, Exhibit 2.1).

Marginal productivity analysis, however, explains only the broad forces that create wage differences. Thus, the MRP model does not predict the actual dollar at which a wage will fall, but rather, a range of wage rates within which the actual wage will fall. It is probably more realistic for the practicing compensation manager to consider MRP theory as illustrated in Exhibit 2.5. MRP theory is able to tell us that the likely wage and employment combination will fall somewhere in the shaded area *ABCD*. Within this range we must turn to structural and institutional considerations and understand wage and employment levels. One of the most important concepts in this regard is John Dunlop's notion of the *wage contour*.[15]

The Wage Contour

Dunlop defines a wage contour as

> a stable group of wage determining units (bargaining units, plants, or firms) which are so linked together by (1) similarity of product markets, (2) resort to similar sources for a labor force, or (3) common market orga-nization (custom) that they have common wage-making characteristics. The wage rates for a particular occupation in a particular firm are not

Exhibit 2.5   Marginal Productivity Theory Predicts Wage and Employment Ranges

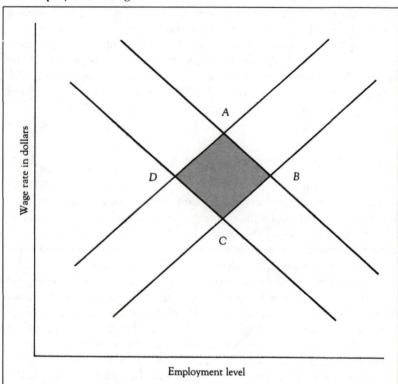

ordinarily independent of all other wage rates; they are more closely related to the wage rates of some firms than to others. A contour for particular occupations is to be defined in terms of both product market and the labor market. A contour, thus, has three dimensions: (1) particular occupations or job clusters, (2) a sector of industry, and (3) a geographical location.[16]

To illustrate the existence of wage contours, Dunlop used the fact that beer truck drivers and laundry truck drivers in Boston are paid different wage rates. In this case, members of the same occupation were in two different contours (determined by industry) in which two different wage rates prevailed. It is important for the compensation manager to pay close attention to external wage contours when trying to bring a company's wage structure into line with the external market. Estimates of market contours must be developed through wage and salary surveys, to be discussed fully in Chapter 6.

Summary

In this chapter we have been concerned with external equity in compensation practice. External equity refers to setting wage rates for jobs that correspond to those prevailing in external markets—markets from which the employer hires. An employer that ignores the external market will not survive for long.

External equity is a complex and sometimes confusing criterion because employers face a variety of external markets. Care must be taken in choosing the criteria (geography, education, industry, experience, and so forth) used to define the boundaries of the market. Movement from one market to the next is quite restricted, especially in the short run. Differing supply and demand characteristics across segmented markets lead to differences in wage rates.

In order to understand why wage rates vary across markets, the manager must thoroughly understand the dynamics of supply and demand within a labor market. These dynamics are essential in answering the following questions: (1) What level will the wage rate be for a given job? (2) How many people will be employed? (3) How much more will an employer have to pay in order to attract additional employees? and (4) How will the number of people a company would employ change if the wage rate were lower or higher?

Marginal Revenue Product (MRP) theory defines a firm's demand for labor as derived from its product demand. Because many firms face a downward-sloping demand for their products and because of the principle of diminishing returns to scale, most compensation managers face a downward-sloping demand for labor, especially in the short run.

We examined three bodies of theory, Reynold's notions of labor scarcity, human capital theory, and labor union behavior, which suggest that in the short run most firms face upward-sloping labor supply functions. Thus, a firm will have to pay more for additional units of labor or employees.

In order to understand wage and employment levels we must consider the interaction of labor demand and supply. We concluded that the intersection of labor demand—what employers are willing to pay—and labor supply—what employees are willing to accept—defines the *exchange rate of labor* and should be considered by the compensation planner as the basis for establishing external equity in setting wage rates for jobs.

Finally, compensation managers should note that a model such as Marginal Revenue Product theory explains only the outer limits of a wage rate. Institutional factors must be considered in addition to supply and demand to get a finer estimate of actual wage rates prevailing in external markets. In this regard, Dunlop's notion of a wage contour is useful. A wage contour is a stable group of wage-determining units (employers) linked by similar product markets and labor markets, and by a common market organization.

Notes

1. Herbert A. Simon, *Administrative Behavior*, 3rd ed. (New York: The Free Press, 1976), p. xxviii.

2. L. G. Reynolds, "Some Aspects of Labor Market Structure," in R. A. Lester and J. Shister (eds.), *Insights into Labor Issues* (New York: Macmillan, 1949); L. G. Reynolds, *The Structure of Labor Markets* (New York: Harper, 1951).

Orme Phelps, "A Structural Model of the U.S. Labor Market," in the President's Committee to Appraise Employment and Unemployment Statistics, *Measuring Employment and Unemployment* (Washington, D.C.: U.S. Government Printing Office, 1962).

3. Ibid.

4. Marc J. Wallace, Jr., N. Fredric Crandall, and Charles H. Fay, *Administering Human Resources: An Introduction to the Profession* (New York: Random House, 1982), Chap. 5.

5. Alan M. Cartter, *Theory of Wages and Employment* (Homewood, Ill.: Richard D. Irwin, 1959).

6. Thomas A. Mahoney, *Compensation and Reward Perspectives* (Homewood, Ill.: Richard D. Irwin, 1979), pp. 118–19.

7. See Alan M. Cartter, ibid., for a more thorough analysis.

8. Lloyd G. Reynolds, "The Supply of Labor to the Firm," *Quarterly Journal of Economics* 60 (1946): 390–411.

9. Ibid.; Adam Smith, *The Wealth of Nations*, 1776 (New York: Random House, 1937, abridged).

10. Thomas A. Mahoney, *Compensation and Reward Perspectives* (Homewood, Ill.: Richard D. Irwin, 1979).

11. Gary S. Becker, *Human Capital* (New York: National Bureau for Economic Research, 1964).

12. Lester C. Thurow, *Generating Inequality* (New York: Basic Books, 1975).

13. Cartter, *Theory of Wages and Employment.*

14. Ibid.

15. John Dunlop, "The Task of Contemporary Wage Theory," in George W. Taylor and Frank C. Pierson (eds.), *New Concepts in Wage Determination* (New York: McGraw Hill, Inc.,1957).

16. Ibid., p. 131.

3

Internal Equity

⌐ The current comparable-worth controversy (discussed in Chapter 1) provides a striking example of the need for managers to keep external and internal equity separate in their thinking about job worth or value. The three recent pay discrimination cases involving sex (*Lemons et al. v. the City and County of Denver, Gunther v. the County of Washington,* and the *International Union of Electrical Workers v. Westinghouse Electrical Corp.*, cited in Chapter 1) have questioned the adequacy of an external market exchange rate (external equity) as a criterion of job worth.[1] In this chapter we will explore several nonmarket bases for valuing jobs.

After reading this chapter you should realize that our knowledge about judging the internal worth of a job, apart from its external exchange value, is far less developed than our knowledge of external markets. Indeed, a major challenge that faces the compensation profession in the 1980s is to develop both the theory and the practice regarding the internal valuing of jobs.

Internal Equity Defined

In Chapter 1, we defined internal equity as the objective of setting wage rates that conform to the job's internal worth to the employer. Indeed, in each of the comparable worth cases, arguments have been made that although the employer may be paying what the job is paid in the marketplace (external equity), women's jobs are still paid less than men's, even though both jobs are of *equal value* or *worth* to the employer (internal equity).

A number of compensation theorists have long pointed out that the exchange rate, presented in Chapter 2, is not a complete criterion for a job's value. Thomas Mahoney, for example, demonstrated that labor's exchange value (the maximum price employers are willing to pay and the minimum labor is willing to accept) equals its use value (the value labor creates for an employer) only if there is (1) long-run general equilibrium and (2) perfect competition in all markets.[2] These assumptions do not coincide with the real world of segmented labor markets as described in Chapter 2.

Lester Thurow also questions the value of an exchange rate as an adequate definition of a job's value.[3] He reasons that very little wage competition actually takes place in contemporary labor markets. He proposes that external wage rates correspond less to the differences in value to employers than they do to cultural norms about fair or equitable distribution of wage rates and incomes across jobs and occupations, an idea, as you will see, that is very similar to the Just Price doctrine of the Middle Ages (see p. 50). Thus, Thurow's ideas lead to the conclusion that a job's external value lies not in an exchange rate, but rather in its relative place in a wage contour (described in Chapter 2, pp. 41–43) reflecting social norms.

Whether we conclude that external equity lies in an exchange rate or in a wage contour defined by society's norms or industry factors, neither criterion defines what value the job is creating for the employer—the central issue in internal equity. Indeed, this is a problem for the compensation profession, because we have very little theory and research to guide us in selecting criteria of internal worth.

Is Job Evaluation the Answer?

Some experts have proposed that job evaluation might be an answer to our problem.[4] Job evaluation is a formal process by which management assigns wage rates to jobs according to some preestablished formula (we will examine such techniques in detail in Chapter 7). Most job evaluation techniques employ *compensable factors* in assessing job worth. A compensable factor provides a base for defining the internal worth of a job. The most commonly employed compensable factors are: (1) responsibility, (2) skill required by the job, (3) effort required, and (4) working conditions.

Those four compensable factors can be traced directly to the U.S. War Labor Board during World War II.[5] One of the Board's major concerns was to make sure that women, who were for the first time moving in large numbers into industrial jobs vacated by men going into uniform, would be paid the same wage as men for work on the "same or similar operations." The four factors of responsibility, skill, effort, and working conditions were adopted as a convenient basis for determining comparability among jobs and subsequently became adopted in almost all job evaluation schemes. Indeed, these four factors were codified in the Equal Pay Act of 1963, a law designed to insure women against sex discrimination in pay. Legal developments subsequent to the Equal Pay Act (to be explored more fully in Chapter 5, pp. 94–95) have set precedents using the four compensable factors to determine pay discrimination against women. Sex-based wage differences have been justified when the jobs in question were demonstrated to be substantially different on one of these dimensions.

It would appear, then, that job evaluation addressing such compensable factors as skill, responsibility, effort, and working conditions might be an answer to the problem of defining internal equity apart from external equity. In practice, though, job evaluation remains a neutral administrative tool for making job evaluation scores (the value assigned to jobs) conform to *any* definition of worth, internal or external.[6] There is an even more difficult problem in practice, however, and that is forcing the compensable factor data in job evaluation to conform to external wage rate data. Donald Schwab, and D. J. Treiman and H. I. Hartman in two recent reviews of job evaluation practices have concluded that it is common among compensation practitioners to use statistical methods (including multiple linear regression) to force internal job evaluation scores to coincide with external market wage rate distributions.[7] This practice obviously confounds external and internal equity and renders job evaluation as a tool merely for bringing internal wage structures into close alignment with external wage structures.[8] Most experts agree, then, that job evaluation as often practiced merely reflects external exchange rates and does not adequately define job worth apart from such external rates.

Economist Ruth Blumrosen points out that the problem of not assessing internal equity apart from external equity is compounded for women to the extent that external wages reflect patterns of long-standing sex discrimination and segregation in external markets.[9] She points out instances in which society valued the work of women less than that of men and those judgments were reflected in the marketplace for jobs. If she is correct, job evaluation schemes that force internal data into line with external data will only perpetuate sex discrimination in pay.

Unfortunately, then, job evaluation is not, in and of itself, an answer to our field's problem with internal equity. At best, it remains a neutral administrative tool for ensuring consistency in managers' judgments about job worth. The field of compensation is just now breaking new ground in a search for bases of job worth internal to the organization. We will examine and integrate several bases in economic and sociological theory for addressing the problem of internal equity in the remainder of this chapter. Such knowledge should prove beneficial for two reasons. First, it will allow us to better explain and understand managers' actual judgments of a job's internal value. Second, it will allow us to ask normative questions about wage setting in organizations. That is, better knowledge about the internal sources of job worth will allow us to ask more readily if specific wage setting practices achieve the norm of internal equity.

Classical Approaches to Job Value

Society's concern with fairness in pay is not new. As early as the Middle Ages religious leaders in Europe were concerned with setting wage rates for crafts and trades. In the eighteenth century, Adam Smith, the intellectual father of market analysis, grappled with the problem of determining the value of labor on a job. And, in the nineteenth century, Karl Marx, the intellectual father of the Communist ethic, extended Smith's ideas about the value created by labor on a job.

The Just Price Doctrine

During the Middle Ages, the Church in Western Europe decreed that occupations should be paid a just price or wage.[10] According to this doctrine, a just price is one that corresponds to the occupation's station in the social hierarchy. The major proposition in the Just Price doctrine is that a job's value derives from the status of the occupation in society (an idea, incidently, that corresponds very closely to Thurow's belief that cultural value, not exchange rates, determine external wage distribution in society).

Strictly speaking, the Just Price doctrine is not a statement of internal equity. It is important in this context, however, because it provides a basis for using social values much broader than an economic exchange for justifying wage differentials. One can see the premises of a just price theory, for example, in charges that it is unfair to pay nurses less than parking meter repairers. Managers should be aware, therefore, that one major source of equity that goes beyond market criteria is a concern with a job's place in the social pecking order.

The Labor Theory of Value

As articulated by Adam Smith, the labor theory of value directly addresses the worth that labor contributes to a job.[11] Smith proposed that commodities gain value according to the amount of labor necessary to produce them. Thus, value is created through the application of labor.

Smith also reasoned that labor's value is measured not only in simple hours but also as a function of five *job characteristics:* (1) hardship or unpleasantness, (2) difficulty of learning the job, (3) stability of employment, (4) responsibility or trust inherent in the job, and (5) chances of success or failure inherent in the work. One should be struck by the similarity between these criteria and the compensable factors of skill, responsibility, effort, and working conditions cited earlier.[12] Smith's reasoning, then, specifies that a job's worth is the amount of labor (including the five compensable factors just cited) required to carry it out.

Karl Marx

In nineteenth-century England, Karl Marx extended Adam Smith's labor theory of value to the extreme position that labor was the *sole* source of value in an economy. Using the ideas of earlier economic thinkers Thomas Malthus and David Ricardo, he reasoned that wages in the labor market tend toward subsistence levels and that the difference between such wages and the full value created by labor was a surplus exploited by capitalists in the form of profits. Managers should note the inference to be drawn from Marx, specifically, that the exchange rate for labor is not an adequate measure of value; it merely reflects a wage at which labor can be sustained.

Contemporary Approaches to Job Value

We will see that contemporary statements of job worth carry over the classical idea that labor on a job creates value. The labor theory of value remains an important legacy of Smith and Marx. We still need, however, to make more explicit what there is about labor that creates value on a job. To accomplish this we must turn to contemporary models of labor demand and supply.

The Need to Distinguish Demand- and Supply-Side Considerations

The Marginal Revenue Product (MRP) model was presented in Chapter 2 as a model of wage and employment levels. The model defines external equity as the exchange value of labor (that is, the intersect of aggregate supply and demand functions in a specific labor market). We have also seen that many experts doubt the adequacy of exchange rates as measures of labor value (especially internal equity). Thurow, specifically, believes that external rates have less to do with demand/supply intersects than shared cultural norms, and Mahoney suggests that exchange value is not the same as use value in the real world.

Wallace and Fay have proposed that to explore internal equity more fully it will be useful to separate demand-side phenomena from supply-side phenomena and address theory on each side separately.[13] A demand-side perspective focuses on *what happens to or for the employer* when a job is performed. Such outcomes might be economic (marginal revenue product is created) or administrative (a process is successfully completed, a decision is made, or discretion over resources is exercised). Demand-side models are concerned with making such bases for job worth explicit in understanding a manager's demand for labor on a job.

A supply-side perspective on job worth focuses on the *sources of labor supply* and any factors that influence such sources, making supply costly to the employer. Such factors include the fact that occupations vary in the amount of training required, the proportion of training costs borne by the employee and the employer, ease of entry into an occupation, differences in quality among members of the same occupation, and any other factor (including geography) that segments a labor market. Such differences may serve as additional bases for judging the internal value of a job to an employer. In effect, a supply-side perspective suggests that jobs can be valued according to the scarcity, the investment value, or the capacity of labor required to perform a job.

Demand-Side Theory

Marginal Revenue Product and Thurow's Job Competition model. In Chapter 2, we examined the MRP model as a theory of wage and employment levels (pp. 31–34). Economists, however, have judged MRP theory most effective not as a complete model of wage and employment but rather as a model of labor demand and labor's use value in a job.[14] One does not need to assume long-run general equilibrium and perfect competition in all markets to use MRP's core thesis: labor in a job is worth the additional value it creates for the employer. The model, further, breaks marginal revenue product (MRP) into two components: (1) the marginal physical product (MPP) produced by the employee, and (2) the marginal revenue (MR) or price per unit generated when the additional product is sold (that is, $MRP = MR \times MPP$).

Managers should carefully consider the internal value implications of marginal revenue and marginal physical product. The marginal revenue component (MR) suggests that the internal worth of a job to a manager is influenced by the revenue or prices the output of the job can command in the employer's product or service market. This leads one to conclude that, in part, the internal value of labor on a job is derived from the product market demand faced by the employer (an idea we made explicit in the course of Chapter 2).

The marginal physical product (MPP) component refers to the productivity of labor, that is, the number of units of product or service the job can be credited with per unit time. We would expect part of the value of a job to a manager to be influenced by productivity.

Again, we mentioned earlier in this chapter that Lester Thurow questions the value of MRP theory as a model of external wage rates, which he claims are set by cultural rather than marginal economic forces. Thurow's Job Competition model still postulates, however, that job value is derived from the value added (marginal revenue product) through employment. Thurow, in fact, goes so far as to maintain that a job's value lies *solely* in the job itself, and is quite distinct from any qualities of the individual person filling the job. [15]

Both the MRP model and Thurow's Job Competition model make important statements about the sources of job value that a manager should consider. Both statements focus the manager's attention on the *economic value of job outcomes* to the manager or the employer as a basis for determining the internal value or worth of a job. In effect, they tell managers that the bottom line (contribution to profit or other managerial financial objectives) is the appropriate measure of a job's internal worth, and that internal equity is achieved when wages are set according to this contribution.

Time span of discretion. Marginal revenue product theory is an economic definition of a job's contribution to an employer. Elliott Jaques provides a noneconomic, administrative definition of use value by capturing the notion of job responsibility in the concept of *time span of discretion*. Time span of discretion is defined by Jaques as "the maximum period of time during which the use of discretion is authorized and expected without review of that discretion by a superior." [16] Jaques' theory is an important alternative statement of job worth for managers to consider. In effect, the model implies that the exercise of discretion over resources is an important job outcome that employers purchase and provides a basis for valuing the work performed in a job. In effect, time span of discretion is one measure of the level of responsibility on a job.

Supply-Side Theory

We have already examined several models of labor supply (Reynolds's theory, the existence of a labor union, and human capital theory) in Chapter 2. We will reexamine them in this chapter for inferences regarding job value that lie not in the job itself (demand-side theory) but in the character and quality of labor seeking work on the job. These supply-side efforts fall into three major groups: (1) those concentrating on labor's *scarcity value*, (2) those concentrating on labor's *human capital* or *investment value,* and (3) those concentrating on variation in labor's *capacity value.*

Labor's scarcity value.   As we mentioned in Chapter 2, economist Lloyd G. Reynolds proposes the following as factors contributing to labor scarcity in the short run under conditions approaching full employment:[17]

the employer's monopsonist influence (when employers in a market are few and large relative to labor supplies)

employees' ignorance of job openings

employees' preferences for monetary and nonmonetary reward combinations

employees' willingness to take on the risk if changing jobs

geographic barriers

Of concern to the compensation manager is that such factors contribute to labor scarcity during periods approaching full employment.

In addition to these factors, union organization contributes to labor scarcity. Alan Cartter's analysis of union leadership preferences in collective bargaining (examined in Chapter 2, pp. 38–40) suggests that union leaders prefer to use increases in labor demand primarily for wage improvements, at the expense of employment, and will resist wage cuts with decreases in labor demand, again at the expense of employment, unless unemployment becomes a long-term and deep problem for the union's membership, as it has in the automobile industry. In most circumstances, then, the result of the union's attempt to place upward pressure on wages is to contribute to labor scarcity.

Labor's human capital value.   The adaptation of financial capital models to labor supply offers a second major supply-side perspective on job worth. Economist Gary Becker and others have developed models of the economic value created by the investment of resources in the development of skills and knowledge required by various jobs.[18] According to human capital theory, wages are in part a return on the investment of resources in developing skills.

Of key importance to the issues of judging job worth is Becker's distinction between *general* and *specific* training.[19] General training contributes marginal revenue product (MRP) in all employment settings. At the extreme, if training were perfectly general, the results would be equally valuable to all employers bidding in the labor market and MRP would be equal for all employers. Firms providing for or investing in such training could not capture any of the return to such equity.

Specific training (as well as employer-specific recruiting, screening, and orientation costs), in contrast, is an investment that contributes to the marginal revenue product of the employer providing it and not to other employers. At the extreme, specific training contributes MRP only to the employer providing it.

Compensation managers should carefully consider the distinction between general and specific training when thinking about the sources of value in a job. In the extreme case of general training, the job applicants pay for all training costs and earns all the equity value of his or her new skills. Employers bid for that value (the wage competition model in Thurow's terms). In this extreme case, value resides solely in the person and not in the job. We would expect, further, that employers would bid for those skills and such value would be an important supply-side basis for valuing a job internally.

In the extreme opposite case of specific training, the employer pays all the development costs and earns the equity in the value created. In fact, this extreme case corresponds to Thurow's job competition model. In this extreme case, labor to a job carries no inherent value and all worth lies in the job itself.

Compensation managers should recognize that in most cases some combination of specific and general training is required to fill a job. Thus, both job factors and individual employee factors become appropriate anchors for making job-worth judgments.

Labor's capacity value.   Human capital theory proposes that job seekers bring valued general skills to the job. In addition, a broad reach of research findings suggest that within a labor or occupational market people vary widely in their skills. Some accountants are more skilled than others. Some electricians are more competent than others. Lester Thurow proposes the interesting idea that labor queues form for each job opening that appears in a market (an idea we explored in detail in Chapter 2, p. 37).[20] He proposes, further, that the employer orders the job applicants in the queue according to each person's skill, and selects the most skilled applicant available. The best prospect will be least costly to train and will be the most productive. More important, people farther back on the ordered queue will be more expensive to train and less productive, even though the same wage is being paid.

The practicing manager should recognize that attending to differences in labor's capacity value will be extremely important when trying to staff jobs that rely highly on general training, such as the jobs of engineers, physicians, attorneys, geologists, or computer systems analysts. Concern with variation in labor's capacity value will not be so great for managers when trying to staff jobs that do not rely heavily on general training, for example, materials handling, low-level clerical work, and unskilled assembly jobs. The point is that jobs do vary in the importance of general training. We would expect among those jobs where general training is critical that labor's capacity value would be an important basis for judging the internal worth of those jobs.

Sociological Views of Job Worth

The demand-side and supply-side models of job worth we have just presented provide a rather narrow economic view of the notion of job worth. Several theorists have provided an additional, broader sociological view of job worth of concern to the compensation manager. The most important work in this regard is that of Thomas Mahoney, who has proposed that a job's place in a formal organizational hierarchy alone, apart from any job content elements, is an important determinant of perceived job worth.[21] He reasons that norms exist in our society regarding the power, influence, and status associated with levels in a formal, organizational hierarchy.

Mahoney cited the work of Herbert Simon in the 1950s as the basis for his ideas.[22] Simon proposed that hierarchical level, apart from any other job or organizational characteristic, is a major factor influencing the level of executive compensation. He specified his ideas in the following model:

$$C = Ab^{L-1}$$

where: C = compensation of the chief executive

A = salary for management trainees

b = proportional compensation difference between adjacent hierarchical levels

L = number of levels in the organization.

Mahoney focused on estimating the coefficient, b, in Simon's model and reports intriguing empirical results. He reported a wide range of data relevant to estimating the coefficient b, including:

United States salary survey data

Canadian salary survey data

judgments of sociology students about what the jobs in a hierarchy should be paid, once the salary of one position is given[23]

similar judgments of business school students[24]

felt fair pay data according to Jaques's notion of time span of discretion

Mahoney reports that there is a striking degree of agreement between what people perceive to be the appropriate differences in pay for adjacent levels in a job hierarchy and what those differences in pay actually are. The data he cites agree closely that the appropriate difference of one rank over another is 30 to 40 percent. That is, the appropriate pay level for one position should be 1.3 to 1.4 times the level set for the next job down in the hierarchy. Mahoney further points out (in line with Simon's original thinking) that the traditional job content factors that are employed in job evaluation, but not associated with hierarchy, could not explain these differences.

Mahoney interprets these data as evidence of social norms regarding the power, influence, and status reflected in a job's place in an organizational hierarchy and advises, "Organizational level of a position, whatever it connotes regarding position content, clearly is a significant influence on the worth or status of positions in organizations."[25]

In this chapter and the last, we have reviewed an extremely broad range of economic and sociological theory regarding the determinants of external and internal equity in managers' thinking about job worth. Exhibit 3.1 summarizes these statements for you. Each theory or model is briefly stated along with its major proposition regarding job worth. The final column in the exhibit states the explicit job-worth inference to be drawn from the proposition. This exhibit is intended to help you organize the information about job worth presented in Chapters 2 and 3.

The Need for Further Study

There is little doubt that the field of compensation needs additional research to provide managers with some direction regarding their practices in valuing jobs. Indeed, the two major professional organizations in the

Exhibit 3.1   Theory Bases for Job Worth

Model	Proposition	Job Worth Implications
Classical Theory		
1. Just Price	A job's value derives from the relative status of the occupation in society. A just wage therefore is one that corresponds to the status distribution in society and preserves customary relationships among classes of workers.	A job derives value from the place of its occupation in society.
2. Labor Theory of Value		
• Smith	A commodity is worth the amount of labor required to produce it.	Labor on a job creates value.
• Marx	Labor is the sole source of value.	
Demand/Supply Theory		
3. Market Exchange Model	Wage and employment levels are determined by labor demand and labor supply intersects.	A job is worth the exchange rate clearing in the market for labor required to fill it.

Model	Proposition	*Job Worth* Implications

Demand-Side Theory

4. Marginal Revenue	$MRP = MPP \times MR$ where: MRP = Marginal Revenue Product MPP = Marginal Physical Product MR = Marginal Revenue	A job is worth the marginal revenue product it generates.
5. Thurow's Job Competition Model	Jobs are training opportunities. Marginal product lies solely in the job.	A job is worth the value of the product it generates.
6. Elliott Jaques	Jobs vary in time span of discretion they demand. People share norms regarding equitable pay according to time span of discretion.	Job value is measured by time span of discretion.

Supply-Side Theory

7. Labor Scarcity Models • Monopsony • Employee preferences for money income and nonmonetary conditions	Additional units of labor become increasingly costly to the employer (upward-sloping supply curve).	Labor to a job (like diamonds) has a scarcity value apart from its use value.

Exhibit 3.1   Theory Bases for Job Worth (*continued*)

Model	Proposition	Job Worth Implications
• Employee preferences for money and risk		
• Collective bargaining		
8. Human Capital Models	Long-run marginal returns to labor will equal the long-run marginal investments made in it.	Wages paid to a job represent, in part, a return on the investments made to develop skills required by a job.
9. Labor Capacity Models	Labor units vary in capacity for carrying out a job.	Labor to a job has value that varies according to capacity.
Sociological Theory		
10. Organizational Hierarchy	Shared norms exist in society regarding the power, influence, and status reflected in a job's place in an organizational hierarchy. Such norms dictate a pay or value differential of between 30 and 40% between adjacent positions.	Organizational level is a determinant of the worth of a job.

Source: Adapted from Marc J. Wallace, Jr. and Charles H. Fay, "Labor Markets, Job Evaluation, and Job Worth: Towards a Model of Managerial Judgements of Job Value," University of Kentucky, *Working Paper in Business Administration*, No. 74, 1982.

field, the American Compensation Association (ACA) and the American Society for Personnel Administration (ASPA) have recently issued a joint policy statement that reflects the dilemma over external equity (Chapter 2) and internal equity (this chapter):

> Regardless of the methodology selected (in job evaluation), pay grades and pay ranges are ultimately determined by:
>
> Market rates for comparable jobs—external competitiveness. This approach is referred to as the "labor market," or "market supply" approach.
>
> Management's judgments as to the relative internal worth of the job's content—internal equity.
>
> Organizations may place different emphasis on either external competitiveness, internal equity, or a blend of the two depending on their objectives or circumstances.[26]

Clearly this statement reflects the dilemma that currently exists in our field regarding the balance to be struck between external and internal criteria in setting wage rates for jobs in organizations. In light of the comparable worth controversy described in Chapters 1 and 3 (and to be discussed in Chapter 5) several important questions arise: (1) Should external market criteria and internal worth criteria be applied in similar fashion across all jobs within an organization, or should market criteria be paramount among one set of jobs and internal equity among another? In practical terms, should management pay more to fill a job with high training requirements than to fill one with no training requirements, even though there is a plentiful supply of applicants for the former job and a severe shortage of candidates for the latter? (2) Should external market criteria and internal worth criteria be applied consistently across different organizations for the same job?

Unfortunately, compensation theory and practice have not yet reached a stage of development sufficient to provide much direction for the compensation manager in resolving these questions. The economic and sociological theory reviewed in this chapter and Chapter 2 take a first step toward increasing our knowledge about how to assess job worth. There remain, however, three immediate needs for future research in compensation theory and practice:

1. to integrate theory further with respect to the valuation of jobs
2. to study the actual job valuations of managers

3. to build an integrative model of job valuation with theoretical and heuristic implications for compensation practice.

Managerial Judgments of Job Worth: A Model and Propositions for Research

The examination of economic and related theory in this chapter has suggested several major classes of variables that are likely to be used as criteria of job worth. These can be organized into the following general model:

$$V_k = W_k C_k + \sum_{i=1}^{I} W_{ik} R_{ik} + \sum_{j=1}^{J} W_{jk} R_{jk} \qquad \text{Eq. 3.1}$$

where:

V_k = value placed on job k

W_k = weight placed on the external wage rate for job k

C_k = prevailing external wage rate for job k

W_{ik} = weight placed on demand-side factor i for job k

R_{ik} = judged amount of supply-side factor j held by job k.

W_{jk} = weight placed on supply-side factor j for job k

R_{jk} = judged amount of supply-side factor j held by job k

The term $W_k C_k$ in Equation 3.1 is an external equity model, proposing that exchange rates in external markets (C_k) will influence the value placed on a job (V_k). The term $\sum_{i=1}^{I} W_{ik} R_{ik} + \sum_{j=1}^{J} W_{jk} R_{jk}$ in Equation 3.1 is an internal equity model consisting of demand-side and supply-side influences on value judgments. Demand-side factors (R_{ik}) are proposed to reside in the job itself and to influence value judgments (V_k) independently from supply-side factors (R_{jk}). Exhibit 3.2 summarizes the theory bases for job worth organized in our model.

Heuristic Value

What inferences can be drawn from the compensation theories integrated in Chapters 2 and 3 for modeling job worth? A starting place would be to test the descriptive accuracy of the external equity and internal equity models in Equation 3.1 in predicting actual job evaluations. Integration

Exhibit 3.2   Alternative Bases for Job Worth Judgments

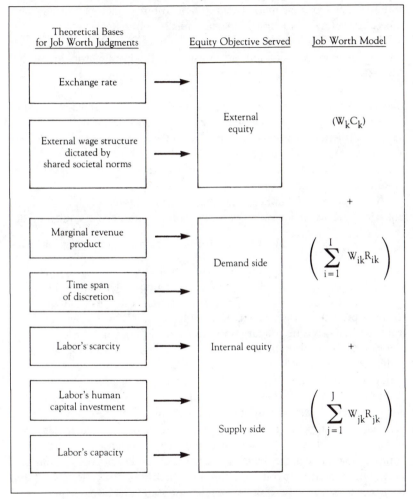

and extension of compensation theory suggests the following empirical propositions for research.

Independence of internal and external equity.   The model in Equation 3.1 reflects the theoretical proposition that external equity and internal equity involve different classes of phenomena. The theories reviewed here suggest specifically that exchange value is independent of use value and supply-side sources of value. This reasoning leads logically to the hypothesis that external market factors and internal factors will have independent effects on managerial estimates of job value.

If subsequent research confirms this proposition, we will have evidence that managers do, indeed, consider nonmarket factors in valuing jobs as suggested in the ACA/ASPA policy statement.

Relative importance of external and internal factors. Compensation theorists have long pointed out that jobs vary in their exposure to external market influences.[27] Entry-level jobs and jobs being used as benchmarks for interfirm pay comparisons, for example, can be expected to provide management with far less latitude in setting wage rates than jobs that are more insulated from the market.

This reasoning implies that the external equity model ($W_k C_k$ in Equation 3.1) will be more powerful than the internal equity model ($\sum_{i=1}^{I} W_{ik} R_{ik} + \sum_{j=1}^{J} W_{jk} R_{jk}$ in Equation 3.1) in predicting job evaluation outcomes and judgments for jobs tied closely to the market. We would expect the weight W_k to be greater, empirically, than weights W_{ik} or W_{jk}. We expect, conversely, that the internal equity model will be the stronger predictor of job evaluation results among jobs that are insulated from the market. The primary importance of testing this hypothesis from a comparable worth perspective will be to confirm or disconfirm empirically whether latitude for making comparable worth judgments independent from the marketplace varies across types of jobs.

Empirical knowledge about the sources of job worth and their influences on actual wage-setting practices will allow compensation theorists to examine compensation policies in the light of pay equity demands. Implicit job valuation policies evident in the weighing of alternative compensable factors can be evaluated, for example, against the fair employment standards of the Equal Pay Act of 1963, Title VII of the Civil Rights Act of 1964, and all other relevant standards of pay equity.

Summary

In this chapter we have examined the problem of internal equity in setting wage rates within organizations. We have reviewed evidence that suggests that external equity (the exchange rate for jobs clearing in external markets) is in many cases different from internal equity and therefore is a poor measure of the internal value of a job.

We have examined a number of theoretical approaches to the definition of a job's internal value. They include the classical principles inherent in the Just Price doctrine of the Middle Ages, and the labor theory of value proposed by Adam Smith and extended by Karl Marx.

Contemporary approaches to the problem of internal worth include the separate examination of demand-size and supply-side influences on job worth. The marginal revenue product (MRP) demand-side model and Thurow's job competition model were examined in this regard. Both theories propose that a job's worth lies in the value created for management when work is performed on the job. Elliott Jaques's concept of time span of discretion was analyzed as a noneconomic, administrative measure of a job's worth.

Three kinds of supply-side theory were examined for propositions regarding a job's worth. These included statements of (1) labor's scarcity value, (2) labor's human capital value, and (3) labor's capacity. In each case, labor to a job was considered to have value, apart from the job itself, that could be considered in establishing the value of the job.

Finally, we examined a sociological view, in which a job's value resides in that job's place in an organizational hierarchy. The premise of this view is that societal norms regarding the power, influence, and status represented by placement in an organization's hierarchy dictate norms regarding fair payment for jobs.

This chapter concluded with the observation that much more research and theory about job worth are needed before practitioners will have any better guides for policy in setting wage rates within organizations.

Notes

1. *Gunther v. County of Washington*, 602 F. 2d. 882 (9th Circuit Court, 1979); *Lemons v. City and County of Denver*, 17 FEP Cases (BNA) 906 (District Court, Colorado, 1978); *International Union of Electrical, Radio, and Machine Workers (IUE) v. Westinghouse Electric Corporation*, 19 FEP Cases 450 (District Court, New Jersey, 1979).

2. Thomas A. Mahoney, "Justice and Equity: A Recurring Theme in Compensation," *Personnel* 52 (1975): 60–66.

3. Lester C. Thurow, *Generating Inequality* (New York: Basic Books, 1975).

4. E. J. McCormick, *Job Analysis: Methods and Applications* (New York: AMACOM,

1979): E. J. McCormick, in D. J. Treiman and H. I. Hartmann, (eds.), *Women, Work, and Wages: Equal Pay for Jobs of Equal Value* (Washington, D.C.: National Academy Press, 1981).

5. 3 War Labor Rep. 321 (1942); 3 War Labor Rep. 348 (1942); 5 War Labor Rep. 461 (1943); 28 War Labor Rep. 666 (1945).

6. Marc J. Wallace, Jr., and Charles H. Fay, *Labor Markets, Job Evaluation, and Job Worth: Towards a Model of Managerial Judgments of Job Value.* Working Paper in Business Administration, BA 74 (Lexington, Ky.: University of Kentucky, 1981).

7. Donald P. Schwab, "Job Evaluation and Pay Setting: Concepts and Practices," in E. R. Livernash (ed.), *Comparable Worth: Issues and Alternatives* (Washington, D.C.: Equal Employment Advisory Council, 1980); Treiman and Hartman, *Women, Work, and Wages.*

8. Wallace and Fay, *Labor Markets, Job Evaluation, and Job Worth.*

9. Ruth G. Blumrosen, "Wage Discrimination, Job Segregation, and Women Workers," *Employee Relations Law Journal* 6 (1980): 77–136; Ruth G. Blumrosen, "Wage Discrimination, Job Segregation, and Title VII of the Civil Rights Act of 1964," 12 *U. Mich. J.L. Ref.* 397 (1979); see Bruce A. Nelson, Edward M. Opton, Jr., and Thomas E. Wilson, "Wage Discrimination and the Comparable Worth Theory in Perspective," 13 *U. Mich. J.L. Ref.* 231 (1980) for an opposing view to those of Blumrosen.

10. Wallace and Fay, *Labor Markets, Job Evaluation, and Job Worth.*

11. Adam Smith, *The Wealth of Nations,* 1776 (New York: Random House, 1937, abridged).

12. Herbert G. Heneman, Jr. and Dale Yoder, *Labor Economics* (Cincinnati: Southwestern Publishing Co., 1965).

13. Wallace and Fay, *Labor Markets, Job Evaluation, and Job Worth.*

14. Alan M. Cartter, *Theory of Wages and Employment* (Homewood, Ill.: Richard D. Irwin, 1959).

15. Thurow, *Generating Inequality.* 1975.

16. Elliott Jaques, *Equitable Payment* (New York: John Wiley and Sons, 1961).

17. Lloyd G. Reynolds, "Some Aspects of Labor Market Structure," in R. A. Lester and J. Shister (eds.), *Insights into Labor Issues* (New York: Macmillan, 1949); Lloyd G. Reynolds, "The Supply of Labor to the Firm," *Quarterly Journal of Economics* 60 (1946): 390–411.

18. Gary S. Becker, *Human Capital* (New York: National Bureau of Economic Research, 1964).

19. Ibid.

20. Thurow, *Generating Inequality,* 1975.

21. Thomas A. Mahoney, "Organizational Hierarchy and Position Worth," *Academy of Management Journal,* 1979, 726–37.

22. Herbert A. Simon, "The Compensation of Executives," *Sociometry* 20 (1957): 32–35.

23. James L. Kuethe and Bernard Levinson, "Conceptions of Organizational Worth," *The American Journal of Sociology,* November 1964, pp. 342–8.

24. Fred Champlin, "An Analysis of the Effects of Organizational Structure on Perceptions of Appropriate Pay," Unpublished paper, University of Minnesota, 1976, cited by Mahoney, 1979; Charles A. Lindberg, "An Empirical Study of the Influence of Structural Variables on Conceptions of Position Worth," Unpublished paper, University of Minnesota, 1975, cited by Mahoney, 1980, op. cit.

25. Mahoney.

26. The American Society for Personnel Administration and the American Compensation Association, *Elements of Sound Base Pay Administration* (Berea, Ohio: ASPA, 1981).

27. E. R. Livernash, "The Internal Wage Structure," in G. W. Taylor and F. C. Pierson (eds.), *New Concepts in Wage Determination* (N.Y.: McGraw-Hill, Inc., 1957), pp. 140–72.

4

Individual Equity

Individual equity has to do with the fairness with which individuals (as opposed to jobs) are paid. It is quite a different concept that either external equity (Chapter 2) or internal equity (Chapter 3) because we are no longer focusing on the job but on the merits of the individual who fills the job. You should think of individual equity as a criterion that requires employers to pay wage rates to individuals—in the simplest case, workers on the same job—according to variation in individual qualities and qualifications. In the equity theory terms we presented in Chapter 1, individual equity is achieved when the input/output ratios for one person and a comparable other person are equal.

This chapter will pursue the notion of individual equity in more detail. We will examine three major research and practical problems that emerge regarding individual equity. First, we will present a conceptual model of individual behavior that will illustrate exactly the way in which success or failure in achieving individual equity will influence employee behavior and performance and all other employee decisions made regarding the employer. Second, we will examine several decisions made by individuals regarding their employers when evaluating their employers against individual equity criteria. Finally, we will show how much pay satisfaction and dissatisfaction affect pay-related individual decisions.

A Review of Equity Theory

The central models for individual equity are those of J. Stacy Adams and Elliott Jaques.[1] Adams's ideas are represented in Exhibit 4.1. According to this model, individuals constantly monitor the exchange relationship with their employer. An exchange relationship (as we pointed out in Chapter 1) involves equity or inequity: people invest inputs (the *I*'s in Exhibit 4.1) and receive outcomes or rewards (the *O*'s). The exchange may or may not be fair.

Of significance to Adams's theory is the concept of distributive justice, an idea originally made formal by sociologist George Homans.[2] This is the condition that is achieved when the ratio of inputs to outcomes for a person is equal to that for some *comparison person*. The comparison person may be another person on the same job, a member of the same occupation, or even some composite of several comparison persons. The experience of inequity is very distressing, according to Adams's theory, and people will try several strategies for bringing the ratios in Exhibit 4.1 back into alignment. Such actions fall into the following categories:

1. adjusting one's outcomes or inputs
2. adjusting the outcomes or inputs of others

Exhibit 4.1 Individual Equity Defined

$$\frac{O_p}{I_p} = \frac{O_o}{I_o}$$

where:

O_p = outcomes (rewards) for the person
I_p = the person's inputs
O_o = outcomes (rewards) for a comparison other
I_o = the comparison other's inputs

3. changing comparison persons

4. leaving the situation

One of the difficulties of translating equity theory into practice so far is confusion over which of these steps a person will take in an actual situation. The employee who experiences inequity, for example, whether over- or underreward, can behave either overtly to reduce inequity—for example, by asking an employer for a raise to bring his or her salary into line with a comparison person's—or psychologically. The latter form of behavior is much more difficult for the manager to detect. In this case, the employee changes a perception of some element in the ratios displayed in Exhibit 4.1. He may, for example, perceptually increase or decrease the valuation of inputs and outcomes. An employee who perceives that he is being paid too much when compared to another employee would tend to rationalize the condition by adding to the perceived value of his own relative inputs, rather than go to the employer and ask for an adjustment in pay.

Perhaps the most important revision of Adams's equity theory has been suggested by Walster, Berscheid, and Walster.[3] Their ideas are represented in Exhibit 4.2 and constitute several important departures from Adams's original notions. The main difference in Exhibit 4.2 from the original equity formulation is that the ratios now have a net return—outcomes or rewards *less* inputs—in the numerator and the absolute value of inputs in the denominator. Computationally, the ratios in Exhibit 4.2 redefine equity as a rate of return or profit on the absolute value of inputs. One of the conditions such a revision allows us to consider is an exchange relationship where a person's inputs are actually negative. According to this reformulation, then, equity is achieved when the rate of return from the employment relationship is equal between an individual employee and a comparison person.

Another departure from traditional equity theory, made by Walster et al., has to do with the notion of distributive justice. Adams's theory proposed that all people seek distributive justice, equality of the comparison ratios in Exhibits 4.1 and 4.2. Although this proposition makes intuitive sense in those cases where the employee perceives that he or she is underrewarded it is not so straightforward in the case of overreward. Equity theory would predict that an employee experiencing overreward would be as distressed as he or she would be if underrewarded, and will act to reduce inequity in both cases. Although some limited experimental

Exhibit 4.2   The Individual Equity Criterion

$$\frac{O_p - I_p}{I_p} = \frac{O_o - I_o}{I_o}$$

Source: Elaine Walster, Ellen Berscheid, and William Walster, "New Directions in Equity Theory," *Journal of Personality and Social Psychology*, 1973, pp. 151–76.

evidence suggests that this is the case, researchers are still doubtful that employees will act altruistically if they perceive that they are being overrewarded.[4]

The Walster, Berscheid, and Walster revision of equity theory proposes that individuals will seek to maximize their individual rates of return (outcomes – inputs/inputs) and will do so if *unchecked by group and social norms*. They propose, further, that work groups develop norms regarding equity among outcome/input ratios and will censure members who seek to violate such norms.

The form of equity theory we have just examined involves social comparison. Equity is defined in terms of one person's comparison of his or her welfare with that of some comparison person. Elliott Jaques proposes an alternative mechanism for defining equity that derives from the following propositions:[5]

1. Every worker is endowed with a specific level of capacity for work and expenditure (C). This capacity varies across people.

2. Each job demands a specific level of capacity. Jaques defines the capacity demanded by a job as its *time span of discretion* (W). Time span is the period of time that elapses between the performance of a task and its review. The longer this span, the greater the capacity demanded by the job. Of course, jobs vary in their time span's of discretion.

3. Any group of individuals will have norms regarding the rate of pay that is fair for each job (Jaques calls this *felt fair pay*); it corresponds to each job's time span of discretion. Surprisingly, strong empirical evidence supports this third proposition.[6]

Exhibit 4.3 presents a sampling of situations that could lead an individual employee to perceive inequity according to Jaques's theory. In the arrays in Exhibit 4.3, C is the individual's own capacity for work, W

Exhibit 4.3   Inequity Defined by Jaques

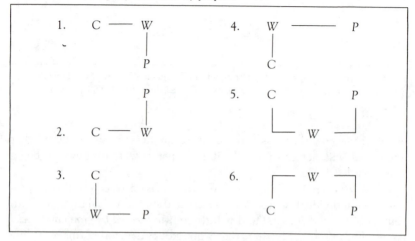

is the level of capacity (time span) demanded by the job, and P is the rate of pay the employer attaches to the job. The case in Exhibit 4.3 show a variety of ways that inequity can develop. In cases 1 and 2, for example, the link between an individual's capacity and the time span demanded by the job is equitable. The person is perfectly qualified for the job. However, inequity exists because in case 1 the job is underpaid and in case 2 the job is overpaid.

Inequity can arise not only from over- and underpayment of a job, however, but also from poor job assignments. In cases 3 and 4, for example, the wage set for the job (P) corresponds equitably to the level of work required (W). Inequity develops, however, because the person assigned to the job is either overqualified (case 3) or underqualified (case 4).

Finally, inequity can arise even when a person is paid according to his or her own personal capacity. In case 5, for example, an employee is being paid a wage that corresponds to his own capacity for work, but his work assignment is below both his capacity for work and the wage being paid. In case 6, finally, inequity exists because a person is being assigned to a job that is both above his capacity to perform and above the rate being paid.

Examination of the possibilities in Exhibit 4.3 should demonstrate that Jaques's theory is rich in implications regarding the variety of ways inequity can arise in compensation:

1. People can be assigned to jobs that do not correspond to their capacities.
2. Wages can be set that do not correspond to the level of work the job demands.
3. Wages can be set that correspond to the level of work demanded by a job but not to the individual's capacity for work.

Although there are differences between Adams's and Jaques's notions of equity, research carried out on these two theories so far should convince the manager that the experience of inequity in rewards is a very powerful influence on employee satisfaction and behavior.[7] The compensation planner cannot ignore the issue of equity (defined in Exhibits 4.1–4.3) in setting wage rates for individual employees.

An Integrative Model of Individual Decisions Influenced by Compensation Practices

What will happen when an employer fails to achieve individual equity in setting individual wage rates? We have already proposed that the results of inequity can be dramatic (people refusing job offers, adjusting performance levels, quitting jobs, and even suing employers). Equity, or inequity, influences employee motivation, and practicing managers should have an intimate knowledge of how this can happen. The model in Exhibit 4.4 summarizes a great deal of theory and research in the field of organizational behavior about employee motivation and behavior.[8] We have adapted it here to the question of behavior in response to rewards.

The first thing to know about the model in Exhibit 4.4 is that it attempts to explain a variety of decisions people make about employers: (1) the decision to enter an occupation, (2) the decision to accept a job offer, (3) the decision to leave or stay once one has been employed by a company, and (4) the level of performance one tries to achieve.

The model specifies, further, that each of these decisions is *motivated through effort*. The work of theorists March, Cyert, and Simon, especially, suggests that effort in the direction of a decision is not spontaneous but, rather, motivated by a process that begins with *search* and *choice*.[9] Ac-

Exhibit 4.4   Integrative Model of Individual Equity

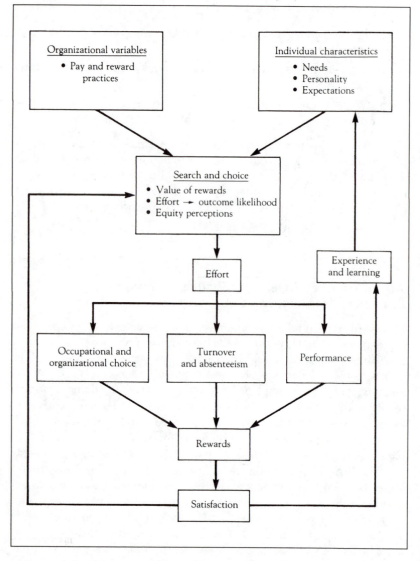

Source: Andrew D. Szilagyi, Jr. and Marc J. Wallace, Jr., *Organizational Behavior and Performance,* 3rd ed. (Glenview, Ill.: Scott, Foresman and Co., forthcoming, 1983). Used by permission.

cording to our model, several mental activities occur during search and choice:

1. Alternative actions are considered and evaluated in terms of the likelihood that each will result in desired outcomes.
2. Outcomes are evaluated in terms of *reward value*.
3. Equity, as defined earlier, is an important component in assessing the reward value of an outcome.
4. The most effort will be expended toward a choice (decision) that maximizes the person's *anticipated satisfaction with rewards*.

Finally, the model in Exhibit 4.4 proposes that search and choice behavior preceding a person's decision is influenced both by organizational variables, including specific pay and reward practices, and by individual characteristics, including experience, needs related to pay, personality characteristics, and expectations about the employers, that have been influenced by previous experience and learning.

What are some of the major implications of the model in Exhibit 4.4 about rewarding people? First, the model specifies that employee behavior and choices regarding the employer—for example, the choice of a job, the decision to remain, the decision to perform—are *motivated* in part by some anticipated satisfaction with rewards. In other words, people will behave and choose in directions that maximize anticipated satisfaction. Second, the way employers reward or fail to reward specific behavior will have a direct influence on actual satisfaction. Third, experienced levels of satisfaction or dissatisfaction will add to an individual's experience and learning. If dissatisfaction with rewards becomes sufficiently intense, we can expect that search and choice behavior will be motivated, and behavior will change.

We should note that satisfaction with compensation plays two extremely important roles in employee behavior. First, anticipated satisfaction with compensation plays an important role in directing a person's current behavior. The actual satisfaction with compensation achieved affects subsequent decisions and adjustments in behavior. Finally, the model predicts that individuals quickly learn the intentional or unintentional reward contingencies that an employer's reward policies imply and behave accordingly. Thus, for example, an employer might not want employees to be sloppy in their work, but may have a piece rate incentive system that rewards only quantity, not quality and cleanliness. As indicated by the model in Exhibit 4.4, it should be no surprise that employees will generally maximize quantity at the expense of quality and cleanliness.

The integrative model in Exhibit 4.4 is general: it addresses all the possible decisions people might make about employers that are influenced by compensation practices. We will see in the next section that such decisions are quite different from each other and should be analyzed separately by compensation practitioners.

Decisions Influenced by Compensation

Compensation theorist Thomas Mahoney has distinguished five decisions that are influenced by compensation policies.[10] He speculates, further, that they occur in the sequence outlined in Exhibit 4.5: (1) the decision to enter the labor force and seek work, (2) the decision to seek work in a given occupation (that is, vocational choice), (3) the choice of an employer, (4) the choice of a job assignment, and (5) the choice regarding level of performance. Mahoney notes that although some of the decisions in this sequence may be contingent on others (for example, the choice of an occupation might be influenced by employment opportunities already offered in the occupation by specific employers), it is convenient to consider each individually in a sequence that goes from very general (the decision to work) to very specific (the decision to perform at a given level).[11] We will examine here three of the decisions influenced by compensation policy: (1) the decision to accept a job offer, or, from the other side of the coin, (2) the decision to leave or to remain with the employer, and (3) the decision to perform. Decisions (1) and (2) are both aspects of the decision that Mahoney places third in his sequence. Decision (3), of course, is Mahoney's fifth and most specific, the level of performance decision.

The Decision to Accept a Job Offer

The decision to accept a job offer is a fairly infrequent one according to Mahoney.[12] Employers compete by offering job opportunities to an external market consisting of applicants for such opportunities. Economists differ in their opinion of how important wage competition is in bringing together job offers with those seeking work. Classical economic theorists would suggest that within broad limits wage competition does take place

Exhibit 4.5   The Sequence of Pay-Related Behaviors

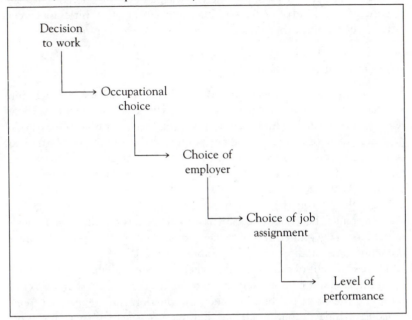

Decision
to work

→ Occupational
choice

→ Choice of
employer

→ Choice of job
assignment

→ Level of
performance

Source: Thomas A. Mahoney, *Compensation and Reward Perspectives* (Homewood, Ill.: Richard D. Irwin, Inc., 1979), p. 368. Used by permission.

among employers when bidding for employees, and that the management of a wage offer would directly influence an employer's success in attracting qualified job applicants.[13] Economist Lester Thurow disagrees with this logic, however.[14] He believes that wages are set by social forces rather than by competition among employers. He proposes that people seeking work in the labor force do not compete for wages, but rather for *job opportunities*. Thus, employers will come to the market with a variety of job opportunities that can be ranked in terms of attractiveness. People in the labor force compete for these opportunities and form a queue or line. Employers order the members of the queue in terms of their qualifications in a way that will minimize anticipated training and orientation costs. They will offer the opportunity to the most qualified person in the queue.

The model in Exhibit 4.4 suggests that an individual in the labor force will accept the job offer that maximizes anticipated satisfaction with rewards.[15] The rewards will include the wage rate being offered, but may also include the kind of work, working conditions, opportunities for career advancement, and other elements of importance to the job seeker.

The Decision to Remain

Mahoney makes a significant distinction between an outsider's decision to accept or reject a job offer and an insider's decision to stay with or leave an employer.[16] This distinction parallels that between the external and internal labor market. Mahoney points out that "individuals attracted to join a specific organization are removed from competition in the broader, external marketplace, and subsequent decisions and behavior are more a function of influences within the organization than of competing influences in the external market."[17]

Several implications for compensation managers arise from Mahoney's ideas. First, job competition, or wage competition, in the external market does not have a direct and constant effect on people once they are employed and out of the external market. Information about external job opportunities and competing wage rates takes time and resources to obtain, and the effort in obtaining such information is not expended spontaneously. Indeed, our model in Exhibit 4.4 suggests that the effort involved in considering the decision to leave an employer will be expended only if the employee experiences *sufficient levels of dissatisfaction* with current employment, not the attraction of alternative employment. What this means as a practical matter for managers is that most employees who leave are rarely *attracted* away by better job offers, but rather are *driven* away by sufficient levels of dissatisfaction with their current employment. Compensation planners should routinely audit all aspects of the compensation package and the way it is administered to determine if any practices provide sufficient grounds for dissatisfaction to encourage a significant number of valued employees to seek job opportunities in external markets.

It is significant that both the decision to accept a job offer and the decision to seek employment elsewhere are very infrequent. Mahoney, for example, points out that it is unrealistic to believe that typical employees constantly consider whether or not they should seek outside employment opportunities. He notes that mobility within the organization is far greater than mobility between organizations for most employees. The decision to leave an employer is likely to be motivated only when dissatisfaction with current rewards becomes great enough to energize a search for alternative employment in the external labor market. March and Simon, in their analysis of the decision to leave, predict that the likelihood of a person's leaving will be a function of not only perceived dissatisfaction with current employment but also the number of perceived job opportunities outside the current employer. General economic conditions, including unemployment rates in the person's occupation and area, will influence such perceptions.[18]

Decisions regarding performance levels, in contrast, are far more frequent, and are most likely to be made on a continuous basis as people perform their jobs. We will now use our rewards model to analyze the decision to perform.

The Decision to Perform

Mahoney has pointed out that the structure of wage rates, that is, differences in individual pay, influences the equity perceived by a group of employees. An equitable distribution, or lack thereof, may well influence pay dissatisfaction and the desire to leave, but it does not guarantee that employees will perform at high levels: "The provision of an equitable compensation structure is a necessary, but not sufficient condition, for the motivation of task performance."[19] Theoretically, the connection between compensation and performance should be as simple in our model (see Exhibit 4.4) as the connection with the decision to join and the decision to leave. In practice, however, performance is far more complex and difficult to predict than decisions to join or to leave.

The model in Exhibit 4.4 would predict that an employee's maximum effort would be directed at the level of performance that maximizes anticipated satisfaction with rewards. It would appear from this analysis that an employer could maximize performance through the use of wage incentives. If a person's pay could be tied directly to performance level, then we would expect the highest level of effort to be directed toward maximizing performance. Several facts of life in the real world of organizations, however, make this logic difficult to apply in compensation practices:

1. Simply creating equity in a wage distribution does not guarantee high levels of performance. Specific incentives have to be tied to specific levels of performance in order to influence performance.

2. Frequently, rewards, in addition to straight earnings, are important to employees (for example, the opportunity to pursue valued friendships with coworkers). High earnings may conflict with other valued outcomes and prevent an employee from responding to a wage incentive with maximum performance.

3. Work groups have been found to develop informal norms about the "proper" work pace, and to take very painful sanctions against members who are rate busters, that is, people who respond to wage incentives and violate group norms.

4. Although many firms *believe* that they have tied wages or earnings to performance, in fact they have failed to make the connection in their practices.

5. Performance outcomes must be under the direct and individual control of employees if wage incentives can be expected to have an effect. If an employee has to depend on another employee to complete a task, or if events beyond the control of the employee also influence results, a pay system's effect as an incentive toward a high performance is bound to fail.

Each of these factors leads to the conclusion that four conditions must be met in a compensation system if it can be hoped to have any incentive effect on performance:[20]

1. Employees must strongly believe that high performance will lead to high levels of reward.

2. The perceived negative consequences of performing at high levels (for example, fatigue, being labeled a rate buster) must be minimized in the anticipations of the employee.

3. Positively valued outcomes other than money (including praise, promotions, recognition) must also be tied directly to high levels of individual performance.

4. Employees must perceive a direct and independent connection between their efforts and the rewards for their efforts.

When these conditions are met simultaneously, compensation can have an impressive effect on the incentive towards performance. Edward Lawler has summarized the most common forms of compensation in terms of their effect on performance.[21] Exhibit 4.6 contains a classification of major pay plans, including payment by straight salary and bonus. Within each of these types, payment on an individual, group, and organization-wide basis is considered. Each type of plan is examined with respect to (1) the performance measure employed, (2) the type of reward employed, (3) the quality of perceived pay–performance linkage, (4) the quality of minimizing negative side-effects, and (5) the quality of the perceived relationship between other rewards and performance.

Exhibit 4.6 should impress managers with the fact that not all forms of compensation are equally effective in creating incentives for maximizing performance, and most salary systems, the most common form of compensation, are at best fair in tying pay to performance.

Finally, much has been made of the problem of pay secrecy in setting up monetary incentives for performance. Theoretically, pay secrecy would make it impossible for a pay system to act as an incentive, because employees would have no way to evaluate the size of a wage rate relative to individual performance or merit. In addition, research suggests that under conditions of secrecy employees tend to misperceive fellow employees' actual pay rates. One study, for example, found that managers tend to overestimate the salaries of other managers in the organization.[22] Such misperception can lead to intense dissatisfaction with pay and negate the positive influence of any incentive system, no matter how well designed. Pay secrecy, however, is not bad in all cases. We are quick to caution a practicing manager against reading this passage and making public what has been a secret pay structure without auditing that structure for external and internal equity. Secrecy may be the best policy for a structure that grossly deviated from external and internal equity criteria, especially where the problem involves the compression of wages being paid to newly hired people and long-term employees.

The Importance of Pay Satisfaction

Our integrative model of rewards and performance in Exhibit 4.4 points to the great role pay satisfaction or dissatisfaction plays in motivation. Satisfaction is an evaluative reaction, an attitude, that determines the degree of like or dislike for an employer's compensation policies and practices. The research we have reviewed in this chapter suggests that pay satisfaction operates in two major ways. The *anticipation of reward satisfaction* will act as an incentive influencing a number of employment decisions, including decisions to accept a job offer, to remain employed,

Exhibit 4.6   Classification and Ratings of Various Pay Plans

Type of Pay Plan	Performance Measure	Type of Rewards		Perceived Pay-Performance Linkage	Miminization of Negative Consequences	Perceived Relationship Between Other Rewards and Performance
		Salary Increase	Cash Bonus			
Salary						
For Individuals	Productivity	—	—	Good	Neutral	Neutral
	Cost effectiveness	Merit rating	Piece rate	Fair	Neutral	Neutral
	Superior's rating	—	—	Fair	Neutral	Fair
For Group	Productivity	Productivity	—	Fair	Neutral	Fair
	Cost effectiveness	—	—	Fair	Neutral	Fair
	Superior's rating	—	—	Fair	Neutral	Fair
For Total Organization	Productivity	Productivity	—	Fair	Neutral	Fair
	Cost effectiveness	Bargaining	—	Fair	Neutral	Fair
	Profits	—	—	Neutral	Neutral	Fair

Exhibit 4.6 Classification and Ratings of Various Pay Plans
(*continued*)

		Type of Rewards					
Type of Pay Plan	Performance Measure	Salary Increase	Cash Bonus	Perceived Pay-Performance Linkage	Miminization of Negative Consequences	Perceived Relationship Between Other Rewards and Performance
Bonus						
For Individuals	Productivity	Piece rate	—	Excellent	Poor	Neutral
	Cost effectiveness	—	Sales	Good	Poor	Neutral
	Superior's rating	—	Commission	Good	Poor	Fair
For Group	Productivity	—	Group incentive	Good	Neutral	Fair
	Cost effectiveness	—	—	Good	Neutral	Fair
	Superior's rating	—	—	Good	Neutral	Fair
For Total Organization	Productivity	—	Kaiser,	Good	Neutral	Fair
	Cost effectiveness	—	Scanlon,	Good	Neutral	Fair
	Profits	—	Profit sharing	Fair	Neutral	Fair

Source: Adapted from Edward E. Lawler, III, *Pay and Organizational Effectiveness* (New York: McGraw-Hill, Inc., 1971), pp. 164–65. Used by permission.

and to improve performance. Motivational theory and research also suggests that *actual rewards influence satisfaction* and thereby provide feedback that inclines employees to adjust their behavior. Thus, we can expect reward practices to influence changes in behavior and performance.

What is pay or reward satisfaction? Research on its content is not very well developed. It is safe to conclude at this point, however, that pay satisfaction has many dimensions. The fact that an organization offers many rewards implies that there are just as many possibilities for satisfaction or dissatisfaction. Thus, for example, an employee may be very happy with his hourly pay rate but very dissatisfied with his benefit package. Although pay satisfaction is many-faceted, most research shows that equity is one of its more important determinants.

Edward Lawler has recently proposed a model explaining the causes of pay satisfaction or dissatisfaction.[23] His schema is displayed in Exhibit 4.7. According to Lawler's thinking, the immediate cause of satisfaction or dissatisfaction with pay is the distinction between the amount employees think they should receive and the amount they think they are actually receiving relative to others. An equality between these two amounts creates an equitable situation and leads to satisfaction with pay. His model relies on an equity theory framework (see pp. 69–73, this chapter) to explain why employees think they should receive a certain amount and how they perceive what they actually do earn.

The amount of pay an individual judges that he should be paid depends upon the amount of input he sees himself contributing as compared to the input of another. Perceived inputs include personal characteristics — for example, skills, experience level, age, seniority, and others as shown in Exhibit 4.7 — as well as the demands made by the job: the level of difficulty, the time span of discretion, and the amount of responsibility demanded, for example. Such inputs are not considered alone, according to the model, but in comparison to the inputs being demanded of another person.

The perceived amount of received pay is a relative amount, based on a comparison of the perceived pay of referent others to the actual pay one receives. Actually, Lawler has merely transformed the terms of the ratios in Adams's original formulation as indicated in Exhibit 4.8. In this case, the ratios defining equity have been transformed into a comparison between an outcome/outcome ratio (O_p/O_o) and an input/input ratio (I_p/I_o).

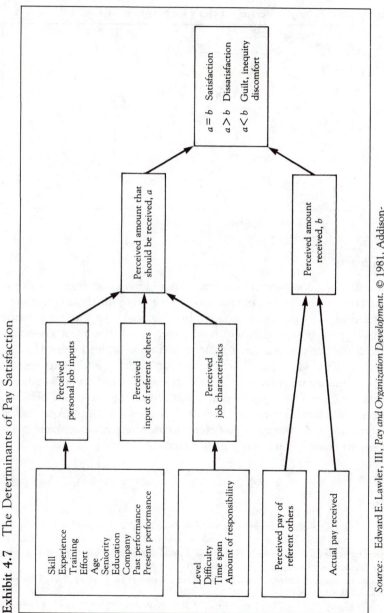

Exhibit 4.7 The Determinants of Pay Satisfaction

Source: Edward E. Lawler, III, *Pay and Organization Development.* © 1981, Addison-Wesley, Reading, Ma., p. 13. Reprinted with permission.

Exhibit 4.8   Adams's Versus Lawler's Conception of Equity

Adams

$$\frac{O_p}{I_p} = \frac{O_o}{I_o}$$

Lawler

$$\frac{O_p}{O_o} = \frac{I_p}{I_o}$$

Summary

The practicing compensation manager should pay close attention to pay satisfaction in his or her organization, particularly to those dimensions which deal with individual equity. If individual equity is consistently denied, pay dissatisfaction will result, and it will become increasingly difficult for the organization to attract and retain valued employees. In addition, individual equity is a necessary, *although not sufficient* condition for performance incentives. If individual equity norms are violated, pay incentives cannot have any measurable effects on the decision to perform. Beyond individual equity, however, pay systems actually linking pay to performance and integrating noncompensation rewards must be in place for pay to positively influence performance.

Notes

1. J. Stacy Adams, "Injustice In Social Exchange," in L. Berkowitz (ed.), *Advances In Experimental Social Psychology* (New York: Academic Press, 1965), pp. 267–99; Elliott Jaques, *Equitable Payment* (New York: John Wiley and Sons, 1961); Elliott Jaques, "Taking Time Seriously In Evaluating Jobs," *Harvard Business Review*, 1979, pp. 124–32.

2. George C. Homans, *Social Behavior in its Elementary Forms* (New York: Harcourt, Brace and World, 1961).

3. Elaine Walster, Ellen Berscheid, and William Walster, "New Directions In Equity Research," *Journal of Personality and Social Psychology*, 1973, pp. 151–76.

4. Robert D. Prichard, "Equity Theory: A Review and Critique," *Organizational Behavior and Human Performance*, 1969, pp. 172–211.

5. Jaques, *Equitable Payment*, 1961.

6. Roy Richardson, Unpublished Ph.D. dissertation, Industrial Relations Center, University of Minnesota.

7. Thomas A. Mahoney, "Towards an Integrated Theory of Compensation," in T. A. Mahoney (ed.), *Compensation and Reward Perspectives* (Homewood, Ill.: Richard D. Irwin, 1979), pp. 367–81.

8. Andrew D. Szilagyi, Jr. and Marc J. Wallace, Jr., *Organizational Behavior and Performance*, 3rd ed. (Glenview, Ill.: Scott, Foresman, forthcoming, 1983).

9. James G. March and Herbert A. Simon, *Organizations* (New York: John Wiley and Sons, 1958); Richard M. Cyert and James G. March, *A Behavioral Theory of the Firm* (Englewood Cliffs, N.J.: Prentice-Hall, 1963); Herbert A. Simon, *Administrative Behavior* (New York: Macmillan, 1957).

10. Mahoney, *Compensation and Reward Perspectives*.

11. Ibid.

12. Ibid.

13. Alan M. Cartter, *Theory of Wages and Employment* (Homewood, Ill.: Richard D. Irwin, 1959).

14. Lester Thurow, *Generating Inequality* (New York: Basic Books, 1975).

15. Donald P. Schwab, "Organizational Recruiting and the Decision to Participate," in K. Rowland and G. Ferris (eds.), *Personnel Management: New Perspectives* (Boston: Allyn and Bacon, 1982).

16. Mahoney, *Compensation and Reward Perspectives*.

17. Ibid., p. 369.

18. March and Simon, *Organizations*.

19. Mahoney, *Compensation and Reward Perspectives*.

20. See, for example, Fred Luthans, Robert Paul, and Douglas Baker, "An Experimental Analysis of the Impact of Contingent Reinforcement on Salesperson's Performance," *Journal of Applied Psychology*, 1981, pp. 314–323.

21. Edward E. Lawler, III, *Pay and Organizational Effectiveness: A Psychological View* (New York: McGraw-Hill, 1971).

22. George T. Milkovich and P. H. Anderson, "Management Compensation and Pay Secrecy Policies," *Personnel Psychology*, 1972, pp. 293–302.

23. Edward E. Lawler, III, *Pay and Organizational Development* (Reading, Mass.: Addison-Wesley, 1981).

II

Compensation Practice

5

Constraints on Compensation Practice

$\mathbf{A}$lthough the major determinants of compensation and benefit levels are economic, for example, market forces, value added through job performance, and the organization's ability to pay, as well as sociopsychological, as with felt fair pay and motivational needs, there are also a number of constraints that prevent the organization from responding to shifts in these factors with like adjustments in the compensation program. These constraints are of three major types. The first, and most severe, constraints are legal. There are major federal laws restricting amount, type, and administration of both salaries and benefits. Additional state laws constrain the compensation administrator.

The second major constraint is found in the various tax laws of the federal and state governments. Though akin to legal constraints, they neither require nor forbid any particular administration, amount, or type, of salary or benefit, but rather make it costly to both employer and employee to follow what might otherwise be a preferred course of action. The final major constraint, which tends to be more of a short-run problem, arises from the contracts employers enter into with unions representing some or all of their employees. Although contracts can be renegotiated, in the short run, at least, they prevent some kinds of adjustments in the compensation program, and even in the long run provide a major barrier to change, at least in ways sometimes desired by the compensation manager.

Compensation Laws

Minimum wage, FICA deductions, comparable worth, garnishment, vesting requirements, overtime, prevailing wage: these are only a few of the words that are part of the compensation analyst's language as a result of the many federal and state laws governing compensation practices. The variety of regulations can be confusing. Many of the major laws deal with several areas of compensation regulation at once; thus, no classification scheme can be entirely satisfactory. In this section we will discuss each of the major laws affecting compensation. Not all parts of every law are discussed but only those sections relating directly to compensation issues. We will conclude with a summary of different aspects of compensation systems and which law or laws affect each aspect.

The Fair Labor Standards Act–1938

The Fair Labor Standards Act (FLSA) contains five major provisions: minimum wage, overtime pay, equal pay (the Equal Pay Act of 1963 is an amendment to FLSA), record-keeping requirements, and child labor laws. All of these except the child labor laws have a major effect on compensation programs.

Minimum wage. Minimum-wage provisions set a floor on the amount of base pay an employer can offer an employee. The minimum wage was raised to $3.35 per hour starting January 1, 1981; currently (1982), there is no legislation mandating increases in the minimum-wage level.

Almost all employers are covered by minimum-wage requirements. FLSA was made possible by the authority of Congress under the Constitution to regulate interstate commerce; thus, it regulates all employers engaged in interstate commerce, producing goods for interstate commerce, or having employees who handle, sell, or otherwise work on goods or materials produced for or moved in interstate commerce. This has been interpreted to include organizations involved in construction; hospitals or other resident health care institutions; educational institutions, including preschools, elementary and high schools, institutions of higher education, and schools for the mentally or physically handicapped; laundries and cleaners; retail or service establishments with an annual gross (as of January 1, 1982) of $362,500; the federal government; state and local governments, although coverage is not in fact extended to all workers; and employers of domestic workers who receive at least $100 per calendar year from the employer.

However, not all workers are covered by minimum-wage provisions. Some employees are exempt, and the distinction made by personnel managers between exempt and nonexempt employees is based on this fact. Exempt employees include executives, administrative and professional employees (for example, teachers), outside salespersons, fishermen, seasonal employees of amusement or recreational organizations, some farm workers, and casual baby-sitters and companions.[1] Given permission of the Wage and Hour Division of the Department of Labor, which is responsible for enforcement of FLSA, employers need not pay the minimum wage to apprentices, handicapped workers, or full-time students working in certain retail or service establishments, in agricultural enterprises, or in institutions of higher education. Under some circumstances the value of room, board, or other facilities may be considered part of wages when calculating wages paid for minimum-wage purposes. If employees receive tips in excess of thirty dollars per month, employers may include those tips when calculating the wages paid for minimum wage purposes. However, the amount used in calculations cannot exceed 40 percent of the minimum wage for the period.

Overtime. FLSA overtime provisions do two things: specify a normal workweek and mandate a pay rate of 150 percent of regular pay for all hours worked in excess of the norm. The workweek is defined as a period of 168 hours during seven consecutive 24 hour periods. An employer may arbitrarily decide on the day and hour when the workweek begins. An employee may be expected to work 40 hours during the workweek at a regular rate of pay. For every hour in excess of 40 worked the employee must be paid 150 percent of his or her regular wage. Hours cannot be shifted from one week to another by the employer. An exception to this rule is the hospital; hospitals may set up 14-day periods and must pay employees 150 percent of regular wages for all hours worked in excess of 80 in the work period.

Calculating overtime pay is not as easy in all cases as it would seem. For hourly workers the calculations are straightforward. If an employee is ordinarily paid $8.00 per hour and works 48 hours in one workweek, then the pay earned is 40 hours at $8.00 per hour, or $320 plus 8 hours at $12.00 per hour (base rate of $8.00 per hour and overtime of $4.00 per hour), or $96 for a total of $416 for the week.

Things become more complicated when the worker is paid on a piecework basis. In this case there is no hourly rate. There are two methods of calculating overtime for piecework employees. One is to increase the piecerate for parts completed during overtime. Thus if a worker receives $2.00 per piece for parts completed during the regular workweek, he receives $3.00 for any part completed during overtime. A second method of calculating overtime due the piecework employee is to convert the piece rate earned to hourly earnings and base overtime on that. If, for example, an employee works 48 hours in a week and produces enough pieces to earn $400, then her average hourly earnings would be $8.33. Her total pay would then be $400 plus one-half of the hourly rate times the overtime hours worked ($\frac{1}{2} \times 8.33 \times 8 = 33.32$), or $433.32.

Salaried nonexempt employees present similar problems. To calculate overtime for these employees it is necessary to convert monthly salary to weekly salary. This is done by multiplying the monthly rate by 12 to get an annual rate and then dividing by 52 to get a weekly rate. This conversion takes care of differences in length of month. The appropriate overtime rate can then be calculated.

As with the minimum-wage provisions, the overtime provisions of FLSA do not apply to all workers. All employees exempt under minimum-wage coverage are also exempt under overtime provisions. Employers may, if they wish, pay overtime to these exempt employees but are not required to do so by the FLSA. Additional employees exempt under overtime provisions include farm workers, motion picture theater employees, some employees of some nonmetropolitan broadcasting stations, sales employees paid on a commission basis, employees of railroads and air carriers, domestic workers residing in the house of their employer, taxi drivers, and seamen on American vessels.

Equal pay.   The Equal Pay Act of 1963 was passed as an amendment to FLSA. Basically, the Equal Pay Act prohibits wage differentials based on sex between men and women employed in the same establishment when they have jobs that require equal skill, effort, and responsibility, and that are performed under similar working conditions. It is under the Equal Pay

Act that some of the "comparable worth" lawsuits have been pursued; these suits have not generally been successful. The most successful case for advocates of the notion of comparable worth, *Gunther v. County of Washington,* was brought under Title VII of the Civil Rights Act, discussed in Chapter 1 and later in this chapter. There are several reasons why the Equal Pay Act is not conducive to comparable worth ideas. The requirement of equal skill, effort, and responsibility means that all three factors must be equal. Equal skill refers to the experience, training, ability, and education required to perform a job. Equal effort does not occur if the more highly paid job has tasks requiring greater effort or if the more highly paid job requires a greater amount of time for such tasks. Equal effort is not the sole criterion of job value, however. If tasks of similar effort result in significantly different economic values to the employer (for example, making computer components versus making nails), the employer may be justified in paying different rates. Minor differences in responsibility do not generally justify pay differentials. Likewise, working conditions must differ significantly if pay differentials are to be justified.

Some conditions that may lead to lower pay for women than for men are specifically approved under the Equal Pay Act. Wage differentials resulting from legitimate seniority systems, merit systems, or any system that ties earnings directly to quantity or quality of production (for example, commission sales, piecework) are permissible. Part-time workers need not be paid as much as full-time workers. Even differentials paid to heads of families are permitted, as long as female heads of families are paid the differential as well as males.

Employers who are in violation of the Equal Pay Act's prohibition on sex-related pay differentials may not lower pay to correct the violation. Instead, the pay of the affected group must be raised to meet that of the favored group. There are no exempt employees under the Equal Pay Act. Nearly all employers and labor unions negotiating for employees are subject to the provisions of the Equal Pay Act.

Record-keeping requirements.   Under the FLSA, employers must collect, store, and report great quantities of information about their compensation system and wage and hour data on nonexempt employees to the Wage and Hour Division of the Department of Labor. Included for nonexempt employees are:

   1. Employee name, address, occupation, and sex

2. Hour and day when workweek begins
3. Total hours worked each workday and workweek
4. Total basic pay on daily or weekly basis
5. Regular hourly pay rate for any week when the employee works overtime
6. Total overtime pay for the workweek
7. Deductions from or additions to wages
8. Total wages paid during the pay period
9. Date of payment and pay period covered
10. Special information when uncommon pay arrangements exist (for example, estimated tips) or when board, lodging, or other facilities are counted as part of pay.

Acts Concerning the Prevailing Wage

There are three acts, The Davis-Bacon Act of 1931, The Walsh-Healy Public Contracts Act of 1936, and the McNamara-O'Hara Service Contract Act of 1965, that, though passed at separate times, all have one goal in common: when organizations do work for the United States government they must pay the "prevailing" wages to their employees. These laws, particularly the Davis-Bacon Act, have been under fire by business organizations in the last several years and have been just as heatedly defended by labor organizations. The primary issue is what a "prevailing" wage is. The Department of Labor is authorized to make this decision; its determination has generally been whatever union workers in the area get. (In the case of Walsh-Healy, wages throughout the industry rather than in one area are used.) Since union workers tend to make more than nonunion workers, businessmen argue that the law helps to establish unions and forces nonunion contractors either to pay higher wages than they otherwise would to workers on government jobs, thereby causing internal or individual inequity in the organization, or to avoid government contracts, or to pay artificially high wages. Labor leaders argue that repeal of the laws, or changes in the interpretation of prevailing wage, would weaken or destroy unions and union contractors. This issue is likely to remain with compensation administrators for some time.

The Davis-Bacon Act of 1931.   Davis-Bacon applies to all contractors holding federal or federally assisted contracts in excess of $2,000 for construction, alteration, repair, painting, or decorating of public buildings or public works. All laborers and mechanics employed under such contracts are covered. The Act requires that wage rates and fringe benefits found by the Department of Labor to prevail in the area be paid. In addition, contractors must submit certified payroll records each week to the contracting agency. An associated law, the Copeland Act of 1934, was passed to prevent abuse of Davis-Bacon wage floors. Under the Copeland Act it is illegal for a Davis-Bacon contractor to demand kickbacks from employees or to make certain prohibited deductions from wages.

The Walsh-Healy Public Contracts Act of 1936.   Walsh-Healy is similar to Davis-Bacon, but it applies to employers holding federal contracts in excess of $10,000 for the manufacture or provision of materials, supplies, and equipment. Among other provisions, Walsh-Healy requires covered employers to pay the wage rate that prevails in the industry, as determined by the Department of Labor, and to pay overtime at not less than one and a half times the basic rate for all hours worked in excess of eight in one day or forty in a workweek, whichever results in greater pay.

The McNamara-O'Hara Service Contract Act of 1965.   This act extends Davis-Bacon concepts to the services sector of government contracting. For employers holding service contracts or subcontracts of $2,500 or less, service employees must be paid not less than minimum wage. For employers holding service contracts or subcontracts in excess of $2,500, employees must be paid not less than the wage rates and fringe benefits found by the Department of Labor to be prevailing in the area, *or* the wage rates and fringe benefits contained in the previous contractor's collective bargaining agreement.

Wage and Price Controls

There have been several attempts to regulate wage increases on the national level in order to control inflation. During World War II, the National War Labor Board was authorized to administer wages and wage changes. During the period of the Korean War, the Wage Stabilization

Board performed similar functions. Peacetime controls have been fewer and less effective. Under the Economic Stabilization Act of 1970, President Nixon was authorized to issue orders and regulations thought necessary to stabilize prices, rents, wages, and salaries at levels not less than those prevailing on May 25, 1970. Running through several phases, the Nixon controls were unpopular and largely unworkable. Even less effective at controlling inflation was the program created under the Carter administration. A Council on Wage and Price Stability was formed, but with no real enforcement powers. The program died when President Reagan took office in 1981. Currently there are no wage or price controls in effect, but compensation analysts should be aware that such programs might be legislated in the future. People who feel that government can effectively control wages and prices continue, under conditions of high inflation, to lobby for such legislation. Even some businessmen, who note that in the past wages always seemed to be more effectively frozen than prices, push for regulation in this area.

The Consumer Credit Protection Act of 1968

Title III of the Consumer Credit Protection Act of 1968 deals with wage garnishment. Wage garnishment occurs when a creditor goes to court and gets a garnishment order. The order, which as the force of law, requires the employer of the debtor to deduct some portion of the debtor's pay and to deliver it to the creditor. Prior to passage of the law, some employers simply fired any employees against whom a garnishment order had been obtained.

Under the law, a court cannot order a garnishment on the aggregate disposable earnings of a debtor for any workweek in excess of the lesser of either (1) 25 percent of the debtor's disposable earnings for the workweek, or (2) the amount by which the debtor's disposable earnings for the week exceed thirty times the minimum wage authorized under FLSA. Disposable earnings are defined as compensation less legally required withholdings (that is, FICA, income tax, and so on).

Garnishment restrictions do not apply to all debts. Federal and state tax debts, alimony and child support, and orders under Chapter XIII bankruptcy filings are exempt from Title III. The law also allows for the preemption of state law. If state laws allow larger garnishments than the federal law then federal law preempts state law. But on the other hand, if the state law restricts the court to even smaller garnishments, then *it* preempts the federal law. The law also forbids employers to fire debtors because of a single garnishment order. If the debtor has a second garnishment order, then the employer is free to fire him.

Old Age, Survivors, Disability, and Health Insurance Program (OASDHI)

The OASDHI is perhaps the most pervasive of all compensation-related legislation in the United States. More than nine out of ten workers are covered by its provisions, which form the base of most benefit programs. The only workers not covered are federal civilian employees covered by other United States retirement systems, employees of state and local governments when those government units choose not to participate, some agricultural and domestic workers, and employees of some nonprofit organizations that have chosen not to arrange coverage.

The programs legislated under OASDHI are the base of most benefit packages and form the backbone of the social programs in the United States. Included are retirement, survivors, and disability insurance, known collectively as Social Security; hospital and medical insurance for the aged and disabled, known as Medicare/Medicaid; black lung benefits for coal miners; Supplemental Security Income; unemployment insurance; and public assistance and welfare services, including aid to families with dependent children, or AFDC. The principal programs of interest to employers, because they are directly taxed to support them, are Social Security, Medicare/Medicaid, and unemployment insurance.

Social Security, Medicare, Medicaid.   Social Security—retirement, survivors, and disability insurance—and hospital and medical insurance for the aged and disabled are paid for by a tax on employers and employees. These taxes, authorized by the Federal Insurance Contributions Act, constitute the FICA deductions noted on every paycheck. FICA taxes are not levied on total salary. In 1950, for example, the wage limit for deductions was only $3,000. As demands for benefits have risen and as the costs for those benefits have risen on a per unit basis, both the salary subject to FICA tax and the tax rate itself have increased. In 1975, for example, the levy was 4.95 percent for Social Security plus 0.90 percent for Medicare/Medicaid, or a total levy of 5.85 percent. This levy was applied against the first $14,100 earned by the employee. In contrast, in 1982 the combined FICA levy is 6.70 percent, and it is being applied against the first $32,400 earned.

Not only the employee pays FICA taxes. The employer pays in an equal amount. Thus, the real tax rate for FICA needed to support these programs is 13.40 percent of the first $32,400 earned by each employee or as much as $4,341.60 per employee. Rates and the levy base are likely to rise as benefit costs and the number of individuals qualifying for benefits continues to grow.

OASDHI places other constraints on employers besides direct taxes. Employees who receive tips are required to pay FICA on those tips. Employers are required to collect data on tips and deduct the tax due on those tips from regular wages. Record-keeping requirements also exist. The employer must keep track of, and report, the amounts and dates of wage payments (including tips), the name, address, occupation, and social security number of each employee receiving wages, and employees' periods of employment.

In addition, the employer must provide each employee a W-2 form by January 31 for the previous calendar year. It must show the name, address, and social security identification number of the employer, the name, address, and Social Security number of the employee, the total amount of wages subject to FICA taxes paid to the employee during the year (including tips), and the amount of FICA taxes deducted from wages. If taxes are still owed on tip income, this information must be reported as well.

Unemployment insurance.   The unemployment insurance program is a state-administered program that operates with federal participation under general requirements set out in OASDHI. The function of unemployment insurance is to provide partial income replacement for a limited period when a worker loses his job through no fault of his own.

Funding for unemployment claims comes from a tax levied by states on employing organizations. The amount of tax depends on the benefit levels granted by the state and on the employer's record. That is, the more people who file for and are granted unemployment benefits after being discharged by an employer, the higher the tax the employer must pay. In a few states, employees must also contribute to unemployment funds.

The standard tax rate for unemployment paid by employers is 3.4

percent of the first $6,000 earned by a worker in a calendar year. Of this sum, 2.7 percent goes to the state and 0.7 percent goes to the federal government. This tax base does not include mandatory deductions for OASDHI. This is the rate that would be assigned to an employer just starting business. Generally, after three years a good rating of the employer's record, or "experience rating," will lower this percentage.

There are several ways for states to determine the experience rating. The most common method, used by over thirty states, is an actuarial method that attempts to ensure enough money in the unemployment fund reserve to cover benefit outflow. This reserve ratio formula is based on the difference between the employer's contribution over a period of time and the total benefits received by former workers of that employer. Tax rates are assigned according to a schedule of rates for specified sets of reserve ratios. The higher the ratio, the lower the rate. The ratio itself is calculated by dividing the reserve attributable to the employer by the employer's current payroll.

A second method used in some states is the benefit ratio formula, under which system the ratio used is benefits paid out over the last three years divided by current payroll. Again, a schedule of rates is used to assign tax rates. The third method makes use of a benefit wage ratio. In this system, the number of dismissals per benefit year, weighted by salaries, is divided by total taxable wages. Schedules similar to those used in other plans provides a means of calculating the tax. The simplest method is to calculate the percentage decline in payroll, and use a schedule of rates for different percentages of decline.

Regardless of the method by which the tax is computed, it is crucial for compensation analysts to make sure line managers and other personnel specialists understand how the system works, because the greater the number of successful filers the greater the tax to the organization. The worker must register at a public employment office and file an unemployment claim. The worker's previous job must be a covered job, and there must be some set amount of earnings or employment in some specified base period, usually one year, prior to filing. The worker may not be sick or disabled, but must be able to work. The worker must be available for work and willing to take a suitable job if one is offered. In addition to being available, workers must actively seek work and must not refuse an offer of suitable work.

Workers covered by unemployment insurance must have lost their jobs through circumstances beyond their control; that is, they cannot have quit, without good cause, or have been discharged for a just cause. In most states, workers may not be unemployed because of a labor dispute in which they are participating. We note here that many workers violate one or more of these conditions for receiving unemployment benefits. Both workers and employers have the right to appeal unemployment insurance benefit eligibility decisions, and it is important for the company to challenge claims when appropriate to prevent tax rate increases. It is also important for employers to discharge only those workers who truly warrant it, and to be able to document the misconduct that resulted in discharge.

Workers' Compensation

Workers' compensation programs are operated by the states, and laws vary from state to state. Because of widely varying costs to employers and benefits to workers there have been, from time to time, national commissions that have suggested mandating standards on the federal level. In 1972, a National Commission on State Workmen's Compensation Laws set forth nineteen recommendations aimed at standardizing state laws and reducing the insurance premiums paid by employers.

The goal of worker compensation laws is to provide immediate money for medical care and support to workers who are injured on the job, and to provide support to dependents if the worker is killed. Thus, worker compensation is essentially an insurance program to cover work-related injury and health problems. Some state laws require all employers to pay for such insurance. Other states allow employers to be self-insured. Most states leave workers' compensation coverage to private insurance carriers. In others, including Ohio, Nevada, North Dakota, Washington, West Virginia, and Wyoming, the state is the carrier.[2] In twelve states employers have a choice between state and private carriers.[3]

Benefit payments are usually based on a worker's wages at the time of the injury and the number of dependents. There are maximum and minimum payments for specified injuries and for total claims. Time limits for benefit payments are also common.

Costs to employers are, like any other insurance costs, a function of base rates, influenced by discounts for quantity purchases and the employer's past record. In 1978, average costs to employers noted in one survey ranged from a weekly cost of $0.68 per $100 of payroll in North Carolina to $4.18 per $100 of payroll in the District of Columbia.[4] These costs are likely to have gone up considerably in the last several years. In 1980, for example, forty-five states changed the maximum weekly benefits that were allowed for temporary total disability.[5] Of these changes in maximums, only one was a decrease, Alaska, from $654.30 to $650; all the others were increases, such as Kentucky, from $131 to $217, and Washington, from $186.88 to $221.72.

The Employee Retirement Income Security Act of 1974

The Employee Retirement Income Security Act of 1974 (ERISA) was passed to regulate the pension programs of employers. Although ERISA does not require employers to offer pension programs, it does require employers who do offer pension programs to follow certain rules if they want favorable tax treatment for both their contributions and their employees' deferral of income.

Briefly, ERISA applies to all employees twenty-five years or older who have completed one year or more of service. Some workers can be excluded, primarily those employees under a collective bargaining agreement where pension benefits are the subject of negotiation. Tax benefits for pension plans apply only to ERISA-qualified plans; the plans must cover 70 percent of all employees of the organization, or 80 percent of eligible employees where at least 70 percent of all employees are eligible, or some fair share of employees in a plan that does not favor officers, shareholders, or highly compensated employees. Basically, then, ERISA prohibits pension programs set up to benefit management only. A look at the law's provisions would help to explain the range of its application.

Vesting. Under ERISA, an employee gains ownership of accrued pension rights over a period of employment time, even if he or she then leaves the organization. This process is called vesting. Vesting requirements under ERISA vary, but basically there are three methods an organization can use. The simplest is the ten-year service rule; an employee is fully vested after ten years of service. A second method is the graded five- to fifteen-year service rule, under which the employee first gains 25 percent vesting in accrued pension rights after five years, then gains 5 percent additional vesting for each year of service for years six through ten, and finally 10 percent additional for each year of service in years eleven through fifteen. The third method, the rule of forty-five, requires 50 percent vesting when the sum of the employee's age and years of service equal forty-five (providing at least five years of service have been completed), then 10 percent vesting for each year of service thereafter. An additional limit on this method is that the employee must be 50 percent vested after ten years of service and 100 percent vested after fifteen years of service.

Accrual of benefits.   Computation of accrued benefits is subject to three constraints. Under the 3 percent rule the employee must accrue for each year of service (up to 33⅓ years) at least 3 percent of the benefit payable under the plan if the employee began participation at the earliest age and retired at normal retirement age. Under the 133⅓ percent rule the annual rate of accrual cannot exceed the accrual rate for a prior year by more than one-third (133⅓ percent of the prior year's rate). This prevents employers from backloading pension benefits. Finally, under the fractional rule, the benefits accrued for any year of service should equal an employee's projected benefit at normal retirement age prorated on the basis of the actual years of participation to normal retirement. Thus, if an employee has participated in a retirement program for twenty-five years, and by normal retirement age is expected to have participated a total of fifty years, then he or she should have 50 percent of expected benefits accrued.

Survivor benefits.   Plans qualifying for ERISA tax treatment must provide an option for employees to receive benefits in the form of a 50 percent joint and survivor annuity.

Funding.   ERISA-qualified plans must be funded. That is, employers must actually fund plans, and not simply carry obligations on the books, with a minimum annual contribution equal to a normal cost plus amortization over thirty years of unfunded accrued liabilities for all plan benefits.

Termination insurance.   Under ERISA, the Pension Benefit Guarantee Corporation (PBGC) was set up in the Labor Department. The function of the PBGC is to insure vested benefits in case organizations default on their obligations. A covered employer pays $2.60 per plan participant per year into the PBGC; vested benefits of up to $750 per month are guaranteed.

Benefit limitations.   ERISA restricts the amount of benefits paid to employees. Benefits may not exceed $75,000 per year or 100 percent of the employee's average compensation for the highest three consecutive earnings years, whichever is lower.

The Multiemployer Pension Plan Amendments Act (MPPAA) of 1980

The MPPAA amended the portions of ERISA dealing with the obligations of employers who participate in multiemployer pension plans. These plans are largely the result of collective bargaining agreements. Employers are required to bargain with a union over pension benefits, and a recent court case, *NLRB v. AMAX Coal Co.*, 101S Ct. 2789, June 29, 1981, determined that the union may legally bring pressure on an employer to join a specific multiemployer plan. The MPPAA requires an employer, once in such a plan, to assume the liabilities for the fund, even upon withdrawal. These liabilities may not necessarily be based on rights accrued to the employees of the employer, and they may in fact be completely out of the employer's control. It may be expected that at some point the problems caused by the AMAX decision and the MPPAA will create a push for revised legislation.[6]

Equal Employment Opportunity

The equal employment opportunity programs consist of several laws and executive orders. The principal laws are the Civil Rights Act of 1964, Title VII as amended by the Equal Employment Opportunity Act of 1972, the Age Discrimination in Employment Act of 1967 as amended in 1978, the Vocational Rehabilitation Act of 1973, Section 503, the Vietnam Era Veterans Readjustment Assistance Act of 1974 and Executive Orders 11246 of 1965 and 11375 of 1967. While these laws have an effect on all personnel functions, their major influence to date has been on the selection and placement functions.

Basically, the laws prohibit discrimination based on race, color, sex, religion, age, or national origin in any of the terms, conditions, or privileges of employment by employers, employment agencies, and labor unions. For government contractors, laws and executive orders require that in addition to the above protected groups employers must not discriminate against Vietnam era veterans or the handicapped, and also must take positive steps (or affirmative action) to correct the results of past discrimination. Since compensation decisions are covered by the law, employers must be prepared to justify any differentials between the sexes (the issue of comparable worth), races, or the majority and any protected group, with the same rigor (that is, by means of reliability and validity studies) that would be applied to any other personnel decisions needing justification.

Summary

Although our discussion of legal constraints touched only on the major points of laws, it should be clear that in some areas the compensation specialist has little leeway. FLSA, Davis-Bacon, Walsh-Healy, and McNamara-O'Hara all place lower limits on wage structures. In addition, FLSA defines the legitimate wage–effort bargain in terms of time, and specifies extra payment for work performed beyond that time. At various times, wage and price controls have set ceilings on the wage structure.

Benefit packages are constrained in two ways. OASDHI and worker compensation laws specify that certain benefits will be offered and also specify how much the employer must pay to offer them. ERISA places restrictions on how pension programs must be run, gives employees certain rights that they did not previously enjoy and requires insurance coverage of benefit obligations.

The various equal employment opportunity laws, including the Equal Pay Act of the FLSA, speak to the establishment and administration of pay and benefit systems. Although effects on pay and benefit systems have so far been limited to comparable worth issues, there is pressure to validate pay systems in the same way personnel deparments have been validating recruiting and selection systems. Legal constraints on employers with respect to wages and benefits are likely to become more complex and more stringent. The compensation analyst should be aided by legal specialists, then, to help ensure the legality of decisions made.

The Internal Revenue Code

The Internal Revenue Code (IRC) affects compensation programs in several ways, some of them fairly obvious. Most people know that the Code requires employers to withhold income tax from checks paid to employees, to send that withholding to the IRS, and to report to employees and the IRS the total amounts withheld.

Less familiar are the constraints the Internal Revenue Code places on benefits. Because the compensation package consists of both wages and benefits, and because there is some tradeoff between the two, it might seem reasonable that all benefits be taxed on the same basis as straight salary. In fact, this is not so. First, the IRC does consider some benefits taxable, but not all of them. Second, some benefits providing deferred income are taxed, not when the employer enters into an obligation to provide the benefit, but when the employee actually receives the benefit. This is true of pensions, profit-sharing plans, ESOPs, and TRASOPs, which are discussed further in Chapter 10. The IRC's third influence on benefits is the treatment of the employer's costs in providing benefits. Thus, for example under ERISA, a company for tax purposes may deduct pension payments from income only if that money is being invested to fund future pension benefits; current pension benefit payments may not be deducted.

Under the IRC, the Revenue Act of 1978, the Economic Recovery Tax Act of 1981, and other tax laws, certain benefits are nontaxable. Health, accident, and disability benefits are nontaxable; so is group term life insurance with a value up to $50,000. Services or perquisites may or may not be taxable. Whether they are taxed appears to depend upon the answers to the following questions that the IRS asks when looking at services and perquisites:

1. Is the expense really an expense of doing business and being reimbursed by the employer rather than being borne by the employee?

2. Are the beneficiaries the obvious ones? A country club membership for the director of public relations makes sense; one for the head of research and development may not. In general, services or perquisites provided only to executives will be considered taxable.

3. What costs are involved? Are they significant in comparison with recipient's income? What would be the cost of keeping track of these expenses and charging them to the individual recipients?

4. What do other, similarly situated organizations do?[7]

One other recent law deserves mentioning here, the Economic Recovery Tax Act of 1981. Several provisions of this tax act are likely to have substantial effects on benefit programs.[8] ERTA speaks to the tax treatment of individual retirement accounts (IRAs), incentive stock options, and payroll-based stock ownership plans for employees; it mandates the eventual demise of the Tax Reduction Stock Ownership Plan (TRA-

SOP) in 1983, and changes in the tax treatment of the Keogh plan and the simplified employee pension (SEP) plan; it extends the exclusion from taxable income of contributions to, and benefits provided under, prepaid group legal services; and it declares a moratorium on any changes in the tax status of fringe benefits until December 31, 1983. Although the details of the ERTA are beyond the scope of this book, we hope our brief overview of the subjects touched upon indicate the pervasiveness of IRS constraints on benefits.

The important matter for our purposes is to indicate that an understanding of tax laws is crucial to the construction of a comprehensive compensation program. Benefits that do not receive favorable tax treatment may benefit no one. Deferred income programs not meeting IRS requirements may be so reduced in value both to employer and employee that their power to attract, retain, and motivate may be negative.

Labor Unions

Labor unions place constraints on compensation programs in several ways. There is a supportive interaction between several federal laws and labor unions. Davis-Bacon and similar laws, for example, require that government contractors pay prevailing wages. The Departmnet of Labor determines what the prevailing wage in an area is; the cases in which this prevailing wage is not the union rate are rare. Thus, unions help determine the wages even for nonunionized employees.

Another constraint placed on compensation managers occurs only when a union is running an organization drive against an employer. The Labor Management Relations Act of 1947, also known as the Taft-Hartley Act, makes it an unfair labor practice to change the wage rates or benefits for employees during the organization drive. Thus, under such circumstances the compensation program of the organization is effectively frozen. A second unfair labor practice prohibited by the Taft-Hartley Act is any refusal to bargain over wages or benefits. It is the outcome of and the necessity for such bargaining that place the greatest constraint on compensation programs. It is not so much the actual settlement figure in a contract that constrains the compensation administrator. The constraint lies in the resulting inability of the compensation administrator to manage the compensation program, to make those changes which he or she believes the employer and the employee need, and to adjust the program to maximize its effectiveness in attracting, retaining, and motivating employees.

A look at typical provisions in union contracts, abstracted from *Basic Patterns in Union Contracts*,[9] indicates areas of constraint common in unionized organizations. With respect to wages, aside from the actual wage rate to be paid initially and increases to be made over the life of the agreement, there are frequently clauses for cost-of-living adjustments, and wage-opening provisions allowing the renegotiation of (1) wages during the life of the contract, (2) the status of negotiated increases under federal wage controls, (3) shift differentials, (4) reporting pay, (5) callback pay, (6) pay for temporary transfer, (7) hazardous work premiums, (8) travel expenses, work clothes and tools, and (9) nonperformance bonuses. In some cases there are clauses dictating the form of piecework or incentive rates, time study procedures (determining what a legitimate output for an employee is and thus the base of costing piecerate jobs), job evaluation methods, and job classification procedures. Hiring rates and wage progressions are also frequently specified. Thus, nearly every aspect of the basic wage and wage-setting process is removed from the administrative discretion of the compensation manager.

Employee benefit discretion is equally constrained. Contract clauses frequently specify formulas for determining retirement benefits, with special provisions for disability retirement, early retirement, the financing and funding of pensions, vesting procedures, and the administration and termination of plans. As we noted earlier, under the legal requirements of ERISA, the union may legitimately force bargaining, though it will still have to negotiate any concessions, concerning which multiemployer pension plan a company will join.

Contracts usually include provisions for life insurance, accidental death or dismemberment coverage, sickness and accident insurance, long-term disability, occupational accident insurance, hospitalization, surgical insurance, doctor's visits and major medical, maternity benefits, dental and optical care, prescription drugs, and the administration of insurance benefits. Severance pay, guarantees of work or pay, supplemental unemployment benefits, and other income-maintenance clauses also exist in many contracts. Various premiums for overtime work and weekend work are covered by many contracts along with provisions for paid lunch, rest, cleanup, and other nonproductive times. Holidays and holiday pay (pay for employees who must work on holidays) are specified, as are vacation entitlements and vacation pay.

In summary, when an organization is unionized, it may expect to meet with union demands on every aspect of the wage and benefit package. Because of this, and especially because unions insist that seniority, rather than performance, should be the deciding factor in many matters such as raises and promotions, compensation practices often do not achieve external, internal, or individual equity.

Notes

1. Wage and Hour Division, U.S. Department of Labor, *Handy Reference Guide to the Fair Labor Standards Act.* W.H. Publication 1282 (Washington, D.C.: U.S. Government Printing Office, 1978).

2. "Ohio's Pivotal Contest over Workers' Comp.," *Business Week*, October 26, 1981, p. 68.

3. M. W. Elson and J. F. Burton, Jr., "Workers' Compensation Insurance: Recent Trends in Employee Costs," *Monthly Labor Review*, March 1981, pp. 45–50.

4. Ibid.

5. L. C. Tinsley, "Workers' Compensation in 1980: Summary of Major Enactments," *Monthly Labor Review*, March 1981, pp. 51–57.

6. W. J. Vesely, Jr., R. R. Boisseau, and J. E. Curtis, Jr., "Multiemployer Pension Plan Liability: AMAX Coal and Beyond," *Journal of Pension Planning and Compliance* 1 (1981): 350–64; D. S. Bowling, "The Multiemployer Pension Plan Amendments Act of 1980," *Personnel Journal*, January 1982, pp. 18–20.

7. D. A. Weeks, *Compensating Employees: Lessons of the 1970's.* (New York: Conference Board, 1979), p. 63.

8. T. E. Rhodes and G. G. Quintiere, "Overview of Employee Benefit Changes Under the Economic Recovery Tax Act of 1981," *Journal of Pension Planning and Compliance* 7 (1981): 323–31; A. B. Shidler and D. G. Cziok, "The 1981 Economic Recovery Tax Act: A Stimulus to Employee Benefits, Compensation and Personal Savings Programs," *Journal of Pension Planning and Compliance* 7 (1981): 332–49; "Tax and Regulation Update." *Personnel Journal*, December 1981, pp. 924–27.

9. *Basic Patterns in Union Contracts* (Washington, D.C.: Bureau of National Affairs, 1979).

6

Job Pricing

A major goal of any compensation program is to maintain external equity, that is, to pay employees salaries and benefits equivalent to those paid to similar employees in other organizations. In fact, if there were an ideally efficient labor market, there would be a single wage for any given job, and compensation systems would be based on such rates. The market, however, is not very efficient, and for any given job we find a wide variety of wage/benefit packages, tempered by geographic, industrial, performance, and seniority differentials. A wage and salary survey, then, is designed to help the compensation analyst make informed decisions about wage rates that will more or less maintain external equity in the compensation system, allowing for labor market imperfections.

Wage and salary surveys can be used as a diagnostic tool as well. Behaviorally, compensation systems are designed to attract, retain, and motivate employees. High turnover or job offer rejection rates may be due to compensation levels, or to other factors. Wage and salary survey data can help the staffing manager judge the role that compensation levels play in staffing problems. Such survey data are also very important to labor relations experts preparing to negotiate a new contract.

Regardless of the uses to which the wage and salary survey data are put, the compensation analyst in need of such data has a "make-or-buy" decision. An organization can run its own survey (or take part in a joint effort), or it can use data collected by others. The tradeoff is generally between up-to-date comparisons with jobs of interest (running one's own survey) and lower cost data (data collected by others), which are easier to obtain. In the following sections, we will look first at the development of a custom survey and then at the use of data collected by others.

Wage and Salary Surveys: The In-House Project

There are several standard stages in making a wage and salary survey:

1. selecting jobs to be surveyed
2. defining relevant labor markets
3. selecting firms to be surveyed
4. determining information to ask
5. determining data collection techniques
6. administering the survey

Selecting Jobs to be Surveyed

No wage and salary survey will include data on all jobs in the organization. First of all, many jobs are unique to specific organizations; that is, there is no market. To attempt to get survey information on such jobs would be futile, since no other organization has an equivalent job. In addition, if the survey attempts to get information on too many jobs, the time it takes to complete the survey form becomes so great that many respondents will refuse to cooperate. Finally, the compensation specialist does not need information on every job: as we shall see in the next chapter, job evaluation processes make such information unnecessary.

Key jobs. The jobs that are chosen for the survey are known as key jobs. They make up a sample that reflects the organization as a whole. Most surveys include about twenty-five to thirty jobs as key jobs. In selecting key jobs, the compensation analyst uses a number of guidelines.

1. Key jobs should be readily definable. All aspects of the job should be describable in common English.

2. Many organizations should employ people in a key job. There is no point in surveying for salary data on a job if you are the only organization possessing such a job.

3. Key jobs should vary in terms of job requirements such as education and experience, and in terms of other "compensable factors." This diversity is of primary importance when survey data is combined with job evaluation data to build a salary structure.

4. Likewise, key jobs should represent all salary levels within the organization.

5. Key jobs should not be in the process of changing. If duties, skills, and responsibilities associated with a job are changing, then different organizations will be reporting data on noncomparable jobs.

6. The twenty-five to thirty key jobs should account for a sizable part of the employee population. Given two jobs similar in all other key job criteria, the compensation analyst would ordinarily choose for the survey the job that employs the most workers.

7. Key jobs for an organization will probably include any jobs with which the organization is having problems such as an inability to hire or excessive turnover.

8. Finally, though less important, key jobs should probably include those jobs traditionally used on wage and salary surveys. Inclusion of such jobs increases the probability that respondents will provide the data requested.

Defining Relevant Labor Markets

Having selected a set of key jobs, the compensation analyst must then determine the relevant labor markets for those jobs. For wage and salary surveys, the relevant labor market for a job is (1) the geographic area(s) within which one would ordinarily expect to recruit all potential employees for that job, and (2) the geographic area(s) to which one would ordinarily expect to lose employees in that job. Most of the time these markets are identical, but they need not be. Thus, one might hire mechanical engineers from a national market—this would be the case if recruiting was done primarily at schools of engineering—but lose engineers largely to local and regional competitors.

The relevant labor market is determined by where the major supply is. The labor markets usually differentiated by compensation analysts are local, regional, national, and international.

Local labor markets.   A local labor market is usually defined as being within easy commuting distance of an organization. A secretary, for example, is usually hired from a local labor market; an employer would not normally recruit in another city for secretarial employees. Likewise, a secretary is not likely to commute for two hours to a job, since an equivalent job is likely to be available at a lesser distance. The secretarial salaries of interest to the compensation analyst, then, are those offered by other organizations within that commuting area. Most blue-collar and white-collar jobs compete in the local labor market; external equity may be preserved by paying salaries that are in line with local market data.

Regional markets.   Some jobs have more regional markets. Schoolteachers, for example, tend to think of salary equity in terms of a state, or perhaps several states. Other technical, administrative, and professional jobs also tend to have labor markets that are not national but are broader than local markets. Accountants, MBAs, some engineers, and many technicians will be recruited only from a multistate area; most job movement within such professions will also be confined to regional markets. Thus, the compensation analyst interested in these kinds of jobs will have to determine the relevant region to survey. Recruiting experience and interviews with departing employees will help to place the boundaries on regional markets.

National markets.   There are a few jobs for which truly national job markets exist. These jobs tend to be highly skilled managerial and professional jobs. Doctors, college professors, executives, and some scientists and engineers tend to operate in national job markets. When dealing with national markets, the individual compensation analyst is much less likely to prepare a formal wage survey; he or she will tend to rely more heavily on data collected by others.

International markets.   Fortunately for the compensation analyst, there are few jobs for which there is truly an international market. Some transportation jobs, such as airline piloting, could be considered as such. Generally, analysts will rely on national market data for such jobs.

Selecting Firms to be Surveyed

Having determined the geographic area to which the survey will be restricted, the compensation analyst must then decide which firms within the area will be surveyed. There are several issues the compensation analyst must take into account when selecting firms to survey.

Labor supply competitors. The firms chosen should include those hiring the same kinds of employees as the surveying firm. These firms should be hiring substantial numbers of employees to fill the jobs being surveyed. Interviews with employees who are leaving may supply leads for potential survey firms.

Compensation system similarities. The firms chosen should include some using the same job evaluation system as the surveying firm. Salary similarities will provide some indication of the kind of job evaluation judgments being made. Conversely, comparability of job evaluation practices among employers will help to make surer salary comparisons.

Industry. If possible, some firms chosen should be in the same industry as the surveying firm. This is because wages are influenced by the type of industry; a firm in the same industry is likely to have similar wages, all other things being equal. In addition, a firm in the same industry is likely to have all the jobs being surveyed, and those jobs are more likely to be similar to jobs in the surveying firm than jobs with the same title in a different industry.

Size. Wages and benefits tend to vary according to size of organization. Thus, the compensation analyst will select firms of varying sizes, making sure to get some larger firms that account for substantial numbers of appointments.

Number of firms to survey. The compensation analyst must decide how many firms as well as which firms to survey. There is no magic number. In a small market with a few large employers, two or three firms may provide all the data needed. In larger local markets, as many as 200 or 300 positions may be surveyed within dozens of firms. National labor market surveys and some regional surveys will use sophisticated sampling strategies to ensure representative, "good" data. Such a strategy might require a survey of 1,000 to 1,500 firms.

Determining the Information to Ask

When deciding what information to request of surveyed organizations, the compensation analyst is faced with a choice between incomplete information versus no information at all. A complete but long survey may inadvertently discourage the cooperation of the surveyed organizations because of its length. Thus, what follows is the information the compensation analyst would usually like to know. How *much* information the analyst will actually acquire depends upon the influence he or she has, the number and kinds of jobs being surveyed, the method of data collection, whether other survey requests have been received by the surveyed organization, and random factors beyond the control of the compensation analyst.

The information wanted by the compensation analyst will be one of four kinds. The first is general information about the surveyed organization. The second is its wage and salary policy. The third is its benefits policy. The fourth relates specifically to each job being surveyed.

General information on the surveyed organization.   The first type of information required is general information on the surveyed organization, which will help the compensation analyst to judge whether that organization is similar to his own. This category also includes information that helps the compensation analyst to identify the organization for further contact if necessary. The information requested in this section of the survey would include:

1. Identification Data. The organization's name and address, and the contact person's name, title, and telephone number would be included.

2. Location of organization. If there are several locations, each would be noted and the total number of locations given. If the survey is local, a map might be provided for the respondent to pinpoint his location. This information would help the compensation analyst to determine the effect of commuting ease on salary differentials.

3. Industry. The surveyed organization's principle line(s) of business

should be requested. If possible, Standard Industrial Classification (SIC) codes should be used.

4. Size indicators. This would include sales volume, total number of employees, and number of employees at each location (if it is a multilocation organization).

5. Organization chart. The organization chart should include all jobs being surveyed.

6. Workweek length, hours worked per day.

7. Unions. All union representation should be noted, along with a description of the bargaining units.

Wage and salary policies. Wage and salary policy information is needed by the compensation analyst to understand the context in which specific wage rates operate. All policies affecting work-related pay should be surveyed. Included in such policies are:

1. The job evaluation system in use. A short description is sufficient here. The following chapter describes the four major types of job evaluation systems; in addition, there are several commercial packages used by many organizations.

2. The overall salary structure. An example of a structure is given in Chapter 8. Confidentiality is a major limitation on obtaining this information.

3. Merit adjustments to wages and salaries. The compensation analyst will want to know the basis for merit adjustments, such as supervisory ratings or other performance evaluations, base pay, and the frequency and size of increases. This information will help the analyst judge the stability of the salary data received.

4. Across-the-board increases. Of particular interest to the compensation analyst is any increase tied to cost-of-living adjustments (COLAs), again, to help judge the stability of salary levels. The frequency of such increases is also needed.

5. Miscellaneous performance-related payments. These are payments that, unlike merit adjustments, do not affect base pay. Profit-sharing programs, cost-reduction programs such as the Scanlon Plan, or other bonus systems related to performance and resulting in nonrecurring payments are of interest.

6. Miscellaneous pay differentials. Policies that affect the pay of individual employees, such as overtime, shift differentials, or holiday pay, are included here. Two individuals in the same job may get different take-home pay due to such differentials. In addition, the pay of the individual is likely to change over time.

Benefits policies. The compensation package today includes much more than direct pay. Benefits may, in fact, amount to as much as one-third of the total compensation package. (Benefit packages are described in detail in Chapter 9.) The compensation analyst needs to know benefit levels, because many organizations trade off benefits for direct salary levels; thus, comparison must be made between total compensation packages and not just wage levels. Major benefits that need to be surveyed include:

1. The pension policy. Company contributions (as a percentage of salary), vesting timetables, and retirement policies should be surveyed. If the organization pays the employee's contribution to Social Security (FICA tax) as well as its own, this should be noted.

2. Insurance. The level of contribution to life, health, dental, optical, and other insurance programs is of obvious interest to the compensation analyst.

3. Pay for time not worked. The organization's policies regarding vacations, holidays, and sick leave should be known. It is also important for the compensation analyst to know about conversion policies, carryover policies, and other organizational treatments of such pay for time not worked. Other leaves (jury duty, paternity/maternity leave, mariage leave, and so on) for which employees receive partial or full payment should be described. Information about paid lunches and rest breaks should also be sought.

4. Major miscellaneous benefits. The compensation analyst may wish to survey organizations for their miscellaneous benefits, such as credit unions, reimbursements for education, stock ownership programs, subsidized cafeterias or other services, thrift plans, or any other benefit that has substantial economic worth to the average employee and may have been substituted for direct wage payment.

Individual job data. The compensation analyst will want to evoke a variety of information on each job in the survey. In some cases, the analyst will provide the information and ask for agreement. Thus, a job title and job description will be provided, and in many cases, the *Dictionary* *of Occupational Titles* (DOT) job code will be given too.[1] This information is given to ensure that the organization being surveyed knows exactly what job the analyst is interested in. Space should be provided for the surveyed organization to note major departures from the job description. In addition, the analyst is likely to provide questions about on-the-job relationships, the amount of supervision received, the skills and training required of entry-level employees, and the number of employees supervised (if applicable). With this basic descriptive data ensuring job comparability covered, the analyst will ask for other information including:

1. Job incumbent data. This information includes the number of employees in the job, turnover rates, average seniority levels, average performance ratings, and the age of employees.

2. Wage and salary data. Six figures are frequently asked for. The first three are related to the salary structure ideal: the minimum wage for the job, the maximum for the job, and the midpoint of the range. The other three figures are related to the actual salaries paid: the current starting salary, the average pay given for the job, and the highest pay.

3. Miscellaneous data. This information would include anything that might account for the wage levels attached to the job, such as special perquisites, for example, a company car, or other benefits not given to all the employees of the organization.

Determining the Data Collection Technique

There are basically three methods of collecting wage and salary data: the telephone interview, the mailed questionnaire, and the group meeting. The one chosen by the compensation analyst will depend on the amount of information wanted, the number of organizations to be surveyed, the scope of the relevant labor market, and the time and budget available.

Telephone interviews. Telephone interviews are usually limited to collection of small sets of data from continuing contacts. Any compensation analyst would be unlikely to give out extensive information to an unknown caller. However, the telephone interview is quite useful when conducted within the informal network that exists in a profession.

The mailed questionnaire. Mailed questionnaires are the most common data-collection technique for wage and salary surveys. They allow for the use of a structured format that ensures getting the same information from all participants. Because respondents can fill out the questionnaire at their own pace, more information can be requested. However, it is also much easier for respondents to ignore or put aside the questionnaire.

The group meeting. Some wage and salary surveys, usually in local labor markets, have been done in group meetings. A list of the jobs to be surveyed is distributed beforehand, and compensation analysts taking part can bring relevant information with them to the meeting. The advantages of such a meeting are that gorup discussion and feedback can ensure that all information received is truly comparable, that differences can be ironed out, and that further information can be sought as it is required.

Administering the Survey

The actual structure of the survey used will be determined by the data collection technique decided on and the precise information being sought. However, the administration techniques used for a mail survey are generally applicable to other types. Before sending out a questionnaire (or calling an unknown respondent) one should contact the organization to be surveyed, explain the purpose of the survey, briefly outline the kinds of information that will be requested, and try to get a commitment for cooperation. Confidentiality of individual survey responses is guaranteed; that is, only aggregated or anonymous information will be published. A copy of the results of the survey is promised to those supplying data. This is the inducement that usually leads many of those contacted to cooperate, for the wage and salary information gained from the survey may be of as much use to them as to the initiating organization. And such information is of course obtained at a much lower cost than if they were to conduct the survey themselves.

The compensation analyst then will have to decide how much information he or she can safely ask for and still have other organizations cooperate. The amount of information really needed to solve the problems that required the survey in the first place must also be considered.

A budget for the survey should be drawn up before starting the project. Aside from printing, postage, and telephone costs, the major expense will be the labor of the compensation analyst and the clerical staff in developing and mailing questionnaires, and in tabulating and analyzing the collected information.

When questionnaires are constructed, the compensation analyst should consider both the ease with which respondents can answer questions and the ease with which completed questionnaires can be coded for analysis. It is better to give respondents questions that can be answered by *yes* or *no,* or with a checkmark in a multiple-choice response ("supervises ☐no ☐1–2 ☐3–5 ☐6–10 ☐11 or more employees"), than to use an open-ended question. Although organization charts, the overall salary structure, and some other items will not fit such a format, most information can be gathered in this way.

Outside Wage and Salary Surveys

Many organizations do not have the time or the money to devote to the ongoing collection of wage and salary data. In many cases, they get some or all of the data they need by participating in surveys conducted by other firms. They may also cooperate with other surveying organizations such as the Bureau of Labor Statistics of the U.S. Department of Labor, industry groups, private companies, and local groups such as chambers of commerce. In this section we will look at some of the major outside sources of wage and salary data available to the compensation manager. There are four primary sources: the aforementioned Bureau of Labor Statistics, other federal government groups, trade groups, and private firms. We will also look briefly at maturity curves.

The Bureau of Labor Statistics

The Bureau of Labor Statistics (BLS) is the major publisher of wage and salary survey data. The BLS puts out three major series of survey data: area wage surveys, industry wage surveys, and the National Survey of Professional, Administrative, Technical, and Clerical Pay.

Area wage surveys.   The BLS makes surveys of approximately 100 areas across the United States for a limited number of jobs. These areas are surveyed to provide wage and salary data used in administering the Service Contract Act of 1965, which requires government contractors to pay prevailing wages (see Chapter 5). A sample of the Service Contract Act survey for Lexington-Fayette County, Kentucky, is shown in Exhibit 6.1. Also, more extensive area wage surveys are made for seventy-one Standard Metropolitan Statistical Areas (SMSAs). The more extensive area surveys differ from the Service Contract Act surveys in two ways.

(Text is continued on p. 126.)

Exhibit 6.1   Area Wage Survey: Hourly Earnings[1] of Office and Plant Workers in Lexington–Fayette, Ky., December 1980

Occupation	Number of workers			Hourly earnings (all workers)[1]		
	All	Men	Women	Mean	Median	Middle range
SECRETARIES[2]	420	1	417	$6.72	$6.34	$5.33- $7.93
SECRETARIES, CLASS A	16	–	16	7.60	6.84	6.11- 8.21
SECRETARIES, CLASS b	89	–	89	6.79	5.76	5.37- 7.96
SECRETARIES, CLASS C	161	1	160	7.15	7.75	5.41- 8.45
SECRETARIES, CLASS D	91	–	91	6.58	6.70	5.90- 7.33
SECRETARIES, CLASS E	61	–	61	5.44	5.07	4.61- 5.81
STENOGRAPHERS	64	–	64	6.51	6.92	5.73- 7.18
STENOGRAPHERS, SENIOR	47	–	47	6.75	7.18	6.17- 7.18
STENOGRAPHERS, GENERAL	17	–	17	5.83	5.79	4.83- 6.12
TYPISTS[2]	26	6	20	5.51	4.04	3.65- 5.41
TYPISTS, CLASS B	23	6	17	5.57	3.93	3.61- 7.75
FILE CLERKS	37	–	37	3.76	3.49	3.35- 4.25
FILE CLERKS, CLASS C	37	–	37	3.76	3.49	3.35- 4.25
SWITCHBOARD OPERATORS	35	–	33	4.31	3.93	3.28- 5.15
KEY ENTRY OPERATORS[2]	160	2	158	5.31	4.94	4.60- 5.80
KEY ENTRY OPERATORS, CLASS A	62	2	60	6.15	5.82	4.92- 6.83
KEY ENTRY OPERATORS, CLASS B	97	–	97	4.79	4.65	4.36- 5.25
COMPUTER OPERATORS[2]	131	99	32	7.16	7.44	5.61- 8.65
COMPUTER OPERATORS, CLASS B	85	61	24	6.54	6.35	5.23- 7.98
DRAFTERS[2]	129	104	23	6.38	6.05	5.18- 7.86
DRAFTERS, CLASS A	12	11	1	8.41	–	– –
DRAFTERS, CLASS B	42	36	6	7.32	7.59	5.99- 8.36
DRAFTERS, CLASS C	66	52	12	5.68	5.50	4.63- 6.83
ELECTRONICS TECHNICIANS[2]	64	59	5	8.95	8.80	8.30- 9.37
ELECTRONICS TECHNICIANS, CLASS B.	12	10	2	10.64	–	– –
MAINTENANCE ELECTRICIANS	97	97	–	9.63	9.12	8.85- 11.18
MAINTENANCE MECHANICS (MACHINERY)	264	262	2	9.10	8.86	8.01- 9.61
MAINTENANCE MECHANICS (MOTOR VEHICLES)	80	80	–	8.79	8.00	7.05- 11.18
TOOL AND DIE MAKERS	193	193	–	10.80	10.60	10.00- 11.84
STATIONARY ENGINEERS	7	7	–	8.39	–	– –
BOILER TENDERS	17	17	–	8.52	7.07	7.07- 10.18
TRUCK DRIVERS[2][3]	508	502	6	8.66	7.46	6.70- 11.97
TRACTOR-TRAILER	348	347	1	9.31	8.08	6.85- 11.97
SHIPPING PACKERS	36	21	15	5.79	5.54	4.10- 7.82
MATERIAL HANDLING LABORERS	209	201	8	5.99	5.95	5.67- 6.97
FORKLIFT OPERATORS	395	386	9	6.90	6.79	6.10- 7.41
GUARDS[2]	78	75	3	6.80	7.30	4.90- 8.36
GUARDS, CLASS B	76	73	3	6.86	7.60	4.94- 8.36
JANITORS, PORTERS, AND CLEANERS	523	399	124	4.13	3.50	3.10- 4.85

[1]Excludes premium pay for overtime and for work on weekends, holidays, and late shifts. Incentive payments, such as those resulting from piecework, production bonuses, and commission systems, are included in the wages reported; nonproduction bonuses are excluded. Cost-of-living allowances are considered as part of the workers' regular pay. Hourly earnings reported for salaried workers are derived from regular salaries divided by the corresponding standard hours of work. The wages of learners, apprentices, and handicapped workers are excluded. The mean is computed for each job by totaling the earnings of all workers and dividing by the number of workers. The median designates position — half of the workers receive the same or more and half receive the same or less than the rate shown. The middle range is defined by two rates of pay: a fourth of the workers earn the same or less than the lower of these rates and a fourth earn the same or more than the higher rate.

[2]Includes workers other than those presented separately.

[3]Includes all drivers regardless of size and type of truck operated.

NUMBER OF WORKERS RECEIVING STRAIGHT-TIME HOURLY EARNINGS (IN DOLLARS) OF--

2.80 AND UNDER 3.20	3.20-3.60	3.60-4.00	4.00-4.40	4.40-4.80	4.80-5.20	5.20-5.60	5.60-6.00	6.00-6.40	6.40-6.80	6.80-7.20	7.20-7.60	7.60-8.00	8.00-8.80	8.80-9.60	9.60-10.40	10.40-11.20	11.20-12.00	12.00-12.80	12.80-13.60
-	-	-	12	41	35	40	46	38	24	22	24	38	49	25	16	7	3	-	-
-	-	-	-	-	-	-	1	4	3	1	1	1	2	-	1	-	2	-	-
-	-	-	-	4	10	13	19	15	2	2	-	2	-	3	14	5	-	-	-
-	-	-	1	22	8	13	8	8	2	2	9	23	42	20	1	1	1	-	-
-	-	-	3	4	3	6	9	9	16	15	11	9	5	1	-	-	-	-	-
-	-	-	8	11	14	8	9	2	1	2	3	1	-	1	-	1	-	-	-
-	-	-	5	4	6	-	5	6	6	21	3	3	2	-	3	-	-	-	-
-	-	-	4	3	2	-	2	2	4	21	3	1	2	-	3	-	-	-	-
-	-	-	1	1	4	-	3	4	2	-	-	2	-	-	-	-	-	-	-
-	5	8	2	2	2	1	-	-	-	-	-	-	-	-	6	-	-	-	-
-	5	8	2	1	1	-	-	-	-	-	-	-	-	-	6	-	-	-	-
-	25	2	4	-	6	-	-	-	-	-	-	-	-	-	-	-	-	-	-
-	25	2	4	-	6	-	-	-	-	-	-	-	-	-	-	-	-	-	-
-	15	4	6	-	3	-	1	2	3	-	-	1	-	-	-	-	-	-	-
-	2	8	21	35	29	21	8	10	5	7	2	2	9	-	1	-	-	-	-
-	-	-	2	10	11	6	3	5	4	7	2	2	9	-	1	-	-	-	-
-	2	8	18	25	18	15	5	5	1	-	-	-	-	-	-	-	-	-	-
-	-	-	6	3	11	13	7	10	5	9	8	4	33	15	7	-	-	-	-
-	-	-	6	3	11	11	6	6	3	7	7	4	20	-	1	-	-	-	-
-	-	6	13	6	11	12	14	8	7	9	9	10	13	8	3	-	-	-	-
-	-	-	-	-	-	-	-	2	-	-	-	-	5	3	2	-	-	-	-
-	-	-	-	-	1	3	8	1	4	1	4	7	7	5	1	-	-	-	-
-	-	2	11	6	8	9	5	5	3	8	5	3	1	-	-	-	-	-	-
-	-	-	-	-	-	-	-	1	-	-	4	3	4	6	31	3	10	2	-
-	-	-	-	-	-	-	-	-	-	-	-	-	-	1	-	9	2	-	-
-	-	-	-	-	-	-	-	-	-	-	-	-	19	49	-	8	21	-	-
-	-	-	-	-	-	-	6	-	-	-	-	-	106	63	30	22	26	3	-
-	-	-	-	-	-	-	8	-	-	15	13	-	10	11	-	4	3	16	-
-	-	-	-	-	-	-	-	-	-	-	-	-	3	37	13	59	66	11	4
-	-	-	-	-	-	-	-	-	-	-	-	1	6	-	-	-	-	-	-
-	-	-	-	-	-	-	-	-	-	9	-	-	-	-	8	-	-	-	-
-	10	27	48	4	16	5	-	1	65	76	13	-	9	-	-	-	160	74	-
-	1	6	-	4	1	5	-	1	65	76	13	-	4	-	-	-	98	74	-
8	-	-	6	-	1	7	3	-	-	-	-	5	-	-	6	-	-	-	-
-	3	9	6	11	13	5	64	42	-	12	40	-	-	-	4	-	-	-	-
-	12	-	2	-	4	18	34	111	45	46	53	-	23	3	42	-	2	-	-
-	4	2	-	7	14	2	-	-	6	-	5	2	30	6	-	-	-	-	-
-	4	2	-	5	14	2	-	-	6	-	5	2	30	6	-	-	-	-	-
184	94	49	8	48	42	16	9	24	21	15	9	-	4	-	-	-	-	-	-

Source: Bureau of Labor Statistics, March 1981.

Exhibit 6.2   Jobs Surveyed in an Area Wage Survey

Office Workers

*Occupation
and Industry Division*

Secretaries ....
  Nonmanufacturing ....
    Public utilities ....
  Secretaries, class A ....
    Nonmanufacturing ....
  Secretaries, class B ....
    Nonmanufacturing ....
    Public utilities ....
  Secretaries, class C ....
    Manufacturing ....
    Nonmanufacturing ....
    Public utilities ....
  Secretaries, class D ....
    Nonmanufacturing ....
  Secretaries, class E ....
    Nonmanufacturing ....

Stenographers ....
  Nonmanufacturing ....
    Public utilities ....
  Stenographers, general ....
    Nonmanufacturing ....
    Public utilities ....

Transcribing-machine typists ......
  Nonmanufacturing ....

Typists ....
  Manufacturing ....
  Nonmanufacturing ....
  Typists, class A ....
    Nonmanufacturing ....
  Typists, class B ....
    Nonmanufacturing ....

File clerks ....
  Nonmanufacturing ....
  File clerks, class B ....
    Nonmanufacturing ....
  File clerks, class C ....
    Nonmanufacturing ....

Messengers ....
  Nonmanufacturing ....
    Public utilities ....

Switchboard operators ....
  Nonmanufacturing ....

Switchboard operator-receptionists ..
  Manufacturing ....

Nonmanufacturing ....
  Public utilities ....
Order clerks ....
  Order clerks, class A ....
  Order clerks, class B ....

Accounting clerks ....
  Manufacturing ....
  Nonmanufacturing ....
  Accounting clerks, class A ......
    Manufacturing ....
    Nonmanufacturing ....
  Accounting clerks, class B ......
    Manufacturing ....
    Nonmanufacturing ....
    Public utilities ....

Payroll clerks ....
  Manufacturing ....
  Nonmanufacturing ....
  Public utilities ....

Key entry operators ....
  Manufacturing ....
  Nonmanufacturing ....
  Public utilities ....
  Key entry operators, class A .....
    Nonmanufacturing ....
  Key entry operators, class B .....
    Manufacturing ....
    Nonmanufacturing ....
    Public utilities ....

Professional and Technical Workers

*Occupation
and Industry Division*

Computer systems analysts (business)
  Nonmanufacturing ....
Computer systems analysts (business), class A ....
  Nonmanufacturing ....
Computer systems analysts (business), class B ....
  Nonmanufacturing ....
Computer systems analysts (business), class C ....
  Nonmanufacturing ....

Computer programmers (business) ..
  Manufacturing ....
  Nonmanufacturing ....

Computer programmers (business),
class A ....
Nonmanufacturing ....
Computer programmers (business),
class B ....
Manufacturing ....
Nonmanufacturing ....
Computer programmers (business),
class C ....
Computer operators ....
Manufacturing ....
Nonmanufacturing ....
Public utilities ....
Computer operators, class A ....
Nonmanufacturing ....
Computer operators, class B .....
Manufacturing ....
Nonmanufacturing ....
Computer operators, class C ....
Nonmanufacturing ....
Drafters ....
Nonmanufacturing ....
Drafters, class A ....
Nonmanufacturing ....
Registered industrial nurses ....

Material Movement
and Custodial Workers

*Occupation
and Industry Division*

Truckdrivers ....
Manufacturing ....
Nonmanufacturing ....
Public utilities ....
Truckdrivers, light truck ....
Truckdrivers, medium truck .....
Truckdrivers, heavy truck ....
Truckdrivers, tractor-trailer .....
Manufacturing ....
Nonmanufacturing ....
Public utilities ....
Shippers ....
Receivers ....
Manufacturing ....
Nonmanufacturing ....

Shippers and receivers ....
Nonmanufacturing ....
Warehousemen ....
Manufacturing ....
Nonmanufacturing ....
Public utilities ....
Shipping packers ....
Material handling laborers ....
Nonmanufacturing ....
Public utilities ....
Forklift operators ....
Manufacturing ....
Nonmanufacturing ....
Public utilities ....
Guards ....
Manufacturing ....
Nonmanufacturing ....
Guards, class A ....
Nonmanufacturing ....
Guards, class B ....
Manufacturing ....
Nonmanufacturing ....
Janitors, porters, and cleaners .....
Nonmanufacturing ....
Public utilities ....

Maintenance, Toolroom,
and Powerplant Workers

*Occupation
and Industry Division*

Maintenance machinists ....
Manufacturing ....
Maintenance mechanics (machinery)
Manufacturing ....
Maintenance mechanics (motor
vehicles) ....
Manufacturing ....
Nonmanufacturing ....
Public utilities ....
Maintenance trades helpers ....
Stationary engineers ....
Manufacturing ....
Nonmanufacturing ....

Source: Area Wage Survey: Seattle-Everett, Washington, Metropolitan Area, December 1980. Washington, D.C., U.S. Department of Labor, Bureau of Labor Statistics, April 1981.

First a larger number of jobs are surveyed. For example, Exhibit 6.2 shows the jobs for which wage and salary data were collected for an area wage survey of Seattle-Everett, Washington, in 1980. Second, the kinds of data provided are somewhat different. In addition to the kinds of data shown in Exhibit 6.1 (similar data are provided for all jobs in Exhibit 6.2), indexes of earnings and percentage increases for selected occupational groups are given for selected periods. Average pay relationships within establishments for selected occupations are also provided. Thus, the compensation analyst can discover, for example, that in the Seattle-Everett area in December 1980, the class A secretary earned 40 percent more, on the average, than the class D secretary in the same firm. Likewise, the shippers and receivers earned only 96 percent, on average, of a forklift operator's salary in the same firm.

Additional area wage surveys are available for some areas. To return to the Seattle-Everett area for a moment, the interested compensation analyst could get occupational earnings and supplementary wage provisions for banks and savings and loan associations, and union wage rates for the building trades, printing trades, local transit operating employees, local truck drivers and helpers, and grocery store employees.

Industry wage surveys.   The Bureau of Labor Statistics publishes surveys on approximately seventy industries, both manufacturing and nonmanufacturing. An example is the *Industry Wage Survey: Hospitals and Nursing Homes, September 1978* (published in November 1980). This survey includes wage and salary data for surveyed non-federal hospital workers in twenty-two geographic areas (e.g., Boston, Houston), giving the number of workers, and mean, median, and middle-range salary data. Breakouts are given for union and nonunion hospitals, private and state and local government hospitals, and part-time employees. Earnings distributions are provided for fourteen hospital occupations. Information is also given about minimum entrance salaries, scheduled weekly hours, shift differential policies, paid holidays, paid vacations, health insurance and retirement plans, and uniform allowances.

Similar information, in less detail, is provided for workers in nursing and personal care facilities. Finally, the federal government's hospital policies are noted. (Being consistent with the Federal Wage System, though adjusted by geographic area, Federal hospital pay is much simpler to report.)

The National Survey of Professional, Administrative, Technical, and Clerical Pay (PATC). The PATC covers eleven professional, administrative, technical, and clerical occupations, differentiating these into eighty-nine occupational levels. A sample table from the PATC, showing the occupations and levels surveyed, is presented in Exhibit 6.3. Examination of this exhibit should emphasize the wide variety of jobs included in the PATC survey. The PATC also provides complete information on salary distributions.

Other Government Surveys

Other branches of the federal government conduct, or contract out, wage and salary surveys. One such survey is the *National Survey of Compensation, Paid Scientists and Engineers Engaged in Research and Development Activities* prepared for the U.S. Department of Energy by Battelle Columbus Laboratories. This particular survey is of interest because it utilizes the maturity curve approach to salary structure. Sample data from this survey are presented in Exhibit 6.4. Notice that salary data are presented in terms of years from a terminal degree. This approach is frequently used for professional workers, whose increases come about largely through longevity. Maturity curves as wage-setting devices are further discussed both on p. 138 and in Chapter 8.

Trade Groups

Many trade groups provide wage and salary survey data for specialized occupations, industries, or locales. An example of one local survey is the *Dallas Area Salary Survey* sponsored by the Dallas Personnel Association. This survey, based on data on fourteen jobs from 176 organizations, provides a wide range of data not available in the BLS area wage survey. A sample page, for the position of receptionist/phone console operator, is shown in Exhibit 6.5.

    Another survey conducted jointly by the American Society for Personnel Administrators and A.S. Hansen, Inc., is the *ASPA/Hansen Salary Survey on Personnel and Industrial Relations Positions.* The 1980 data for the position of wage and salary analyst are shown in Exhibit 6.6.

Exhibit 6.3   Jobs Surveyed in PATC

Occupation and Level

Accountants and Auditors:

Accountants I
Accountants II
Accountants III
Accountants IV
Accountants V

Auditors I
Auditors II
Auditors III
Auditors IV

Public Accountants I
Public Accountants II
Public Accountants III
Public Accountants IV

Chief Accountants I
Chief Accountants II
Chief Accountants III
Chief Accountants IV

Attorneys:

Attorneys I
Attorneys II
Attorneys III
Attorneys IV
Attorneys V
Attorneys VI

Buyers:

Buyers I
Buyers II
Buyers III
Buyers IV

Personnel Management:

Job Analysts II
Job Analysts III
Job Analysts IV

Directors of Personnel I
Directors of Personnel II
Directors of Personnel III
Directors of Personnel IV

Chemists and Engineers

Chemists I
Chemists II
Chemists III
Chemists IV
Chemists V
Chemists VI
Chemists VII
Chemists VIII

Engineers I
Engineers II
Engineers III
Engineers IV
Engineers V
Engineers VI
Engineers VII
Engineers VIII

Technical Support:

Engineering Technicians I
Engineering Technicians II
Engineering Technicians III
Engineering Technicians IV
Engineering Technicians V

Drafters I
Drafters II

Technical Support (cont.)

Drafters III
Drafters IV
Drafters V

Computer Operators I
Computer Operators II
Computer Operators III
Computer Operators IV
Computer Operators V

Clerical:

Accounting Clerks I
Accounting Clerks II
Accounting Clerks III
Accounting Clerks IV

File Clerks I
File Clerks II
File Clerks III

Key Entry Operators I
Key Entry Operators II

Messengers

Personnel Clerks I
Personnel Clerks II

Personnel Clerks III
Personnel Clerks IV
Personnel Clerks V

Secretaries I
Secretaries II
Secretaries III
Secretaries IV
Secretaries V

Stenographers, General
Stenographers, Senior

Typists I
Typists II

Source: National Survey of Proessional, Administrative, Technical, and Clerical Pay, March 1979. Washington, D.C.: U.S. Department of Labor, Bureau of Labor Statistics, October 1979.

Private Firms

A large number of private firms provide salary data. A comprehensive listing of these firms and other sources of wage and salary data can be found in the *Prentice-Hall Personnel Policies* series volume on compensation. Compensation analysts should have access to the Prentice-Hall

(Text is continued on p. 138.)

Exhibit 6.4   A Maturity Curve Approach to Salary Surveys: Doctorate Degree—Nonsupervisory Employees—Total Survey: Working As Occupation—Electrical and Electronic Engineering

SALARY	0	1	2	3	4	5	6	7	8	9	10	11	12	13
6551-7550														
6051-6550														
5551-6050														
5051-5550														
4551-5050														
4451-4550														
4351-4450														
4251-4350														
4151-4250														
4051-4150														
3951-4050														
3851-3950														
3751-3850														
3651-3750														
3551-3650														
3451-3550												1	3	
3351-3450												1		
3251-3350												1	1	5
3151-3250												6	1	3
3051-3150											1	1	1	6
2951-3050											1	2	6	7
2851-2950									2	1	5	1	3	12
2751-2850										1	8	5	7	7
2651-2750								2	1	7	9	8	8	11
2551-2650						1	1	5	4	4	9	9	5	11
2451-2550					2	1	5	3	4	10	12	10	15	8
2351-2450							1	6	7	9	15	6	9	9
2251-2350					1	4	7	5	19	13	7	9	10	9
2151-2250					1	4	8	5	8	12	9	7	8	6
2051-2150					1	2	6	6	6	3	7	10	2	5
1951-2050								6	5	4	9	6	3	3
1851-1950						2	1	1	6	2	2	4	3	4
1751-1850								3	2	3	1	3	2	3
1651-1750											2	2	3	2
1551-1650												1	2	1
1451-1550														
1351-1450														
1251-1350														
1151-1250														
1051-1150														
951-1050														
851-950														
751-850														
651-750														
551-650														
SUM					6	13	38	41	66	73	98	85	86	109
%						1	3	6	10	14	19	24	29	36
MEAN					2367	2192	2187	2285	2239	2307	2417	2468	2537	2596
0.90						2342	2494	2628	2560	2660	2827	3100	3006	3101
0.75					2525	2293	2314	2475	2371	2487	2655	2696	2757	2897
0.50					2400	2212	2187	2280	2271	2307	2430	2465	2496	2618
0.25					2200	2112	2041	2087	2075	2160	2188	2182	2295	2319
0.10						1915	1930	1972	1876	1975	1980	1937	2130	2068

YEARS SINCE FIRST DEGREE

14	15	16	17	18–19	20–21	22–23	24–25	26–27	28–29	30–31	32–33	34–35	36–40	41–50	SUM	%
													1		1	100
						1				1	1		1	1	5	
							1	1	1						3	99
				1	1					2			1		5	
					1				2	1				1	5	
						1	1	1	1	1	2		1		8	98
	1			1				1		1		2			6	
		2						1	1	1	1	2			8	
	1		1	1	1	2		1		2	1	1	1		11	97
	1	1	1	1		4	2		1	3		2			15	96
1		1	2	2	2	3		4	1	1	1	1	3	1	24	95
1	2		1	2	2	3		2	3	2	1	1	2		22	
1	1		1	1	4	9	3	5	4	1	1	1	2		38	93
2	4	4	2	2	8	5	7	5	2	3	1		1	1	48	91
2	3	3	4	9	5	5	3	3	6	4	2	2	1		59	88
5	5	4	5	12	17	6	4	1	5	6	2	1	2	2	87	85
4	13	6	5	7	10	7	5	3	4	4	2	1	4		84	80
13	11	6	7	14	17	4	6	5	3	4	2		8	4	120	75
13	6	13	6	10	11	9	2	6	7	2	6	1	5	4	125	68
6	12	8	7	15	10	7	5	1	5	5	6	7	6	2	130	61
12	10	12	5	15	7	4	2	3	8		4	1	2		131	53
13	15	11	7	15	5	6	3	3	5		2	1	1		136	46
10	11	10	8	12	5	1	2			3	3	2	2		139	38
12	6	5	6	7	2	1	4		2	1	2	1	1		112	30
3	9	3	5	6	5	1	2	2	1	1					122	23
7	4	6	4	5	2	2		1			1		1		101	16
3		2	2	3	2			1		1					62	10
5	3			1		1									46	7
2	1	1		1	5	1	1				1			1	37	4
	1														18	2
		1			1										13	1
1															3	
		1													1	
	1														1	
115	121	99	79	142	123	81	59	49	65	50	40	26	46	16	1726	
42	49	55	60	68	75	80	83	86	90	93	95	96	99	100	2747	
2664	2767	2748	2814	2839	2943	3094	3097	3173	3094	3294	3018	3308	3189	3094	2747	
3137	3280	3253	3355	3314	3433	3695	3755	3727	3700	4150	3850	4070	3890	3690	3405	
2944	3055	2970	3095	3100	3210	3458	3410	3505	3345	3700	3250	3825	3475	3200	3047	
2662	2745	2729	2785	2796	2988	3100	3080	3133	3000	3216	2883	3250	3012	2975	2704	
2414	2497	2507	2484	2560	2703	2796	2737	2870	2715	2925	2700	2800	2825	2875	2374	
2157	2273	2231	2288	2336	2296	2568	2397	2580	2560	2516	2450	2610	2780		2136	

Source: *1979 National Survey of Compensation: Paid Scientists and Engineers Engaged in Research and Development Activities.* Prepared by Battelle Columbus Laboratories, Columbus, Ohio, for the U.S. Department of Energy, Office of Industrial Relations, 1979. Page H41.

Exhibit 6.5 Dallas Area Salary Data for Receptionist/Phone Console Operator

	Organizations with Match	Total Employees	Organizations with Salary Range	Total Employees in Position
TOTAL STATISTICS	150	93,324	130	322
Geographic Statistics				
Downtown	24	13,994	21	64
Downtown Dallas to Loop 12	47	17,078	37	86
Loop 12 to Dallas City Limits	24	7,400	21	42
Multiple Locations	18	30,118	16	42
Other Cities:				
Northern	20	10,213	18	49
Western	14	11,544	14	23
Industry Statistics				
Durable Manufacturing	34	19,337	31	52
Non-durable Manufacturing	13	4,909	11	24
Trade, Wholesale, and Retail	12	3,564	8	29
Financial, Real Estate, and Banking	14	3,972	12	39
Insurance	24	8,604	22	32
Utilities, Communications, Publications, Transportation	9	20,760	9	25
Service, Hospitals	11	6,641	9	35
Government (City, County, State, and Federal)	5	19,362	5	32
Other	28	6,175	23	54

	Average Starting*	Highest Actual Starting*	Average	Weighted Average	Average Highest	Average Minimum	Average Midpoint	Average Maximum
TOTAL STATISTICS	775	1,238	872	852	902	746	898	1,050
Geographic Statistics								
Downtown	770	904	868	862	906	722	883	1,045
Downtown Dallas to Loop 12	767	1,220	862	842	890	738	883	1,029
Loop 12 to Dallas City Limits	790	946	866	852	897	745	901	1,058
Multiple Locations	795	1,238	914	897	942	781	928	1,076
Other Cities:								
Northern	773	983	867	828	887	743	894	1,046
Western	765	875	883	884	915	764	931	1,098
Industry Statistics								
Durable Manufacturing	781	983	903	885	917	761	912	1,062
Non-durable Manufacturing	792	1,220	861	872	898	760	917	1,073
Trade, Wholesale, and Retail	770	900	863	884	892	740	920	1,099
Financial, Real Estate, and Banking	733	904	811	806	850	686	832	978
Insurance	742	925	848	847	856	702	860	1,019
Utilities, Communications, Publications, Transportation	810	1,238	1,001	1,002	1,083	822	995	1,167
Service, Hospitals	729	823	796	777	847	690	820	949
Government (City, County, State, and Federal)	689	735	776	713	810	689	799	908
Other	842	1,148	901	890	935	797	947	1,097

*Due to the number of organizations that did not report starting rates, the number of respondents for this calculation is less than for other calculations.

Source: 1980 Dallas Area Salary Survey. Dallas Personnel Association, 1980. Used by permission.

Exhibit 6.6   ASPA/Hansen Survey

POSITION CODE: 401
POSITION TITLE: WAGE AND SALARY ANALYST
POSITION DESCRIPTION:

STUDIES AND ANALYZES HOURLY OR SALARIED POSITIONS AND PREPARES DESCRIPTIONS IN STANDARDIZED FORM; EVALUATES POSITIONS USING ESTABLISHED EVALUATION SYSTEMS, DETERMINES GRADES AND PREPARES RECORDS OF THE VALIDITY OF THE EVALUATIONS; MAY SERVE ON POSITION EVALUATION COMMITTEES; CONDUCTS COMPENSATION SURVEYS AND PARTICIPATES IN COMPENSATION SURVEYS CONDUCTED BY OTHER COMPANIES.

NO. OF FIRMS: 198
NO. OF EES.: 245
PERCT FIRMS PAYING BONUS: 8.1%
PERCT EES. RECEIVING BONUS: 6.9%

SUMMARY OF REPORTED SALARIES & BONUSES

FORM OF COMPENSATION:	NO. OF FIRMS	NO. OF EES.	10TH PERCTL	25TH PERCTL	AVG	50TH PERCTL	75TH PERCTL	90TH PERCTL
SALARY(ALL EES.)	198	245	$ 14.8	$ 16.3	$ 19.7	$ 18.9	$ 22.3	$ 25.3
SALARY(NO BON.EES.)	182	228	14.8	16.2	19.6	18.8	22.0	25.1
SALARY(BONUS EES.)	16	17	13.0	17.5	21.1	20.4	23.5	26.0
BONUS(BONUS EES.)	16	17	.4	.9	2.0	1.6	2.1	2.6
TOTAL(BONUS EES.)	16	17	13.6	19.6	23.1	21.4	25.2	27.8
TOTAL(ALL EES.)	198	245	14.8	16.3	19.8	19.0	22.4	25.4

Exhibit 6.6 *(continued)*

AVERAGE SALARY RANGE MIDPOINT $ 21.4	COMPA-RATIO (AVERAGE SALARY ALL FIRMS/ AVERAGE SALARY RANGE MIDPOINT)	.92
NUMBER OF FIRMS REPORTING RANGE 185	AVERAGE NUMBER OF EMPLOYEES SUPERVISED	

RELATIONSHIP OF COMPENSATION TO SCOPE

SCOPE MEASURE 1: GROSS SALES

RANGE	NO. OF FIRMS	NO. OF EMPLOYEES	AVERAGE SALARY	AVERAGE TOTAL	AVERAGE EMPLOYEES SUPERVISED
UNDER $50 MILLION	14	14	$ 19.3	$ 19.4	
$50 - $125 MILLION	26	27	22.1	22.3	
$125 - $400 MILLION	32	38	21.5	22.0	
OVER $400 MILLION	25	26	20.8	20.9	

SCOPE MEASURE 2: EMPLOYMENT

RANGE	NO. OF FIRMS	NO. OF EMPLOYEES	AVERAGE SALARY	AVERAGE TOTAL	AVERAGE EMPLOYEES SUPERVISED
UNDER 200	11	18	$ 20.5	$ 20.7	
200 - 500	19	19	18.4	18.5	
501 - 1,000	39	43	20.2	20.3	
1,001 - 2,500	73	83	19.9	20.0	
OVER 2,500	56	82	19.3	19.5	

Exhibit 6.6 (*continued*)

FINANCE

SCOPE MEASURE 1: ASSETS

RANGE	NO. OF FIRMS	NO. OF EMPLOYEES	AVERAGE SALARY	AVERAGE TOTAL	AVERAGE EMPLOYEES SUPERVISED
UNDER $500 MILLION	3	4	$	$	
$500 MIL - $1 BILLION	5	6			
OVER $1 BILLION	12	13	19.9	20.4	

INSURANCE

SCOPE MEASURE 1: PREMIUMS PAID

RANGE	NO. OF FIRMS	NO. OF EMPLOYEES	AVERAGE SALARY	AVERAGE TOTAL	AVERAGE EMPLOYEES SUPERVISED
UNDER $100 MILLION	5	7	$	$	
$100 - $500 MILLION	7	8			
OVER $500 MILLION	4	5			

Exhibit 6.6 (continued)

GOVERNMENT

SCOPE MEASURE 1: OPERATING BUDGET

RANGE	NO. OF FIRMS	NO. OF EMPLOYEES	AVERAGE SALARY	AVERAGE TOTAL	AVERAGE EMPLOYEES SUPERVISED
UNDER $100 MILLION	7	13	$ 22.0	$ 22.0	
$100 - $500 MILLION	4	6			
OVER $500 MILLION	1	6			

MISCELLANEOUS SERVICES

SCOPE MEASURE 1: OPERATING BUDGET

RANGE	NO. OF FIRMS	NO. OF EMPLOYEES	AVERAGE SALARY	AVERAGE TOTAL	AVERAGE EMPLOYEES SUPERVISED
UNDER $20 MILLION	13	14	$ 18.5	$ 18.5	
$20 - $50 MILLION	14	18	18.1	18.1	
$50 - $100 MILLION	13	15	18.1	18.1	
OVER $100 MILLION	11	23	16.7	16.7	

Source: ASPA/Hansen *Salary Survey on Personnel and Industrial Relations (PAIR) Positions.* Berea, Ohio: American Society for Personnel Administration, 1980. Reprinted by permission of the American Society for Personnel Administration.

series, and to similar publications from the Bureau of National Affairs and Commerce Clearinghouse.

Maturity Curves

A variant to pricing a specific job in terms of the external market is the maturity curve. A maturity curve represents wage data for a profession, for example, engineers, accountants, or physicians, rather than for specific jobs. A typical maturity curve presents wage or income data for the profession as a function of time since professional degree. An example of a maturity curve is seen in Exhibit 6.7.

In effect, maturity curves are substitutes for wage information about specific jobs. They simply report wage or income trends for professionals as a function of time in the profession. An external equity criterion is served in setting wage rates for employed professionals according to maturity curves to the extent that a firm wants to keep an employed professional on an income par with the rest of his or her profession.

Maturity curves, however, do not address issues of internal and individual equity very well. Income trends in a profession have little or nothing to do with the real value of an employed professional to his or her organization. Similarly, should a company make pay distinctions among those employed in a given profession according to their time at work since their professional degrees, factors such as individual performance and company loyalty (seniority, or time with the employer) are not recognized.

Utilizing Survey Data

Regardless of whether wage and salary data are generated through an in-house survey or purchased from external sources, the compensation analyst needs to compare survey data with the figures from his or her own organization. A number of comparisons are needed; the following exhibits developed for the Heavyweight Manufacturing Company show how both in-house and purchased data can be used.

Heavyweight has a salary structure consisting of nine salary ranges. Adjustments to the midpoints of these salary ranges have been proposed by the compensation analyst; the comparisons to be made are between survey data and the proposed structure. It should be noted that survey

Exhibit 6.7   Maturity Curve—Scientists and Engineers

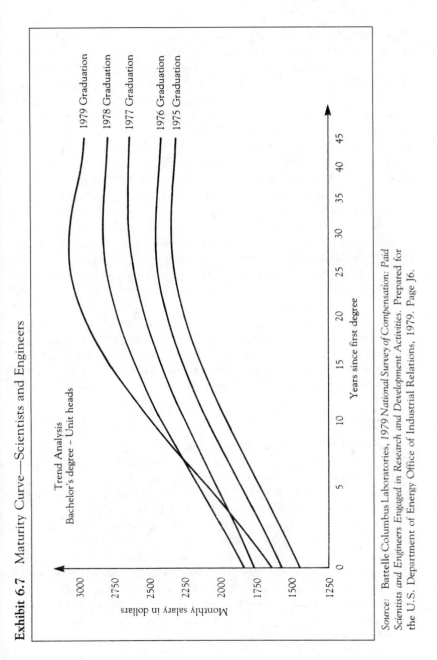

Source: Battelle Columbus Laboratories, *1979 National Survey of Compensation: Paid Scientists and Engineers Engaged in Research and Development Activities.* Prepared for the U.S. Department of Energy Office of Industrial Relations, 1979. Page J6.

data always lag behind current salary levels; the analyst would expect his or her own organization's current salaries to be greater than survey data, and would expect a proposed system to exceed survey levels by a considerable amount (depending on the actual and forecasted levels of inflation). Exhibit 6.8 shows the first comparison, that of Heavyweight's midpoints the survey's midpoints. To help account for the lack of currency of the data, the compensation analyst has obtained the range adjustments contemplated by organizations in the survey; these data are shown in Exhibit 6.9. The analyst has also gotten data from two trade association surveys, also shown in Exhibit 6.9, indicating annual percentage range adjustments for several previous years. Finally, the compensation analyst has graphed comparison data; this comparison is seen in Exhibit 6.10. In this case, the comparisons are between the proposed Heavyweight wage curve, constructed by connecting the midpoints of each pay grade, and (1) current industry wage data from Exhibit 6.8 and (2) industry wage data adjusted for expected increases, based on data in Exhibit 6.9. This comparison indicates that Heavyweight's proposed structure will continue to lead the industry.

Of course, the kinds of comparisons the compensation analyst will make depend on the problems leading the organization to conduct a wage and salary survey in the first place. However, both tabular and graphic presentations of the information received will increase the value of that information and the ease of proposing changes to management.

Summary

It is crucial for the compensation analyst to get wage and salary survey data if external equity is to be maintained. Whether the analyst chooses to do his or her own survey or to acquire survey data from other sources depends on the specific problem(s) facing the organization. Most larger organizations will probably acquire data from both sources.

Naturally, even the most comprehensive survey will not "tell" the analyst what a specific job should be paid. A wide range of salaries exists for most jobs. The median salary for wage and salary analysts, for example, is as low as $12,900, and as high as $21,800, depending upon the industry and other circumstances (see Exhibit 6.6). Wage and salary surveys only provide benchmarks for the compensation analyst. Before setting up a wage structure, the analyst must consider internal equity issues, that is, the relative value of jobs within the organization.

Exhibit 6.8 Heavyweight Manufacturing Company Midpoint Comparison

| | | | | Sample Wage Survey Metalworking Personnel Group—December, 1999 | Salary Proposal July 1, 2000 |
| | | | | Plus or Minus Survey | |
Grade	Survey Population	Heavyweight Midpoint[a]	Survey Midpoint Average[a]	Dollars	Percent
3	33	$4.85	$4.46	$+.39	+8.7%
4	91	5.37	4.93	+.44	+8.9
5	10	5.91	5.44	+.47	+8.6
6	4	6.40	5.87	+.53	+9.0
7	27	7.04	6.46	+.58	+9.0
8	20	7.70	7.08	+.62	+8.8
Overall (Weighted)	185	$5.82	$5.35	$+.47	+8.8% above average of midpoints

(Results of 1998 survey = 11.1% above average of midpoints)

Heavyweight Current Population 384

[a]Midpoints represent midpoint of salary structure ranges.

Source: R. Beatty, N. F. Crandall, C. H. Fay, R. Mathis, G. T. Milkovich, and M. J. Wallace, Jr., *How to Administer Wage-Salary Programs and Perform Job Evaluations.* New York: Penton Learning Systems, 1979, p. 83. Reproduced by permission.

Exhibit 6.9   1999 Midpoint Trend

| Date | Company | Metalworking Sample Survey | Salary Proposal July 1, 2000 |
		Surveyed Employee Population	Actual or Anticipated Range Adjustment
6–1–1999[a]	Zankowski's Metalworks	52	6.0%
9–1–1999	Gama Products	78	5.2
9–1–1999	Mannix, Inc.	57	5.0
2–1–2000	Alpha Manufacturing	145	5.7
1–1–2000	Lumman's Laminations, Inc.	198	5.4
2–1–2000	Tip & Tater Company	86	5.5
3–1–2000	Alco Electronics	123	4.8
7–1–2000[a]	Exco Heavy Construction	—	Unknown
7–1–2000[a]	Machined Tools	—	Unknown
—	Tool & Die Designers	Does not use pay ranges	
Overall		739	5.4%

[a]Unionized Firms—Zankowski's a deferred wage increase and contracts to be negotiated for other two firms.

| Survey | Other Trend Data | | | | |
	1995	1996	1997	1998	1999
AMA Sample Survey Trend	3.7	4.0	4.7	5.6	6.5
Metalworking Trades Survey	2.0	1.6	4.4	7.1	4.7

Source: R. Beatty, N. F. Crandall, C. H. Fay, R. Mathis, G. T. Milkovich, and M. J. Wallace, Jr., *How to Administer Wage-Salary Programs and Perform Job Evaluations.* New York: Penton Learning Systems, 1979. Reproduced by permission.

Exhibit 6.10 Comparison of Proposed Heavyweight Midpoints to Metal-working Survey Midpoints

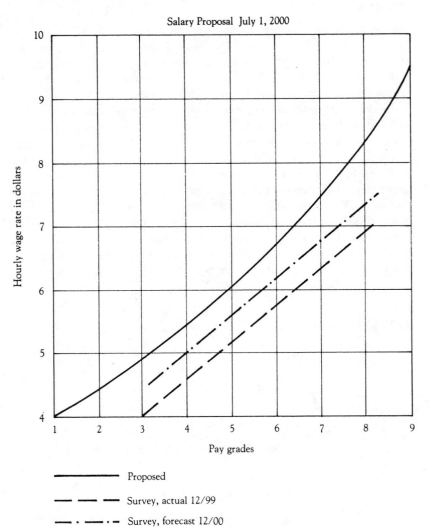

Salary Proposal July 1, 2000

Hourly wage rate in dollars

Pay grades

——————— Proposed

— — — — Survey, actual 12/99

— · —— · — Survey, forecast 12/00

Source: R. Beatty, N. F. Crandall, C. H. Fay, R. Mathis, G. T. Milkovich, and M. J. Wallace, Jr., *How to Administer Wage-Salary Programs and Perform Job Evaluations.* New York: Penton Learning Systems, 1979. Reproduced by permission.

Postscript

We begin our discussion of wage-setting practices and techniques as we began our discussion of the theory of wage determination, with processes related to external rather than internal equity. Although this reverses the order found in most books, we feel it is important to underline the sovereignty of external equity influence on wages over internal equity influence. Certainly the power of a wage or salary to attract employees is based solely on external equity considerations. The retention power of a wage or salary is also influenced heavily by external equity considerations. When external and internal equity considerations are in conflict, we suspect, though lacking scientific evidence, that external equity takes precedence. Comparable worth advocates have certainly found this to be the case. Any organization constructing a wage and salary structure *de novo* is likely to start with market data. In the ongoing organization, of course, internal and external equity processes are likely to be carried out simultaneously, with strong effects upon each other. Such a simultaneous presentation is, unfortunately, not possible in the format of a book.

Notes

1. U.S. Department of Labor, *Dictionary of Occupational Titles,* 4th ed. (Washington, D.C.: U.S. Government Printing Office, 1977).

7

Job Evaluation and the Wage–Salary Structure

As we noted in Chapter 6, it is not enough for the compensation analyst to collect wage and salary data and use it directly as the wage salary structure. First of all, the survey data will not consist of a single wage for any job, but will be made up of a broad range of wages reflecting location, size, industry, employee demographics such as seniority and performance levels, and other factors. Second, it is not possible for any organization to collect wage and salary data for all jobs in the organization. Most jobs in any organization have some characteristics unique to that organization. Secretaries in one organization may be expected to operate automated data retrieval equipment requiring special training; in another organization, secretaries may have to deal with no higher a technology level than the electric typewriter. There are also jobs in many organizations for which there is no market; that is, the job is truly unique to that organization. The so-called administative assistant is a job for which this is frequently the case. The variety of abilities, skills, company-related experiences, and specific training often required belies the generality of the title.

Third, even if single rates (with adjustments for location, and so on) were available for all jobs in the company through surveys, such rates would not satisfy internal equity demands. The value of an engineer to company A and company B relative to the value of a lawyer to those two companies could vary significantly, depending on environmental pressures. If company A has a history of discrimination cases but its products are very successful, and company B has few legal problems but has significant quality control problems, the relative worth of lawyers and engineers may vary considerably.

Thus, lack of information and internal equity considerations require that market data alone not be used to build the wage and salary structure. In fact, the structure is usually built on internal equity considerations and then adjusted to meet market forces. These internal equity decisions, when formalized, become the process known as job evaluation, that is, what jobs are worth to the organization: which jobs are of similar value, which are worth more, and which are worth less. After describing current approaches to job evaluation, we will show how the results of job evaluation are merged with market data to achieve the final wage-salary structure.

Job Evaluation

The immediate purpose of job evaluation is to create a hierarchy of jobs based on their value, or worth, to the organization doing the evaluation. Most job evaluation techniques do not have as their initial result the wage and salary structure, but rather a ranking of jobs by classification, or a ranking in some other format. The jobs then must have prices attached to them within the structure of their ranking.

Job evaluation is the process by which one tries to ensure internal equity—that jobs of comparable worth receive comparable wages. It is not, on the whole, concerned with value of the job in the external market.

Job Families

When undertaking a job evaluation, the compensation analyst first must decide the scope of jobs to which the job evaluation process will be applied, and thus, the number of job-worth structures that will be constructed. There are several arguments for having a single job-worth structure, but most of them are based on one of two factors. First, an organization ends up with a simple wage and salary structure in that one job is paid in one range, and a second job in another range. In the end, jobs are paid in common units, dollars; and the job-worth structure should be common to all jobs too. If different structures are developed, say for managers and supervisiors, points of overlap, between lower managers and upper-level supervisors, for example, may create problems. The compensation analyst will, in any case, have to combine the two or more job-worth systems into a common wage-and-salary structure.

Aside from difficulties from the organization's point of view, employees may not feel internal equity goals are met when they compare their pay to the pay of others whose jobs are valued under a different system, or to the pay they receive when they are moved to a different job which is valued under a different system. This is a litigious age, and an employer may find it difficult to justify valuing one set of jobs on one basis while valuing another on a second basis, particularly if the two systems result in an adverse effect on any legally protected group.

Countering these arguments, proponents of multiple job-worth structures point out that most organizations do have separate pay systems, for example, exempt versus nonexempt, or union versus nonunion, and for a variety of practical reasons often wish to recognize those differences in the job-worth structure. If the compensation analyst does decide on separate job-worth structures, he or she will use a variety of criteria to help determine which jobs should be clustered into *job families*. The job-worth structures will then be constructed for those job families.

Criteria.   The criteria used for clustering are those related to administering wage and salary systems, and those which make building the worth structure easier. Criteria related to ease of job evaluation include:

1. common skills
2. common occupational qualifications
3. common technology
4. common licensing
5. common working conditions.

Criteria related to administering the final wage and salary system include:

1. common union jurisdictions
2. common work place

3. common status with respect to the law (for example, exempt versus nonexempt)
4. common career paths
5. organizational tradition
6. special compensation arrangements (for example, sales personnel and executives).

Typical job families used in job evaluations based on these criteria include sales, managerial, supervisory, production, technical, and clerical, though other categories are sometimes used.

Sources of Value

A second major decision to be made by the compensation analyst (with agreement by the organization) is the source of value in jobs. Some job evaluation techniques require that these sources of value be made explicit, but all job evaluation requires that the organization think about what aspects of a job have value to the organization. These sources of value are known as compensable factors. In the discussion of internal equity in Chapter 3 we noted the demand-side and supply-side aspects of job value. In practice, compensable factors may be classified into job inputs (what employees bring to the job) and job outputs. Inputs, include experience; education; effort; responsibility for people, assets, or workflow; and ability to function under various working conditions. Job outputs include work outcomes such as production, profit, or results.

Job Analysis

Having decided on the sources of job value, the compensation analyst must get job descriptions that will allow him or her to estimate the degree to which jobs possess the factors that create value. This is generally done through job analysis. It is important to differentiate job analysis and job evaluation. Job analysis is a systematic study of the tasks making up a job, the employee skills required to do the job, time factors, situation-specific factors such as the technology used, certain physical aspects (for example, lighting and temperature), information flows, interpersonal and group interactions, and historical traditions. From good job analysis procedures, job descriptions can be written. One reason it is important for the compensation analyst to make decisions about sources of value before selecting a job analysis technique or getting job descriptions is to ensure that the job analysis procedure speaks to those dimensions of jobs which give them value to the organization.

Ordinarily, the compensation analyst will not be the individual doing the job analysis. Because job analysis is the basis for many personnel processes—such as performance appraisal, selection, and training—each of which requires knowledge of different aspects of jobs to different degrees, most organizations have specially trained job analysts who can coordinate the analysis with the needs of other personnel specialists. Thus, the compensation analyst will have as input a series of job descriptions to work with.

A typical job description the compensation analyst might get is shown in Exhibit 7.1. This description, after a general summary of the job, lists the key tasks performed by the employee and the amount of time devoted to each task. A task-statement data sheet at the end of the description notes the equipment used, the knowledge, skills, and abilities required for each task, and the level of difficulty or consequence of error associated with each task.

Further information is provided on supervisory responsibilities, supervision received, external contacts, and equipment used on the job. Finally, different aspects of working conditions are noted and the variety of training (both formal and on-the-job) is listed. Similar data sheets would be provided to the compensation analyst for all jobs in the job family under evaluation.

Job Evaluation Techniques

Hundreds of job evaluation techniques have been developed over the years. The great majority of them belong to four general types. These types can be differentiated by looking at two major lines along which job evaluation systems vary. The first question concerns the directness of the evaluation, whether a job being evaluated is compared to some other job directly (that is, ranking), or whether it is measured against some standard to produce a rating, with the rating then being compared with the ratings of other jobs. The second question concerns the specificity of the evaluation, whether the comparison is made on the basis of the whole job, or whether specific factors in jobs are compared. These characteristics suggest a classification table for the four major types of job evaluation as

Exhibit 7.1   Job Description

Date Issued: _____

Job Title: Secretary II

Summary of Job:

Under general supervision independently performs assigned administrative and secretarial duties. Maintains log of executive staffs' activities and whereabouts. Executes special assignments as requested by various staff personnel.

Job Tasks:

Task 1:   10% — Keeps records of special activities for various staff representatives.

Task 2:   60% — Performs general secretarial duties for all four members of executive staff (correspondence, reports, and telephone duties).

Task 3:   10% — Communicates and answers telephone. Supplies appropriate information when possible and directs caller to appropriate other if not.

Task 4:   10% — Executes special assignments as requested.

Task 5:   10% — Maintains staff appointment calendars and itineraries. Coordinates trip details and schedules with travel department.

Supervisory Responsibilities: None

Supervision Received: Direct 25% — General 25%

External Contacts: Customers, operating managers, travel department

Equipment Used: Telephone, IBM Selectric, Electronic Calculator, Copier, Dictaphone.

Employee: _____
Supervisor: _____

Working Conditions

Hazards: None

Work Environment: Comfortable

Noise Level: Below normal office exposure

Lighting: Excellent

Temperature: Controlled 70–72 degrees

Miscellaneous: —

Job Training

A. Required Experience: (Include other jobs) 2–3 years secretarial exposure

B. Formal Educational Experience: Time in semesters/quarters

Vocational Courses: —

High School Courses: Shorthand, typing

College Courses: —

Continuing Education: —

C. Internal Training Programs: Telephone etiquette/message-taking

Task Statement: 1–5

1. Equipment Utilized: Typewriter, telephone, Dictaphone®, calculator, copier

2. Knowledge Required: Filing, business forms, telephone etiquette, general business experience

3. Skills Required: Typing, shorthand, and mathematical

4. Abilities Required: As indicated, and good at thinking on his/her feet.

5. Time Spent and Frequency of Performance: —

6. Level of Difficulty/Consequence of Error: Varies by particular task/ basically error-free

Source: Adapted from R. Beatty, N. F. Crandall, C. H. Fay, R. Mathis, G. T. Milkovich, and M. J. Wallace, Jr., *How to Administer Wage-Salary Programs and Perform Job Evaluations.* New York: Penton Learning Systems, 1980.

depicted in Exhibit 7.2. We shall look at all four types: first at the two whole job systems, then at the two systems utilizing specific job factors.

Ranking. The ranking of jobs is the simplest evaluation system available. When there are fewer than twenty jobs, ranking is probably an acceptable method. It is simple, fast, and inexpensive. There are two ways of ranking jobs. The first is a forced ranking, done either by one individual or a committee. In either case, one job is chosen as having most value to the organization, a second as having next most value, and so forth, until one job is chosen as having the least value to the organization. There are several problems inherent in this technique. There are no standards for comparison. Job A may be seen as more valuable than job B because it requires much more responsibility; job B may be seen as more valuable than job C because of educational differentials, and so on. This lack of standards makes rankings particularly vulnerable to bias when most of the job incumbents are women or minorities. In addition, forced rankings do not allow for jobs having equal value. Nor are changes in job value readily accommodated by the ranking method. Ranking does not indicate how much *more* value job A has than job B, and value differentials are essential if internal equity is to be preserved. Most individuals appear to have trouble ranking many jobs: most can agree on which jobs have most value and which have least, but the mid-level jobs are difficult to differentiate.

To get around this, proponents of ranking techniques have used paired comparisons, in which each job is compared to every other job and the job of most value in each pair is noted. The score for a job is the

Exhibit 7.2   Four Approaches to Job Evaluation

	Whole Job	*Specific Job Factors*
Job vs. Job	ranking method	factor comparison method
Job vs. Standards	classification method	point method

Source: Adapted from R. Beatty, N. F. Crandall, C. H. Fay, R. Mathis, G. T. Milkovich, and M. J. Wallace, Jr., *How to Administer Wage-Salary Programs and Perform Job Evaluations.* New York: Penton Learning Systems, 1980.

number of times it is considered the most valuable; ranks are based on these scores. There are two drawbacks to the paired-comparison technique. First, there is still no guarantee that comparisons are made on the same basis. A second equally serious drawback is that as the number of jobs to be ranked rises arithmetically, the number of paired comparisons to be made rises geometrically. The formula showing the number of comparison decisions to be made is $CD = \frac{N(N-1)}{2}$, where N is the number of jobs to be ranked. Thus, with seven jobs to be ranked, the analyst must make $\frac{(7)(6)}{2} = 21$ comparison decisions; with twenty jobs to be ranked, the number of comparison decisions rises to $\frac{(20)(19)}{2} =$ 190! On the whole, then, ranking is simply not a very satisfactory method of evaluating jobs.

Classification. The classification method of job evaluation is a job-to-standard comparison technique that solves a number of the problems inherent in simple job ranking. The compensation analyst using the classification method first decides into how many categories, or classification steps, the job value structure is to be broken. A typical number of classes is around eight; the number might very from five to fifteen.

The second step in the classification method is writing definitions for each class. These definitions are the standards against which the jobs will be compared. Exhibit 7.3 shows a part of a classification system

Exhibit 7.3 Clerical Worker Classification System

CLASS I	Simple work, no supervisory responsibility, no public contact
CLASS II	Simple work, no supervisory responsibility, public contact
CLASS III	Work of medium complexity, no supervisory responsibility, public contact
CLASS IV	Work of medium complexity, supervisory responsibility, public contact
CLASS V	Complex work, supervisory responsibility, public contact

developed for clerical workers. Notice that although several factors are used to define class levels, a job is compared to these standards on the whole-job basis, not on a factor-by-factor basis. The compensation analyst compares the jobs to be evaluated with the class definitions, placing jobs in appropriate classifications.

Although classification does provide specific standards for comparison and does accommodate changes in the value of individual jobs, it too has some drawbacks. There is still not much detail in the standards, and a rigid relationship between job factors of value is assumed. In Exhibit 7.3, for example, it is assumed that no clerical job will exist that entails complex work and supervisiory responsibility but has no public contact. As a result, many jobs in a large organization using a classification method are likely to be forced to fit into the classes when it comes to job evaluation. The fact that some jobs do not exactly fit their classes may lead to some disagreement about the equity of the final value structure.

A related problem is tied to the decision as to how many classifications there should be. If there are too few classes for the number of jobs in an organization, it will be difficult to differentiate job value, and thus wage levels, sufficiently. If there are too many, the drafting of class definitions will be difficult, and the results of placing particular jobs in certain classes will be more open to dispute. On the positive side, a classification system can be constructed simply, quickly, and inexpensively. It is also an easy system to understand (if not to get agreement on); organizations that have open pay plans may find that a classification system helps in its communications with its employees.

The factor comparison method.   In factor comparison, jobs are compared against other jobs on the basis of how much of some desired factor they possess. It therefore ranks certain aspects of jobs rather than whole jobs. It is also one of the most complex of job evaluation systems and requires considerable training if it is to be done well.

The first step is for the compensation analyst to get job descriptions that will allow him to make judgments about factors the jobs possess. Traditionally, five factors are used in the factor comparison method: the mental, physical, and skill requirements of the job, the responsibility entailed by the job, and the working conditions.

From the entire set of jobs to be evaluated, the compensation analyst then selects ten to fifteen key jobs. The nature of key jobs was more fully discussed in Chapter 6. For factor comparison, the primary requirements are two: key jobs must show considerable variation on the five factors, and there must be well-defined market rates, which the organization considers legitimate.

To start the actual evaluation process, each job is ranked on each factor. This stage is conventionally done vertically; an abbreviated version is shown in Exhibit 7.4. The vertical ranking is identical to whole-job ranking except that factors are used.

The next stage is to take the market rate for each of the key jobs and apportion that rate across factors. An example of this apportionment is shown in Exhibit 7.5. In this stage, the compensation analyst is deciding how much of the salary associated with a specific key job is being paid for mental requirements, how much for physical requirements, and so on. This allocation is made for each key job. When allocations have been made for all key jobs, the dollar figures for each factor are ranked across jobs. These rankings are shown in Exhibit 7.5 in parentheses. For example, job F has more allocated to mental requirements than any other job, so it recieves the highest rank of 6.

The purpose of this ranking becmes clearer in Exhibit 7.6. In Exhibit 7.6, a comparison of the two rankings is presented. The vertical rankings are based on the factors' importance to the jobs, or on the extent to which they form a basis for the jobs' value. The allocation rankings indicate the relative pay currently given the jobs for each factor. If the jobs are truly key jobs, there should be little or no difference between the two sets of numbers. The reconciliation shown in Exhibit 7.6, then, is basically a validity check on whether the jobs chosen are truly key jobs. It can be seen in the exhibit that generally there is no difference in the two sets of rankings, except with respect to skill requirements for job C. The current market rate allocated to those skills is considerably higher than the skill requirements would indicate. It may be that these skills are currently in short supply or that union pressure has forced up wages. Regardless of the reason, job C is not a key job, and must be discarded from the evaluation for the time being. The elimination of job C brings the rest of the rankings into exact agreement.

The compensation analyst is then ready to set up a job evaluation scale to be used in evaluating the other jobs in the organization. An example of such a scale constructed from the data from Exhibit 7.5 is shown in Exhibit 7.7. The data from Exhibit 7.5 have been rearranged to show ascending dollar values for each factor. The amount allocated to each factor for key jobs is indicated by the anchoring of value levels

Exhibit 7.4   Factor Comparison Method
Step 1 — Vertical Ranking

			Factors		
Key Jobs	Mental Requirements	Physical Requirements	Skill Requirements	Responsibility	Working Conditions
Job A	1	5	2	3	3
Job B	2	4	4	1	6
Job C	3	6	1	6	4
Job D	4	1	6	2	1
Job E	5	3	5	5	2
Job F	6	2	3	4	5

NOTE: The rank of 6 is highest.

Source: Adapted from: R. Beatty, N. F. Crandall, C. H. Fay, R. Mathis, G. T. Milkovich, and M. J. Wallace, Jr. *How to Administer Wage-Salary Programs and Perform Job Evaluations.* New York: Penton Learning Systems, 1980.

Exhibit 7.5 Factor Comparison Method
Step 2 — Allocation of Wage Across Factors
Step 3 — Ranking of Allocations Across Jobs

Key Jobs	Factors					Current Market Rate (Dollars/Hour)
	Mental Requirements	*Physical Requirements*	*Skill Requirements*	*Responsibility*	*Working Conditions*	
Job A	.40 (1)	2.00 (5)	0.40 (1)	0.75 (3)	0.30 (4)	3.85
Job B	1.75 (2)	1.50 (4)	1.95 (3)	0.20 (1)	2.20 (6)	7.60
Job C	2.15 (3)	2.05 (6)	2.70 (5)	4.10 (6)	0.35 (3)	11.35
Job D	3.00 (4)	0.25 (1)	2.80 (6)	0.40 (2)	0.10 (1)	6.55
Job E	3.20 (5)	1.35 (3)	2.50 (4)	2.50 (5)	0.25 (2)	9.80
Job F	4.10 (6)	0.75 (2)	1.80 (2)	2.10 (4)	0.70 (5)	9.45

NOTE: The rank of 6 is highest.

Source: Adapted from: R. Beatty, N. F. Crandall, C. H. Fay, R. Mathis, G. T. Milkovich, and M. J. Wallace, Jr. *How to Administer Wage-Salary Programs and Perform Job Evaluations.* New York: Penton Learning Systems, 1980.

Exhibit 7.6 Reconciliation of Vertical Ranking and Allocation of Wages Ranking

| | Factors | | | | |
Key Jobs	Mental Requirements	Physical Requirements	Skill Requirements	Responsibility	Working Conditions
Job A	V-1 / A-1	V-5 / A-5	V-2 / A-1	V-3 / A-3	V-3 / A-4
Job B	V-2 / A-2	V-4 / A-4	V-4 / A-3	V-1 / A-1	V-6 / A-6
Job C	V-3 / A-3	V-6 / A-6	V-1 / A-5	V-6 / A-6	V-4 / A-3
Job D	V-4 / A-4	V-1 / A-1	V-6 / A-6	V-2 / A-2	V-1 / A-1
Job E	V-5 / A-5	V-3 / A-3	V-5 / A-4	V-5 / A-5	V-2 / A-2
Job F	V-6 / A-6	V-2 / A-2	V-3 / A-2	V-4 / A-4	V-5 / A-5

Source: Adapted from: R. Beatty, N. F. Crandall, C. H. Fay, R. Mathis, G. T. Milkovich, and M. J. Wallace, Jr. *How to Administer Wage-Salary Programs and Perform Job Evaluations.* New York: Penton Learning Systems, 1980.

Exhibit 7.7 Job Evaluation Scale for Additional Jobs

Job Value	Mental Requirements	Physical Requirements	Skill Requirements	Responsibility	Working Conditions
.00					
.20					
.40	Job A	Job D		Job B	Job D
.60				Job D	Job E/Job A
.80		Job F	Job A	Job A	Job F
1.00					
.20		Job E			
.40		Job B			
.60					
.80	Job B		Job F		
2.00		Job A	Job B	Job F	Job B
.20					
.40					
.60			Job E	Job E	
.80			Job D		
3.00	Job D				
.20	Job E				
.40					
.60					
.80					
4.00					
.20	Job F				
.40					

Column group heading: Factors

Source: Adapted from: R. Beatty, N. F. Crandall, C. H. Fay, R. Mathis, G. T. Milkovich, and M. J. Wallace, Jr. *How to Administer Wage-Salary Programs and Perform Job Evaluations.* New York: Penton Learning Systems, 1980.

by the key jobs. It is for this reason that the validation of key jobs in the previous stage is so important. As another check, the compensation analyst will take an additional set of key jobs and value them using the scales. That is, key job G will be compared on each factor with respect to jobs A through F and a value level determined. Total value assigned to the job will be summed, and that value will be compared with market data. There should be a close match for the additional set of key jobs. If there is, the compensation analyst can then use the scales, with the additional key jobs as further anchors of value to evaluate the rest of the jobs in the organization.

Factor comparison does have some advantages over both ranking and classification systems. It is much more reliable than either because of the two rankings made. It also speaks to internal and external equity issues at the same time. However, there are some major drawbacks to the use of this system. To use it requires extensive training. As dollar values change, particularly in periods of inflation, the whole system needs to be changed. More seriously, market rates tend to change differently for different jobs. These differential changes require extensive reworking of the system. Some compensation analysts argue that not all jobs can be analyzed accurately in terms of the five factors traditionally used. Finally, as the example of job C indicates, the reconciliation of internal and external equity issues is incomplete. In the balance, the factor comparison system of job evaluation is cumbersome and not appropriate when labor markets have any instability. As a final note, consider yourself in the position of a compensation analyst trying to explain to a worker why a job is valued as it is under this system.

The point factor method.   The point factor method, or one of its variations, is the most commonly used job evaluation method, and the one that seems most sensible for use by most organizations. The first step in the point factor method is to choose the factors that will be used to rate each job. Some typical compensable factors are education, experience required, need to work independently, physical demands, visual/mental demand, responsibility for equipment, responsibility for material, responsibility for safety of others, supervisory responsibility, working conditions, accident and health hazards, contact with public, and manual dexterity. In fact, any aspect of a job for which a company is willing to pay can be a compensable factor.

Exhibit 7.8   Point Factor Method Compensable Factor Scale

Education — 300 points

This factor measures the amount of formal education required to satisfactorily perform the job. Experience or knowledge received through experience is not to be considered in evaluating jobs on this scale.

Points

20	Level 1	Eighth-grade education
90	Level 2	High school diploma or eighth-grade education and four years of formal apprenticeship
160	Level 3	Two-year college degree or high school diploma and three years of formal apprenticeship
230	Level 4	Four-year college degree
300	Level 5	Graduate degree

Having chosen the compensable factors, the compensation analyst must define each factor in some detail and then develop a scale for each factor. A sample factor scale, for education, is shown in Exhibit 7.8. Notice that besides the definition of the factor itself, there is a definition for each level of the scale. There is no optimal number of scale levels, nor do all factor scales have to have the same number of levels.

The compensation analyst then decides how many points will be used in the system as a whole. Although this is an arbitrary number, we recommend the use of 1000 since it is easy to work with and provides enough points to make meaningful differentiations. The total number of points must be allocated across factors. Given the factors education, experience, physical demands, responsibility, and working conditions, the analyst might decide to have education worth 300 points, experience worth 300 points, responsibility worth 200 points, and physical demands and working conditions each worth 100 points. This weighting of factor value cannot be done in an entirely arbitrary fashion. Rather, the analyst will look at key jobs in the organization and will decide how much each of the factors contributes to the value (note, not the wage) of the job to the organization. Although only rough estimates can be made, it is clear that in most organizations education is of much more value than the ability to tolerate poor working conditions.

When points have been assigned to each factor, the points assigned to each level of a factor must be determined. Our education scale, for example, has been weighted fairly heavily: 300 points out of 1,000. The analyst must now decide how many points to assign each level. The highest level of a scale is always assigned the full number of points allocated to the factor; thus, a graduate degree would be assigned 300 points. The lowest level on a factor scale is usually assigned some points, since an eighth-grade education is not equivalent to no education at all. For the job family we are considering, it seems equitable to value an eighth-grade educational level at 20 points. Scale levels between the base level and the top level can be assigned points on the basis of rational argument, or levels can be assigned such that the differences between levels are (in terms of points assigned) equal. We have assigned equal intervals to this scale; thus the intermediate levels are assigned 90, 160, and 230 points.

A similar process is carried out for each factor scale. Jobs are then compared to scales and points assigned to the job for each factor. Factor points are totaled, and the resulting scores may be compared to show the relative value of each job.

The advantages of the point factor system lie in its reliability and its immunity to the fluctuations in market rates. Changes in jobs may be accommodated. Once created, the scales are relatively easy to use. The points assigned to jobs not only give differences in value, but also indicate the size of those differences. On the other hand, the point method is expensive and time-consuming to develop. The accuracy of the scales may be questioned, for although they are based on the judgment of the compensation analyst, there is no way to "prove" that they accurately reflect value. However, some statistical checks (for example, against employee perceptions) can be used to support factor scales. Finally, we should note that the analyst has only a set of points reflecting the internal equity value of a set of jobs, and not a wage and salary structure. It remains for these values to be translated into such a structure.

Administering the Job Evaluation Process

The discussion of job evaluation so far has been written as if it were a one-person job, that is, as if the compensation analyst handled all aspects of the process. In fact, nothing could be further from reality, especially in larger organizations.

Even in using the simple whole-job ranking method, a committee usually does the ranking. Compensable factors are usually developed by a committee consisting of management, compensation specialists, and representatives of at least some of the jobs in the job family being evaluated. When a job family is represented by a union, there will usually be an official of the union on the committee.

The same kind of participation takes place when jobs are actually being evaluated. The inclusion of some job-knowledgeable people on the committee is useful, because written job descriptions may be misleading to individuals not familiar with the way the jobs are actually done. Finally, it is important for all decisions of the job evaluation committee (or of the compensation analyst) to be written down in a job evaluation manual. In this way, consistency between committee members and consistency over time can be ensured. The manual also provides important documentation in the event of a comparable worth lawsuit.

Miscellaneous Job Evaluation System

There are a variety of commercial job evaluation systems in use in many types of organizations. The leading systems in terms of popularity are the Hay system, the NMTA's National Position Evaluation Plan, EVALU-COMP, the PAQ, and Management Compensation Services' Project 777.

The Hay system. The Hay system is essentially a point factor system that evaluates jobs with respect to "know-how," "problem-solving," and "accountability." It is aimed at evaluation of upper-level jobs in organizations, both professional and managerial. Hay utilizes standardized "Guide Charts" but does customize them to fit the needs of individaul clients.

National Position Evaluation Plan. The National Position Evaluation Plan has evolved from the old National Electrical Manufacturers Association (NEMA) job evaluation system. Sponsored by eleven management/manufacturers associations, the plan is offered under the umbrella group known as NMTA Associates. The plan is a point-factor system with four units, each utilizing common criteria, which can be used to evaluate all jobs in an organization. Unit I is used to evaluate manufacturing, warehousing, service, distribution, and maintenance jobs. Unit II evaluates nonexempt clerical, technical, and administrative jobs. Unit III is used in evaluating exempt professional, techical, administrative, sales, and supervisory jobs. Executive jobs are evaluated using unit IV. The commonality of criteria used in the units is a strength of the NMTA Associates plan, since it allows for a single hierarchy of job evaluation points for all jobs in an organization.

EVALUCOMP.   EVALUCOMP is a job evaluation plan for office personnel, technicians, professional and scientific personnel, and all levels of management. Developed and offered by the American Management Associations, EVALUCOMP differs from traditional job evaluation systems in that no effort is made to construct an internal hierarchy of jobs on the basis of job characteristics. Rather, an extensive description of each job is provided (to allow for matching) along with EVALUCOMP wage survey data. Users of the system can ensure external equity, but unless adjustments are made on some consistent basis, internal equity may not be achieved.

The Position Analysis Questionnaire (PAQ).   The PAQ, developed by Ernest McCormick and his associates, is a job analysis technique that captures more than 150 aspects of a job. PAQ results can be regressed against market data to provide the dollar value of each level of each of these aspects. Additional jobs can then be analyzed with respect to level of these aspects and valued using weights from the regression equation. Like EVALUCOMP, the PAQ does not speak to internal equity so much as external equity, and its value as a job evaluation system is therefore limited.

Project 777.   A third market-based system is Management Compensation Services' Project 777 and supplements such as MR/MA (multiple regression/multifactor analysis). Salary survey data for executives is related to sales, number of employees, net income, stock value, and other relevant organizational variables. By matching organizations, a compensation specialist can maintain external equity. Because of restrictions on participants, however, use of Project 777 is limited. (A participant must be a manufacturer with sales in excess of $100 million per year, not a division or subsidiary of another organization.) Again, internal equity is not served except by accident, and it is questionable whether such systems should be considered job evaluation systems.

Building the Wage and Salary Structure

At this point, if the compensation analyst used the point factor method, he or she has the number of points assigned to the jobs in the organization and, on the basis of wage and salary surveys discussed in Chapter 6, has reliable market data for a variety of key jobs. What is needed is to construct a wage structure from these two data sets. Although a wage structure might be constructed which provides a specific range of wages for each job in the organization (including a starting, midpoint, and high wage figure) such a structure is inadvisable for several reasons.

1. In a company with many jobs the structure would be unwieldy and possibly unworkable.

2. Neither job evaluation nor wage survey data are sufficiently precise, reliable (having agreement between sources), or stable (over time) to justify such a structure.

3. Internal equity issues are unlikely to be served by such a structure, because of the problems noted in 2. Aggregation is likely to smooth over small inconsistencies in survey and evaluation rankings.

In brief, neither survey nor job evaluation data are good enough to create one salary range per job. Therefore, organizations create wage structures with a number of ranges, into which are aggregated all the jobs in the organization. This structure will have several characteristics controlling its construction; these are the questions the compensation analyst must keep in mind when building the structure:

1. How many classes (or ranges) is the structure to have?

2. How far apart should the midpoints of those ranges be?

3. How wide should each range be?

4. How much should the ranges overlap?

To answer these questions, the compensation analyst will also have to know the answer to some additional questions:

5. How is the organization going to relate to the market with respect to pay levels? Will it exceed, fall short of, or match the market?

6. On what basis is the organization going to make individual pay decisions? Will all incumbents receive the same salary, or will there be differentials for seniority, performance, or some other factor?

Number of Ranges

The number of ranges to be used depends on several things. A major determinant is the number of jobs evaluated, their hierarchical level in the organization, and their reporting relationships. That is, a supervisor and subordinate would not ordinarily be in the same pay range. The more layers an organization has, the more pay ranges it will require. Career development issues also influence the number of ranges. When an individual is promoted to a new job, a raise is expected; career paths can typically be mapped by moves between ranges.

Range Parameters

The distance between midpoints will be largely determined by the number of classes. When the number of ranges has been determined, the compensation analyst can look at job evaluation points assigned to various jobs and see if there are obvious breaks. Another method is to divide the total number of job evaluation points possible (under the example used for the point factor system there were 1000) by the number of ranges decided on. Thus, if it were decided to have ten ranges, range 1 would consist of all jobs receiving between one and 100 points; range 2 would consist of all jobs receiving between 101 and 200 points, and so on.

The midpoints would be based on salary survey data for the jobs in the range in this case; thus, the distance between midpoints would be derived from marketplace differentials.

The Range Spread

The width of a given range, or the rate range spread, can be determined in different ways. One way is to look at market rate data of jobs falling within the classification and to base rate ranges on those data. A second way is to use a percentage band (usually between 5 percent and 20 percent) above and below the midpoint of each range. When this is done, the smaller percentages are used on lower ranges, and the larger percentages for the upper classes.

The midpoints and ranges chosen will depend on the policies of the organization reflected in questions 5 and 6. The organization must decide if it is going to exceed or fall below the market, or just match it. To implement this policy, the organization will choose a survey statistic (median, upper quartile, lower quartile) and consistently use that statistic for each key job surveyed. It may choose to adjust these figures in a consistent fashion; for example, it may say, "We will pay 15 percent above the median salary reported for this class."

Individual pay policies will influence range spreads. If the organization is going to pay for performance, then a wider range is needed to reflect differentials than if no merit pay is given. The same is true of seniority payments. In the typical organization, employees are brought into the lower end of a range and move to the midpoint in two or three years if performance is satisfactory; movement thereafter is less rapid. Promotion policies also influence range spreads. If most people in a job will be promoted to the next level within three years or fired, the range need not be broad.

Range Overlap

Many of the same issues governing range width influence ideal range overlap. As with range spread, there is no "right" overlap. The problems that occur when overlap exists include:

1. A promoted employee who was at the top of the old range must be placed above the base of the new range, or receive a cut in salary.

2. Supervisors may have employees working for them who make more money than they do. This can cause morale problems.

However, to avoid overlap completely creates an alternative problem: jobs will have artificial constraints on pay ceilings. All other factors being equal, organizations with more classifications can expect more overlap; each organization will have to judge the degree of overlap acceptable on the basis of the issues noted. An example of a typical wage structure is shown in Exhibit 7.9.

In building the wage structure, the compensation analyst must relate

Exhibit 7.9   Wage Chart

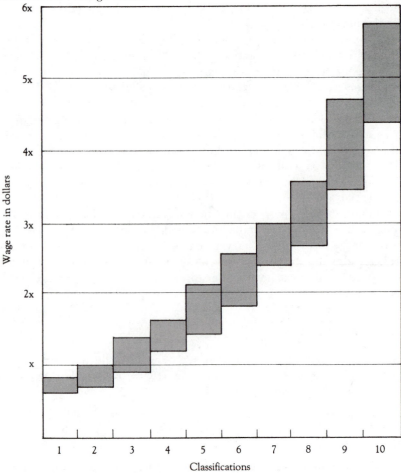

job evaluation points and wage survey data. Salary data for key jobs in each point range are noted. Some analysts average out salary data to arrive at a midpoint. Others use more complex statistical techniques to derive not only the midpoint but also the minimum and the maximum of the range. Actual range construction is an art; it is an iterative process in which the compensation analyst tries to meet the constraints of internal policy and still allow the organization to provide external equity.

Adjustments to the Structure

From time to time, adjustments will need to be made to the structure. Inflation drives labor prices upward, jobs change in their relative value to the organization, and jobs themselves change as technology changes. Employees entering jobs change as well. The wage structure will have to be adjusted to meet these changes. In some cases, the compensable factors and their weightings will be questioned; in other cases, scale values will need to be changed. These kinds of changes will make it necessary to reevaluate all jobs. A more normal situation will be the need to reevaluate selected jobs.

Adjustments that should be made are adjustments to movements in labor markets and to major changes in the organization. Adjustments that should be avoided are general cost of living adjustments, whether they are simple across-the-board adjustments or formal programs tied to the Consumer Price Index.

Finally, the structure should be taken seriously, but not as a straight-jacket. Job evaluation is a tool, and wage survey data are estimates and averages. Building the structure is a matter of judgement, not a precise science. If done carefully, the structure should handle almost all jobs and the base salary for all but a few employees. There will always be a few employees who require special treatment. The compensation analyst, recognizing the uniqueness of these situations, should handle them outside the wage and salary structure and not distort the structure to accommodate these few cases. In short, adjustments to the structure should not be confused with individual employee adjustments.

8

Individual Wage Determination

Even though the compensation analyst has completed the wage and salary structure as envisioned in Chapter 7, he or she is still a long way from being able to say what pay an individual in a job is to receive, unless the decision has been made to pay all job incumbents the same wage. A single-rate wage structure is uncommon, and the reasons for such a structure's variety center on individual equity needs. To preserve individual equity, some consideration must be given to individual contribution of job incumbents in similar positions.

In fact, individual pay decisions are not always made on such rational grounds. Merit, whether in terms of performance or organizational loyalty (seniority), is usually recognized as a basis for individual pay differences. Those with organizational experience recognize other factors as well. Some forms of compensation are distributed on an equal basis: health insurance and the Christmas turkey are examples. Other forms are allocated on the basis on need. These are usually benefits, such as counseling, but some individual wage decisions are based on need ("We should give

Jones that raise; they just had triplets"). All cost of living adjustments are in response to employee need.

A third type of individual pay decision not based on merit is that based on power. In some cases, the power is market-based ("The competition has just offered me a job at 20 percent more than I make now; if you can't meet that I'm going to have to accept their offer."). In other cases, the power is based on intraorganizational relationships: if your inlaws are major stockholders in a corporation you will probably be paid a higher salary than merit would justify. The fourth nonrational determinant of individual pay differences is luck. A few good breaks (the boss happens to be at the office the one Saturday you dropped in to catch up on some work; a client gets angry at the competitor and places a large order with you) or bad breaks (the boss has a hot domestic dispute going at review time and is in a rotten mood; cash flow problems of a client cause them to cancel the large order they placed with you) can have significant effects on individual salaries.

There is not much the compensation analyst can do about nonrational determinants of individual pay. They certainly cannot be programmed. The best approach is to control them as much as possible; those which cannot be controlled should be recognized for what they are, and the entire system should not be distorted to justify a few exceptions.

The best way for the organization to manage individual pay decisions is to set out policies governing individual pay and to draw up procedures to implement those policies. In this chapter, we will look at the two major determinants of individual pay: seniority and performance. A means of adjusting for each is shown individually, and a joint adjustment is also shown.

Seniority

There are two ways in which an organization can adjust for seniority. The more common way is to reward employees for loyalty to the organization; that is, employees receive a pay increment for every year they have served the company. Typically these pay increments are tied to grade: an employee in job A who has worked in that job longer than a second employee will be paid more. However, when the first employee is promoted to job B, he will make less than an employee, X, who had filled job B longer, even if that employee, X, has worked for the organization for a shorter time than the first employee. Seniority in this case works *within* a grade and not across grades. A second way organizations pay for seniority is not to make adjustments to the pay structure to account for service, but to develop and use what is called a maturity curve.

Pay Adjustments for Seniority

The first step for the compensation analyst preparing pay adjustments for seniority is to draw up a policy providing guidelines for such adjustments. Options to be considered include:

1. How long an employee has to work before receiving a seniority adjustment.

2. The number of adjustments possible in a single job (i.e., shall seniority be rewarded indefinitely, or is there a limt?).

3. Size of the seniority adjustment, and differential adjustments across job levels and years of service.

Exhibit 8.1 shows a seniority pay adjustment guideline that takes these options into account. Annual increases are given to employees, but only through the tenth year of service in the same job classification. Adjustments shrink as a percentage of total salary both with years of service and with increase in salary classification. The philosophy behind this adjustment policy is that the organization believes that employees who perform well will be promoted to higher pay grades. Since the adjustment made after year one creates a higher base for year two adjustment, a lower adjustment, in terms of percentage increase, can be made in year two. Note that these adjustments are independent of any other adjustments made to the structure. Midpoints and entire ranges may be shifted to respond to changes in the labor market, the inflation rate, or changes in the company's technology level, size, or location.

A different form of adjustment may be embodied in the salary structure itself. A good example of this is the general schedule (GS) pay system of the United States government, seen in Exhibit 8.2. The GS pay system takes the adjustment policy shown in Exhibit 8.1 and constructs a graded pay structure with seniority adjustments built in. Either system is satisfactory; however, the GS pay system must be revised frequently to accommodate market and inflationary influences. A percentage table of seniority adjustments need not be revised so frequently.

Exhibit 8.1 Seniority Pay-Adjustment Policy (Percentage increase)

Classification	*Years of Service*									
	1	*2*	*3*	*4*	*5*	*6*	*7*	*8*	*9*	*10*
1	4.5	4.4	4.2	4.0	3.8	3.6	3.4	3.2	3.0	2.8
2	4.5	4.4	4.2	4.0	3.8	3.6	3.4	3.2	3.0	2.8
3	4.5	4.4	4.2	4.0	3.8	3.6	3.4	3.2	3.0	2.8
4	4.4	4.3	4.1	3.9	3.7	3.5	3.3	3.1	2.9	2.7
5	4.4	4.3	4.1	3.9	3.7	3.5	3.3	3.1	2.9	2.7
6	4.4	4.3	4.1	3.9	3.7	3.5	3.3	3.1	2.9	2.7
7	4.3	4.2	4.0	3.8	3.6	3.4	3.2	3.0	2.8	2.6
8	4.3	4.2	4.0	3.8	3.6	3.4	3.2	3.0	2.8	2.6
9	4.3	4.2	4.0	3.8	3.6	3.4	3.2	3.0	2.8	2.6
10	4.2	4.1	3.9	3.7	3.5	3.3	3.1	2.9	2.7	2.5

Maturity Curves

Maturity curves, discussed as a method for pricing jobs in Chapter 6, are sometimes adapted as a variant in making individual pay distinctions among professionals such as scientists and engineers. The underlying assumption of the maturity curve is that value of a worker to an organization increases with years in the field. Maturity curves reward not organizational loyalty but professional longevity.

Maturity curves usually reflect market values more closely than other seniority adjustments. The major differences between maturity curves and regular pay adjustments for seniority are two. The first, as noted above, is that maturity curves reward seniority in the field, not the organization. A more important difference for the compensation analyst is that maturity curves do not speak to internal equity at all. External equity is served by use of wage survey data, and individual equity is served (in part, at least)

Exhibit 8.2 General Schedule Pay System

GS–1	$ 8,342	$ 8,620	$ 8,898	$ 9,175	$ 9,453	$ 9,615	$ 9,890	$10,165	$10,178	$10,439
2	9,381	9,603	9,913	10,178	10,292	10,595	10,898	11,201	11,504	11,807
3	10,235	10,576	10,917	11,258	11,599	11,940	12,281	12,622	12,963	13,304
4	11,490	11,873	12,256	12,639	13,022	13,405	13,788	14,171	14,554	14,937
5	12,354	13,282	13,710	14,138	14,566	14,994	15,422	15,850	16,279	16,706
6	14,328	14,806	15,284	15,762	16,240	16,718	17,196	17,674	18,152	18,630
7	15,922	16,453	16,984	17,515	18,046	18,577	19,108	19,639	20,170	20,701
8	17,634	18,222	18,810	19,398	19,986	20,574	21,162	21,750	22,338	22,926
9	19,477	20,126	20,775	21,424	22,073	22,722	23,371	24,020	24,669	25,318
10	21,449	22,164	22,879	23,594	24,309	25,024	25,739	26,454	27,169	27,884
11	23,566	24,352	25,138	25,924	26,710	27,496	28,282	29,068	29,854	30,640
12	28,245	29,187	30,129	31,071	32,013	32,955	33,897	34,839	35,731	36,723
13	33,586	34,706	35,826	36,946	38,066	39,186	40,306	41,426	42,546	43,666

14	39,689	41,012	42,335	43,658	44,981	46,004	47,627	48,950	50,273	51,696
15	46,485	48,241	49,797	51,353	52,909	54,465	56,021	57,577	59,133	60,689
16	54,765	56,580	58,405	60,230	62,055	63,390	65,705	67,530	69,055	
17	64,142	66,280	68,418	70,656	72,694					
18	75,177									

Source: *Federal Register*, Vol. 46, No. 200, Friday, October 16, 1981, p. 50922.

through the curve itself. No provision is made for internal equity: there is no job evaluation. For this reason, maturity curves tend to be confined to professional jobs for which there is a very clear market rate. They are not suitable for most jobs in most organizations.

Pay Adjustments for Performance

We saw in Chapter 4 that pay can affect performance. Performance can also affect pay. The focus of this section is on adjustments to base pay rates as a result of some level of performance. A second means of paying for performance, which we will look at later in this chapter, is to give one-time payments as a reward for performance. These one-time payments do not affect base pay, nor is any adjustment made to the pay structure. Typically, performance adjustments to base pay rates are based on individual performance appraisal systems.

Bonus systems, on the other hand, may be individual, group, or company-wide plans and are typically based not on performance appraisal systems but on dollar measures of productivity or cost savings.

In either case, several conditions must exist before a pay for performance system can work. Organizations in which any of these conditions are missing will find that performance-based pay systems have little effect except for the expenditure of money and employee morale.

Required Conditions for a Performance-Based Pay System

The first condition is that employees must have some control over their performance, and be able, either individually or as a group, to perform better or worse. It would be hard to justify a merit system for assembly-line workers based on amount of output, since the speed of the line is typically set by an engineer, and the employee cannot produce more than is sent past the work station. Likewise, about the only conrol a gate guard has over performance is showing up. Many workers are so dependent on the actions of others that they have little control over their individual performance. In such cases, group performance may be the basis for merit pay decisions.

A second condition for merit pay is that any performance differential must be important to the organization. It may be that the organization requires only minimal levels of performance; higher levels are irrelevant or even undesirable. A cleaning service, for example, may only need the halls swept and the wastepaper baskets emptied in a client's office. The same degree of shine and polish that one might desire at home are not required.

The third condition is that the organization must be able to measure performance in a valid and reliable way. This is probably the most difficult condition for most organizations to meet; for that reason a section on performance appraisal systems follows.

The other conditions for a workable merit pay system center on the compensation system itself. First, the organization must be willing to budget enough money to the system so that changes in pay will be meaningful to employees. Second, the pay system must truly match performance differentials with pay differentials. High performance must be well rewarded; mediocre performance must not be well rewarded. Employees must accept the performance measurement system and the links between performance and pay as fair and equitable. This means that employees must have some realistic information about what the organization considers good performance, what linkages exist between performance and pay, and what pay levels exist in the organization.

Performance Appraisal

Performance appraisal is a major area of personnel administration, and it is obviously beyond the scope of this book to give it comprehensive treatment. Three recent books that do treat the area comprehensively are: R. W. Beatty and H. J. Bernardin, *Appraising Human Performance* (Boston: Kent Publishing Co., 1982); G. P. Latham and K. N. Wexley, *Increasing Productivity Through Performance Appraisal* (Reading, Mass.: Addison Wesley, 1981); and L. S. Baird, R. W. Beatty, and C. E. Schneier, *Performance Appraisal Sourcebook* (Human Resource Development Press, 1982).

There are a number of appraisal decisions that must be made; we will look at those decisions only as they affect compensation systems. The first issue to be decided is the use to which appraisal data shall be put. There are three broad categories of use: to make personnel decisions, to help develop employees, and to conduct research. The compensation analyst is not interested in development of employees; thus, the requirements placed on appraisal systems by developmental uses (that is, the output of information telling the employee areas of excellence, areas of shortcomings, and ways to improve) will not be covered here. Research uses of appraisal data may be important to the compensation analyst who wants to see what aspects of performance respond to merit pay systems, and to experiment with the effects of pay adjustment on performance level. However, it is the effect on personnel decisions that is of primary concern to the compensation analyst. That decision aspect places one major constraint on performance appraisal systems: data output from the system must have the capability of being summarized in a single number, which can be compared against standards for a specific job and across all employees regardless of job or level in the pay structure. For example, employee A, a forklift truck operator with a performance appraisal rating of 7, is a better employee than B, an administrative assistant to the vice president of sales with a rating of 5.

Who should be appraised? From the point of view of the compensation analyst, it is only necessary to appraise employees for whom merit adjustments are to be made. Thus, salesmen on straight commission and unionized workers paid flat rate plus seniority adjustment need not be appraised.

What performance should be appraised? There is no such thing as an objective performance waiting to be appraised. The organization must define performance for each job in terms of overall organizational goals. In addition, the definition of "effective" performance on a job is likely to change as organizational goals and requirements change, and as the environmental pressures on the organization change.

For the compensation analyst, performance is whatever aspect of employee behavior, makeup, or job outcomes the organization wishes to increase by rewarding it. Compensation definitions of performance may not always agree with other organizational definitions. Thus, individuals caught in illegal activities on behalf of the organization frequently say that although the organization may pay lip service to legal and ethical practices, raises come to the employee who price fixes, bribes government officials, or makes payoffs to corrupt union officials. The compensation analyst will have to reconcile these differences, making sure that the organization rewards what it really wishes to motivate. The compensation analyst must thus make sure that the performance appraisal system captures those aspects of performance on which rewards should be based.

Four criteria the compensation ananlyst will use to judge the performance appraisal system are its relevance, reliability, freedom from bias, and practicality. Evidence of relevance, or validity, would indicate that appraisal measures are in fact tapping those aspects of performance the organization wishes to reward. Thus, the compensation analyst might compare appraisal systems with management statements of what it wishes to reward to look for similarities and differences. For the compensation analyst, the reliability that is of interest is interobserver reliability. An employee should receive the same score on the appraisal system regardless of the appraiser. The appraisal system is most likely to fail in reliability because of rater bias. Rater bias refers to information processing errors all managers are subject to making rather than to blatant prejudice. Major rater errors include:

Restriction of range errors. Some managers, especially with salary increases at stake, give all their subordinates high ratings. This is known as leniency error. Other managers like to make their employees "reach." "After all," they say, "no one is really that good." Other managers, to avoid offending anyone, rate everyone about the same.

Contrast error. Some managers will not rate their subordinates against standards, but contrast them with other employees. The major problem with this practice is that most of us are so inbued with the idea of the normal distribution that we force small sets of employees into such distributions. Thus, one outstanding employee may be compared to several good ones, and the good employees marked down to average as a result.

Weighting errors. Several errors result from improper weighting of appraisal data. Managers tend to rate individuals similar to themselves in background or attitude higher than other individuals with comparable performance. Irrelevant data, which should be weighted zero, enters into the appraisal. Many managers are apt to take into account more recent performance, which accounts for the tendency of some workers to go all out just prior to a performance review. "Halo" error occurs when a manager is so impressed with one aspect of a subordinate's performance that he reates the subordinate highly overall. Thus, a faculty member with a high research output is likely to be rated as a good teacher. Poor student evaluations may be excused, or even taken as evidence that the faculty member is really making the students learn, rather than just amusing them. Regardless of its source, rater bias gets in the way of linking performance and merit correctly, and appraisal systems must be as impervious to it as possible.

Practicality of the performance appraisal system, as far as the compensation analyst is concerned, has two components. The first is the acceptance of the system by raters and ratees. Rater acceptance is necessary if the system is to be taken seriously. Raters must see that use of the appraisal system allows them to reward employees they view as high performers and withhold rewards from employees they view as mediocre. Ratee acceptance of the system is necessary if employees are to make performance–reward linkages. The other area of practicality is the degree to which the system will stand up under legal scrutiny. Merit pay decisions, like all other personnel decisions, are subject to the requirements laid down by Title VII of the Civil Rights Act and the administrative interpretation of that Title by the Equal Employment Opportunity Commission.

Systems for appraising performance.   There are five systems used to measure performance for pay adjustment purposes: global ratings, comparative procedures, cost-related outcomes, traits, and behavioral systems. Each of these will be discussed in terms of its value for merit pay uses.

Global rating. A manager making a global rating simply assigns to each employee a number that represents overall performance level. Such systems are only as good as the manager doing the ratings. Global ratings are likely to show the effects of bias, and this bias will detract from both the reliability and the relevance of the ratings. Resulting data will be as much a measure of the manager making it as the employees on whom it is made. From a compensation point of view, global appraisal measures are more likely to be used after raise decisions are made than before them ("Joe deserves a 10 percent raise; that means I'll have to give him a 7 on the appraisal.") Preserving individual equity, especially across departments, while using global ratings is not likely. It is equally unlikely that one could successfully defend the organization in a pay discrimination suit in which global appraisals are a contested issue.

Comparative ratings. Although methods differ, all comparative rating procedures end up with a ranking of some set of employees. Comparative ratings are not much of an improvement over global measures from a compensation point of view. First of all, these procedures use global measures and thus are subject to all of their problems. However, there are additional problems. Ranks are not comparable from one rating unit to another. Being the third best employee in one unit is not the same as being third in another unit. Rankings also have no absolute meaning. All employees in a unit may be superb; ranking will force some employees to the bottom raise classification. In another unit, all employees may be wretched beyond belief, yet the best of these misfits will recieve the same raise as the best worker in another unit. Any attempt to preserve internal equity through a comparative system such as this in hopeless.

Cost-related outcomes including Management by Objectives (MBO). Cost-related outcomes are all the kinds of hard data management uses to judge the effectiveness of the organization. Examples are profit, scrap rates, net sales, cost of goods sold, maintenance costs, and age of accounts receivable. There is no doubt that these bottom-line data are crucial for measuring organizational performance. Their use in measuring individual performance, unfortunately, is questionable, especially when compensation adjustments are the result of such measures.

The major problem of cost-related outcomes as a performance measure lies in the nature of work in our society. There are simply too few jobs for which cost-related outcomes can be generated. Sales jobs are compensated solely on the basis of cost-related outcomes. This is the commission system. Piecerate systems are also rewarded on the basis of cost-related outcomes. However, most jobs in this society are not independent, but are tied in closely with many other jobs. Isolating the effect of one worker would be impossible. Consider a planning group drawing up long-range plans for a hospital system. Such a group might consist of managers, health care economists, a human-resource planning specialist, union representatives, and even representatives of city government or patient groups. How would you isolate the contribution of the human resource planner on some basis that would allow equitable annual salary adjustments? When cost-related outcomes are available for a job and the effects of one individual on those outcomes can be isolated, they are an excellent basis for merit adjustments. Because this can be done so rarely, they are not of much use for individual merit adjustments. However, as we shall see, they do form the basis of most pay-for-performance schemes that do not involve adjustments to individual base rates.

Trait systems. Trait systems are undoubtedly the most widely used performance appraisal system. Usually the appear as graphic rating scales. Such scales typically begin with ratings of quality and quantity of work (not traits, but rather quasiglobal measures) and continue with ratings of initiative, cooperation, judgment, leadership, creativity, responsibility, commitment, tact, mental alertness, and decisiveness. Trait scales, though widely used, are inadequate in terms of the four criteria mentioned earlier. They are particularly subject to rater bias and thus to lack of reliability. Most psychologists now question the ability of managers to make clinical decisions about traits. The relationship of traits to the job is difficult to demonstrate anyway. An employee might demonstrate excellent leadership qualities in organizing fellow workers for a union; but management is unlikely to consider this good performance.

Trait ratings have little practicality. Although easy to construct and use (badly), they are not likely to stand up to court challenges. For the compensation analyst, trait ratings have another, equally serious, flaw. Most traits are, by definition, stable behavioral patterns not likely to change. A good leader, for example, is likely to remain so; an individual with no initiative is unlikely to change suddenly. If the function of merit adjustments to base salary is to motivate specific behaviors, those systems should operate at those levels. Adjustments to base pay should not be made for an unchangeable characteristic of an employee; doing so would be equivalent to making continuous adjustments because the employee has red hair. If the trait can be said to exist, and is measurable, then employees should be selected on the basis of the trait.

Behavioral systems. Behavioral systems are based on employee behaviors rather than global comparisons with other employees, outputs, or traits. They can avoid the problems of other systems, because they are less subject to rater error than are traits or comparative systems. Unlike cost-related outcomes, behaviors can be associated with the individual performance of any job. Properly constructed, a behaviorally based appraisal system can be relevant, reliable, and relatively free from error. Such a system is likely to be upheld if challenged in court.

A behaviorally based system is also of greater benefit to a compensation analyst than previously mentioned systems. Because behaviors can be associated with an individual employee, the appraisal system can be used as a basis for individual pay adjustments. In addition, an employee has more control over individual behaviors than over traits or outcomes. Performance standards stated in behavioral terms can be readily communicated to employees; thus it is possible for employees to see linkages between what they do, the performance ratings they get, and the salary adjustments they receive.

There are two major forms of behavioral systems commonly used today. The first is the behavioral expectation scale, or BES. The second is the behavioral observation scale, or BOS.

Behavioral Expectation Scales. BES development is based on the critical incident technique, a job analysis procedure. A sample of job-knowledgeable people provide examples of effective, ineffective, and neutral behaviors. These incidents are clustered by content area, and the clustered dimensions are named and defined.

The incidents defined by this first group of job-knowlegeable people are placed in random order. A second sample of job-knowledgeable people takes the dimensions defined by the first group and assigns each incident to one of them. This process is called "retranslation," and serves as a validity check on the relationship of incidents and dimensions. Only those incidents matched with the same dimension they were connected with by the first group are retained.

These incidents are not important in themselves but, as examples of behavior, they indicate some level of effectiveness on a dimension. A group of employees rates each incident for effectiveness in terms of the dimension. Only those incidents whose effectiveness is agreed on are retained. Of the incidents left, between five and seven are chosen that illustrate different levels of effectiveness with respect to the dimension. Since the behaviors used are illustrative, raters need not have seen the actual behavior performed; anchor behaviors serve as examples of many behaviors of equal effectiveness of ineffectiveness. The usual practice is to state the anchor behaviors in terms of expectations. A sample of a BES is shown in Exhibit 8.3.

Raters using BES typically are required to write down one or more behaviors observed by the rater during the rating period justifying the BES score given the employee. There are usually eight to twelve different BES used in this system. For compensation purposes, scores on each dimension are averaged. The BES will be different for each job, but the average score will be comparable across all jobs as a measure of performance.

Behavioral Observation Scales. The other major appraisal based on behaviors is the behavioral observation scale. Also known as a summated rating scale or behavioral checklist, the BOS differs from the BES both in method of development and appearance of the final scale. A BOS is similar to a BES in that they are based on the same job analysis technique, critical incidents.

A sample of job-knowledgeable people provide critical incidents related to job performance. For the generation of a BOS, only effective and

Exhibit 8.3   A Behavioral Expectation Scale for a Retail Clerk

Customer relations — includes all those behaviors the clerk displays when dealing with customers.

```
7 ─┬
   ├─ If a customer asked this clerk for merchandise the store does not
   │  carry, you could expect this clerk to telephone other stores and find
   │  where the customer could purchase it.
6 ─┤
   ├─ You could expect this clerk to help a hesitant customer by giving
   │  advice on the relative merits of similar products.
5 ─┤


4 ─┬─ This clerk could be expected to chat with customers while waiting
   │  on them.


3 ─┤
   ├─ When customers ask questions about merchandise, you can expect
   │  this clerk always to reply, "I don't know."
2 ─┬─ You could expect all customers to have to ask this clerk for help.


   ├─ You could expect this clerk to refuse to serve minority customers.
1 ─┴
```

Source: M. J. Wallace, Jr., N. F. Crandall, and C. H. Fay, *Administering Human Resources: An Introduction to the Profession* (New York: Random House, 1982), p. 483. Used with permission.

ineffective incidents are sought, not neutral ones. A job analyst takes all the critical incidents generated and clusters similar incidents into behavioral items. Thus, four specific incidents relating to lateness would be generalized to "Arrives to work on time." The behavioral items are then categorized into job dimensions. Thus, "Arrives to work on time" would be placed in a category with other similar aspects of "work habits."

A second analyst, taking the behavioral items and performance dimensions, tries to duplicate the first analyst's judgments about the relations of incidents to items and items to dimensions. This step, similar to retranslation, provides a check on the reasonableness of the items and dimensions. In addition, two checks are made on content validity of the items and dimensions. A preliminary appraisal instrument is a five-point Likert scale in which each item indicates the frequency of a behavior for the person being appraised. A sample of one dimension and its associated items is shown in Exhibit 8.4.

The preliminary appraisal instrument is then used to rate employees. Item analysis or factor analysis is used to refine the instrument, eliminating behaviors that do not differentiate effective from ineffective performances. When a manager uses the BOS to rate an employee, the employee's scores are averaged to give an overall rating of performance.

How To Make Adjustments for Performance

Adjusting pay for performance is similar to adjusting for seniority. Such adjustments can be made either in terms of percentage increases to base pay or in terms of relationship to midpoint. Typically, no differentiation in grade is made; if a 4 on a five-point performance scale gets an 8 percent raise, that will hold true whether the employee is in class 1 or class 6 of the salary structure. An example of a range placement policy is shown in Exhibit 8.5. In fact, this adjustment is not determined strictly by merit, for a distinction is made based on experience in the job. In a sense, this matrix simply has different definitions of performance depending on experience: performance considered "acceptable" for someone just learning the job differs from that considered "acceptable" for someone fully experienced in all functions of the job. The fully experienced "acceptable" performer is thought to contribute more to the organization and is therefore worth more.

Combined Adjustments for Performance and Seniority

Many organizations make adjustments for both seniority and performance. This is typically done through a placement-in-range matrix, an example of which is shown in Exhibit 8.6. In this system, even unsatisfactory employees can reach the range midpoint, through seniority, though it takes five years. The excellent employee can get to the midpoint of the

Exhibit 8.4

A Behavioral Observation Scale

Work Habits
1. Argues with a foreman in front of others.
   Almost always   1   2   3   4   5   Almost never
2. When unsure about a problem, discusses it with supervisor.
   Almost never   1   2   3   4   5   Almost always
3. Knows the information provided in technical bulletins and manuals on the equipment in his area.
   Almost never   1   2   3   4   5   Almost always
4. Knows where to get special equipment or supplies to get the job done.
   Almost never   1   2   3   4   5   Almost always
5. Is ignorant of the capabilities and limitations of equipment.
   Almost always   1   2   3   4   5   Almost never
6. Arrives to work on time (e.g., no later than 6 A.M.).
   Almost never   1   2   3   4   5   Almost always
7. Stays on the job.
   Almost never   1   2   3   4   5   Almost always
8. Meets deadlines with minimum overtime (if possible).
   Almost never   1   2   3   4   5   Almost always
9. Keeps a sense of humor (smiles) even in difficult situations.
   Almost never   1   2   3   4   5   Almost always
10. Has the smell of liquor on his breath.
    Almost always   1   2   3   4   5   Almost never
11. Spends more time behind the desk than in the work area.
    Almost always   1   2   3   4   5   Almost never
12. Resists change, complains, and/or is slow to implement it.
    Almost always   1   2   3   4   5   Almost never
13. Does not delegate work (must do everything himself).
    Almost never   1   2   3   4   5   Almost always
14. Does not check to see that a job area is clean after completion of the job.
    Almost always   1   2   3   4   5   Almost never
15. Does not get written reports in on time.
    Almost always   1   2   3   4   5   Almost never

Source: M. J. Wallace, Jr., N. F. Crandall, and C. H. Fay, *Administering Human Resources: An Introduction to the Profession* (N.Y.: Random House, 1982), p. 485.

Exhibit 8.5 Guide to Salary Placement in Range

	Performance				
	Unsatisfactory	*Acceptable*	*Fully Satisfactory*	*Excellent*	*Highly Exceptional*
4. Fully experienced and trained in several functions of higher-level position(s)	Employee	100% of midpoint	105% of midpoint	110% of midpoint	115% of midpoint to maximum
3. Fully experienced in all functions of job	on	95% of midpoint	100% of midpoint	105–110% of midpoint	110–115% of midpoint
2. Experienced in most functions of job	Probation or	90% of midpoint	95% of midpoint	100% of midpoint	105% of midpoint
1. Still learning basic functions of job	Terminated	Minimum	80–85% of midpoint	85–90% of midpoint	90–95% of midpoint

Source: R. Beatty, N. F. Crandall, C. H. Fay, R. Mathis, G. T. Milkovich, and M. J. Wallace, Jr., *How to Administer Wage Salary Programs and Perform Job Evaluations* (New York: Penton Learning Systems, 1980).

Exhibit 8.6   Guide to Placement in Range Based on Seniority and Performance (Percentage of midpoint)

Years in position	Performance level				
	1	**2**	**3**	**4**	**5**
1	80%	82%	84%	86%	88%
2		86	88	90	100
3	Probation	90	94	100	104
4	————	95	100	104	108
5	T	100	102	108	110
6	E R	100	103	110	112
7	M I	100	104	112	114
8	N A	100	105	114	116
9	T E	100	105	116	118
10		100	105	118	120

range in two years, but it takes ten years to reach the top of the range.

Three problems arrive from using a matrix such as this. The most serious problem is the need to adjust the entire structure in response to market fluctuations. If employees are brought in at 80 percent of the midpoint, then the midpoint must rise when market rates do, and everyone in that classification must be raised. A second problem arises from fluctuations in performance level. A third-year employee who earned a 5 the previous year but performed at a 3 level in the third year should be placed at 94 percent of the midpoint. This obviously will not occur. The final problem is the reaction of many managements to a lack of freedom in setting individual salary levels. Although use of a matrix tends to ensure internal equity, it also removes management discretion with respect to salary levels. If the appraisal system is reliable and valid, this problem is not serious.

Direct Performance Payments

The individual adjustment techniques we have reviewed so far in this chapter result in a permanent adjustment in an employee's base pay as well as the relation of that employee's pay rate to the internal wage structure. An alternative to such procedures is individual pay policies that make no permanent adjustment in a person's base pay but, rather, allow a person's earnings to vary directly and continuously with some measure of work output. Some of these direct performance systems are based on individual performance; others are based on group, or even organization-wide effort.

Individual Direct Performance Payments

Individual direct performance payments take on three basic forms; (1) piecerate incentives, (2) sales commissions, and (3) bonuses. All three result in direct income to the employee based on individual achievement and vary directly with performance.

Piecerates. Under most circumstances, piecerates are designed to take external market rates for a job into account in determining a piecerate formula under which a worker will be paid. Usually managment establishes the external market rate as the "fair" rate a person of average skill working at a normal amount of effort should make on the job. A job analysis is then carried out to determine how many units of acceptable quality a person should be able to turn out per hour. This work rate is then defined as a standard.

Suppose, for example, that an employer is attempting to set a piecerate for machinests turning out a part on a lathe. A market survey indicates that machinest on such a job earn $10 per hour. A job analysis is carried out that determines that a machinist of average skill working at a normal rate should be able to turn out 10 units per hour. The piece rate for the job is then calculated by dividing the market rate ($10 per hour) by the output standard (10 units per hour) to get a piecerate of $1 per unit. The machinist who produces 10 units per hour earns $10 for that hour. The machinist who produces 20 units per hour earns $20 that hour.

In practice, piecerates are most ofen set up in a way that guarantees some minimum hourly wage rate. Thus, for example, a typical piecerate will guarantee a machinist $10 per hour but will pay earnings based on the piecerate when such earnings exceed $10 per hour.

Piecerates are not without problems. First, the nature of the job must be such that a single output measure (quantity *alone*) is sufficient to measure performance. Where jobs involve complex dimensions of performance piecerates will be impossible. Second, employees (and unions) often come to mistrust management's intentions in setting the work output standard. Suppose in our earlier example, that management sets the output standard at 10 units per hour and finds that 90 percent of the machinists within two weeks are producing 40 units per hour and earning $40 per hour. Management will very likely reanalyze the job and determine that 20 or 30 units per hour is a more reasonable standard. Thus, they reduce the piece rate from $1.00 per unit to $0.50 or $0.33 per unit. The machinists thus end up working harder to earn the base wage of $10 per hour. In many cases, employees and management have come to distrust each other, destroying the incentive effects of a piecerate system. Indeed, many labor unions are on record against piecerate systems, because they claim such policies do not protect the economic interests of the worker.

A third problem with a piecerate system is that employees can sometimes work themselves out of a job and into a layoff. In this case employees respond to the piecerate and perhaps double their hourly earnings until management finds itself with an inventory of output that will last for the next four months. Their reaction is to lay the employees off for this period, having no more work for them. Many employees in this situation will gladly trade off maximum hourly earnings in the short run for long-run employment stability.

Finally, piecerates have the potential of disrupting informal status systems within a work group. Social scientists for many years have recognized the informal group problems that develop when traditional relationships between earnings of traditional work groupings are disrupted when a particularly eager worker maximizes his or her earnings.[1] A great deal of formal research and informal managerial experience suggests that informal groups develop extremely effective sanctions to discourage such "rate busters."

Commissions. Commissions are almost exclusively used as a form of payment for sales representatives. A simple sales commission formula would set a representative's commission as some percentage of the gross or net sales for which he or she is responsible. Thus, a person on a 5 percent commission who generates $500,000 in sales would earn $25,000. Other commission formulas can be more complex. Suppose, for example, that a company wanted to (1) ensure a sales representative of some base amount of annual earnings and (2) create an incentive to expand sales in a representative's territory. The company is in the chemical business, and a sales representative's performance is measured by the number of gallons he or she is responsible for selling. The commission formula may look like this:

Base: $18,000 per year
Commission: 1¢ per gallon on the first 2 million gallons
2¢ per gallon on additional gallons

If the sales representative sold three million gallons her earnings would be:

$ 18,000   (Base)
  20,000   (1¢ commission × the first 2 million gallons)
+ 20,000   (2¢ commission × the third million gallons)
$ 58,000   (total earnings)

The problems, in setting fair rates and readjusting them, inherent in piece rates apply to commissions, as well. Compensation planners must be very careful to set commission rates in line with the specific kinds of behaviors they wish to influence.

Bonuses. A third form of individual, direct, performance payment is a bonus. A bonus is simply a lump sum payment made on top of a base salary. Bonuses can be tied to any aspect of performance, and specific bonus formulas take on a wide variety of forms.

A sales bonus, for example, may take the following form. A sales representative's base annual salary is set at $15,000 per year. A bonus formula is set up that provides an additional payment of $10,000 if a particular sales objective is met. If the objective is met, the sales representative earns a total of $25,000. Very often, bonuses are set up on a sliding scale with increasingly difficult targets. The greater the performance, the higher the bonus.

One-Time Performance Payments

There are a number of performance-related payments that are not the result of adjustments to the wage-salary structure and that have no effect on that structure. Some of these payments are made on the basis of individual performance; others are based on group, or even organization-wide effort. The base usually depends on the degree to which rewarded performance can be associated with the individual, the group, or the organization.

Individual One-Time Performance Payments

The most frequent form of individual one-time performance payment is some form of piecerate or commission statement. Such payments are possible only in situations where performance can be well-defined in terms of output (sales dollars generated, number of items completed) and where employees work independently of other workers. In some cases there is a basic wage paid, with set production rates or net sales expected as a minimum, and then a bonus paid for production or sales in excess of the base. If the organization is going to make individual performance payments of this kind it should have those employees affected in a separate wage and salary structure, because the flexibility required for such systems is not possible in the standard wage and salary structure. Job evaluation in traditional terms is not applicable to these jobs; the output possible is the only factor of interest. A commission or piecerate system must be explained in detail to employees since income will fluctuate from pay period to pay period.

Determining the size of commissions or piecerates is a different process from making other pay decisions. Wage survey information is still necessary in terms of external equity considerations. The primary set of data used for both internal and individual equity is economic: value added by the employee, based on accounting information. It is necessary to find out, for example, what an additional unit of sales is worth to the organization. The commission paid to the sales personnel will be some portion of that average marginal net revenue to provide an income for the salesperson which is competitive with income provided by similar jobs.

Direct Performance Payments to Groups

Direct performance payments to groups are similar to those to individuals. That is, in some cases there is a group, such as a small sales team or an assembly team, performing with well-defined outputs and with relative independence from other workers or groups of workers. In such cases, group piecerates or bonuses are paid on a basis similar to that of individual payments.

An additional factor enters in if the group is not homogenous, as a sales team for a computer company may be made up of a hardware specialist, an accountant, and a management analyst. The organization must find a way to factor out the contributions of each member of the team in a way that is satisfactory to all group members. One-time performance payments are, for this reason, not much used unless all members of the group do obviously comparable work.

Organization-Wide Direct Performance Payments

Much more widespread are payments shared by all members of the organization. Generally these payments are based on one of two performance concepts: a sharing of profits generated by the efforts of employees or a sharing of money saved as a result of employees' cost-reduction efforts.

Profit-sharing programs. Some compensation specialists argue that profit-sharing programs are membership benefits like insurance or pensions. This is largely because the linkage between performance and reward for the individual is so weak. Like almost all group or organization-wide plans, an individual's share of the total profit-sharing pool is based on salary as a percentage of total payroll; that is, if the total annual profit-sharing pool were equal to the total annual payroll, each employee would recieve a bonus equal to his or her annual salary. Even though profit-sharing programs may not be effective motivators of performance, most companies using them as immediate salary supplements act as if they are, and the rhetoric accompanying payouts refers to rewards for performance, not to membership. Of course, many organizations use profit sharing as a source of deferred income for employees in connection with, or as a substitute for, other pension programs: these "profit-sharing" programs are a membership reward and will be discussed in Chapter 9. However, the profit-sharing programs designed for annual payouts are part of pay for performance.

These profit-sharing programs are probably most effective in a small organization, where organizational performance is largely dependent on close cooperation between members of the organization. Advertising agencies, brokerage houses, accounting firms, and similar service organizations where professional and managerial effort is the bulk of expense for the organization are more likely to use profit sharing than are manufacturing organizations.

The key issue for management in a profit-sharing program of this nature is what proportion of net is to be taken to form the pool for distribution to employees. There is no set answer for this, obviously; labor market pressures, other organizational needs, and tradition will provide guidelines.

Cost-reduction programs.   Cost-reduction programs are much more numerous than profit-sharing plans with an annual payout. There are several well-known cost reduction programs in use, including the Scanlon Plan, the Rucker Share of Production Plan, and the Kaiser Plan. All these programs have shared features. They tend to work best in smaller to medium-size firms (under 1000 employees). They appear to be applicable more to manufacturing operations than to service. They tend to work best in organizations where the work of the firm requires cooperation. Finally, they tend to work best in organizations where there is a high level of trust between workers and management.

The mechanics of these programs require that a ratio of labor costs to sales be calculated for some base period. Over the year (as frequently as bimonthly, as infrequently as semiannually) the ratio for the most recent period is calculated. If the ratio drops (labor decreases as a percentage of sales) savings go into a cost-reduction pool. This bonus pool is then divided between the organization and the employees, with 25 percent going to the organization. Typically, 25 percent of the employee's share goes into a reserve (in case, during later periods, labor costs rise above the base rate), and the rest is shared among employees.

The other feature of cost-reduction plans is the set of suggestion committees designed to have employees give input on means of reducing costs. This participative feature, with screening of ideas by management and employee representatives is what makes it probable that cost can, in fact, be reduced. The advantages of cost-reduction plans are the employees' lack of resistance to change and their active involvement in keeping costs down.

Miscellaneous Payments

Several miscellaneous payments made to employees are not permanent adjustments to the wage and salary structure, but are more stable add-ons to individual pay. The two most common add-ons are shift differentials and differentials for temporarily unpleasant or hazardous working conditions.

Shift differentials are based on the feelings of many employees that they deserve an extra bonus for working during periods other than Monday through Friday from nine to five. In most cases, unorthodox work hours are rewarded by extra pay per hour; in some cases additional benefits, such as a paid "lunch" hour, are given.

Some jobs have occasional temporary duty (usually at a different location) that is unpleasant, hazardous, or both. An example would be a maintenance operator, one of several who worked in a main plant, who on occasion would be required to visit remote sites. Since the amount of time spent at such sites would vary, and since assignment would vary with who was present when maintenance was required, how many remote-site visits were required at one time, and so forth, the organization might provide an add-on hourly pay for those times. These differentials should not be used when the hazard or unpleasant working condition is a standard, daily feature of the job; in these cases, job evaluation builds rewards into the wage and salary structure.

Finally, some organizations set up pay bonuses for special situations. A company with recruiting problems might offer a "bounty" to employees who refer qualified applicants who are subsequently hired. Rewards might be offered to employees with records of no, or low, absenteeism. Specific suggestions are rewarded by many organizations with one-time bonuses. Certainly all of these bonuses are "pay for performance," yet they are rarely the work of the compensation specialist. The compensation administrator will have to coordinate these payments with the compensation program in general.

Notes

1. William F. Whyte, *Money and Motivation* (New York: Harper and Row, 1955).

9

Benefit Programs

The compensation analyst who has developed a salary structure with policies for individual placement in the structure based on merit, seniority, or some combination of the two, has half the compensation job done. The other half is creating a benefit structure which will complete the compensation package. The goals of the benefit structure are similar to those for the wage and salary structure, in that they should also attract, retain, and motivate employees, and should do this in the least costly fashion for the employer. The benefit structure should also be complementary to the wage and salary structure and planned with the wage and salary structure in mind; many benefit levels (for example, life insurance and pensions) are a function of salary level.

Salaries and Benefits

Why not just pay people salaries and let it go at that? There are a variety of reasons why benefits are popular, and popular they are. (One survey of 186 companies, for example, shows a growth in benefits from 1959 to 1980 from being 24.7% of payroll to being 41.4% of payroll.)[1] The reasons for their popularity are as follows:

196

1. During World War II wage controls made it difficult to use salaries as a means of attracting, motivating, or retaining employees. Changes in benefits were easier to make, and employers started to compete in terms of benefits.

2. For many benefits, it is more cost efficient if a company provides them. Group coverage for insurance, for example, is cheaper per dollar protection bought than individual coverage.

3. Internal Revenue Code treatment of benefits makes them preferable to wages. Many benefits are nontaxable to the employee and are deductible by the employer. With other benefits, taxes are deferred. In addition, inflation has caused "bracket creep" for most employees. That is, salaries themselves have grown artificially high because the dollar is worth less; employees must pay taxes at a higher rate for the same purchasing power. Inflation, then, tends to make benefits preferable to wages, too.

4. Unions have found it profitable to bargain over benefits. If a union gains certain benefits, say total dental care, and the benefit is granted in terms of services given, any price increases are likely to be absorbed by the employer with no further bargaining necessary. This is also the case in nonunion situations. A benefit (such as a company car or cafeteria service) once granted is unlikely to be withdrawn.

5. Management finds it convenient to bargain over benefits, or to grant benefits in nonunion organizations. In a sense, the granting of benefits confers an aura of social responsibility on employers; they are "taking care of" their employees.

6. Many benefits, such as Social Security, are mandated by the federal government. Others may be required under state law. There are other benefits, such as pensions, that are controlled under federal and state law, as noted in Chapter 5 (pp. 92–108).

Benefit Surveys

Before starting to set up a benefit structure, the compensation analyst will want to obtain the same type of survey data for benefits as he or she obtained for salaries. In Chapter 6 we indicated the necessity of asking surveyed organizations for levels of various benefits granted. The information is needed both for interpreting wage-level data and for determining benefit levels needed to be competitive. Factors such as labor market or industry type that are used in determining the scope of the survey are noted in Chapter 6. If the purpose of the survey is to gather information only on benefits, key jobs will not be used. This is because benefits tend to be distributed fairly equally across the organizations; if one worker gets dental insurance, all do. The exceptions to this general rule are executive perquisites and certain deferred income programs. Thus, surveys such as the *U.S. Chamber of Commerce Employee Benefits Survey* concentrate on nonexecutive employees; other, such as *The Hay/Huggins Non-Cash Compensation Comparison*, concentrate on managers.

Outside Surveys

Because benefits tend to be given by organization rather than by job (as are salaries), and because organizations tend not to compete over benefit packages as much as they do over salary levels, much more published information seems to be available to compensation analysts on benefits than on wages. An additional cause of this greater availability of information is that many benefits are supplied to organizations by outside companies; these vendors are willing to supply whatever information they have as part of the sales effort.

The standard survey of employee benefits is published annually by the U.S. Chamber of Commerce. Exhibits 9.1 and 9.2 show the basic kinds of information contained in the survey. The benefit data in the Chamber of Commerce survey are conservative with respect to benefits actually paid by organizations. Except for the data on banks, financial institutions, and some hospitals, these data do not include benefits paid to managerial or professional employees, but only those paid to hourly employees and salaried employees whose pay varies with the number of hours worked. Managerial and professional employees tend to get higher benefits, both absolutely and as a percentage of base pay. A second point to note is the chamber's use of "percent of payroll." When it is stated that total benefits for all industries were 40 *percent* of payroll, that means that for every dollar spent for direct wages or salary, an additional $0.40 was spent on benefits. Thus, benefits in this case amounted to about 28.5 percent of the total compensation package. The third point is that not all benefits are included in the Chamber of Commerce survey. These benefits, which are primarily services, may or may not be mentioned by survey respondents in miscellaneous categories. Nevertheless, this survey is the basic survey; any compensation specialist should obtain it as a matter of course.

There are many other sources of benefit survey data. The three loose-leaf services (Bureau of National Affairs, Commerce Clearinghouse, Prentice-Hall) all have one or more volumes including coverage of current benefit practices; survey data are reported by these services on a timely basis. *Compensation Review* frequently publishes articles relating current practices data; in addition, there is a front section called "Compensation Currents" that provides summary information from many commercial benefit surveys. *Personnel Administrator* and *Personnel Journal* have articles and issues devoted to benefit levels. Finally, many of the wage and salary surveys discussed in Chapter 6 provide information on benefits as well. Regardless of the source of information, it is important for the compensation specialist to obtain survey data on benefits just as on wage levels, and for the same reason: if external equity in the compensation package is to be preserved, the benefit portion of that package must be planned in relation to the market.

Benefits Policy

If it is important for the compensation specialist to know what the average organization in the market is offering in the way of benefits and benefit levels, it is crucial that he or she not follow such averages slavishly, but rather build a benefits program based on organizational policy. There are many decisions to be made on benefits policy; some are similar to policy decisions for wages and salaries. In the most general form, a benefits policy must address the following questions:

1. What benefit goals does the organization have? Benefit programs may be used to ensure employee security and health, provide deferred income, reward employee loyalty, fulfill the social obligations of the organization, underline status differences between different groups of employees, or provide an incentive to join the organization.

2. What benefit levels will the organization provide? It may choose to meet, exceed, or follow the market, just as it may with wages. There may be a tradeoff between wage and benefit levels.

3. What specific benefits will the organization provide? Will em-

Exhibit 9.1   Employee Benefits as Dollars per Year per Employee, by Type of Benefit and Industry Groups, 1980 (Excerpt from Table)

Type of benefit	Total, all industries	Total, all manufacturing	Food, beverages, and tobacco	Textile products and apparel	Pulp, paper, lumber, and furniture	Printing and publishing	Chemicals and allied products	Petroleum industry	Rubber, leather, and plastic products	Stone, clay, and glass products
					Manufacturing industries					
Total employee benefits as dollars per year per employee	6,084	6,314	5,808	3,534	5,427	5,954	7,493	10,578	5,562	5,769
1. Legally required payments (employer's share only)	1,446	1,633	1,611	1,064	1,601	1,500	1,389	1,817	1,755	1,528
a. Old-Age, Survivors, Disability, and Health Insurance (FICA taxes)	954	974	949	666	900	966	1,012	1,266	915	897
b. Unemployment Compensation	223	280	276	247	286	357	178	225	321	248
c. Workers' compensation (including estimated cost of self-insured)	261	370	385	151	413	165	198	313	502	380
d. Railroad Retirement Tax, Railroad Unemployment and Cash Sickness Insurance, state sickness benefits insurance, etc.*	8	9	1	**	2	12	1	13	17	3
2. Pension, insurance, and other agreed-upon payments (employer's share only)	2,066	2,126	1,869	924	1,877	1,735	2,590	4,396	1,628	1,957
a. Pension plan premiums and pension payments not covered by insurance-type plan (net)	888	794	814	225	714	784	1,257	2,507	564	756
b. Life insurance premiums; death benefits; hospital, surgical, medical, and major medical insurance premiums, etc. (net)	950	1,121	853	606	963	809	1,051	1,427	941	1,041
c. Short-term disability	58	76	72	23	75	47	86	119	55	52
d. Salary continuation or long-term disability	41	32	32	18	29	18	46	71	33	10
e. Dental insurance premiums	55	64	68	20	25	42	102	99	8	62
f. Discounts on goods and services purchased from company by employees	22	8	13	15	15	24	5	18	8	4
g. Employee meals furnished by company	29	10	9	**	12	7	29	46	1	3

*Figure is considerably less than legal rate, because most reporting companies had only a small proportion of employees covered by tax.
**Less than 50¢.

Source: Survey Research Center, U.S. Chamber of Commerce, *Employee Benefits 1980*, Washington, D.C., 1981. Used with permission.

Exhibit 9.2 Employee Benefits as Percent of Payroll, by Type of Benefit and Industry Groups, 1980 (Excerpt from Table)

Type of benefit	Total, all industries	Total, all manufacturing	Food, beverages, and tobacco	Textile products and apparel	Pulp, paper, lumber, and furniture	Printing and publishing	Chemicals and allied products	Petroleum industry	Rubber, leather, and plastic products	Stone, clay, and glass products
					Manufacturing industries					
Total employee benefits as percent of payroll	37.1	38.2	36.4	31.9	35.0	35.7	43.3	48.0	36.7	37.8
1. Legally required payments (employer's share only)	8.9	9.9	10.0	9.6	10.3	9.0	7.9	8.2	11.5	10.0
a. Old-Age, Survivors, Disability, and Health Insurance (FICA taxes)	5.8	5.9	5.9	6.0	5.8	5.8	5.8	5.7	6.0	5.9
b. Unemployment Compensation....	1.4	1.7	1.7	2.2	1.8	2.1	1.0	1.0	2.1	1.6
c. Workers' compensation (including estimated cost of self-insured).	1.6	2.2	2.4	1.4	2.7	1.0	1.1	1.4	3.3	2.5
d. Railroad Retirement Tax, Railroad Unemployment and Cash Sickness Insurance, state sickness benefits insurance, etc.* .	0.1	0.1	**	**	**	0.1	**	0.1	0.1	**
2. Pension, insurance, and other agreed-upon payments (employer's share only)	12.6	13.0	11.8	8.4	12.2	10.3	15.1	20.0	10.8	12.8
a. Pension plan premiums and pension payments not covered by insurance-type plan (net)	5.4	4.8	5.1	2.0	4.6	4.7	7.3	11.4	3.7	5.0
b. Life insurance premiums; death benefits; hospital, surgical, medical, and major medical insurance premiums, etc. (net)...	5.8	6.8	5.3	5.5	6.2	4.8	6.1	6.5	6.2	6.8
c. Short-term disability	0.4	0.5	0.5	0.2	0.5	0.3	0.5	0.5	0.4	0.3
d. Salary continuation or long-term disability	0.3	0.2	0.2	0.2	0.2	0.1	0.3	0.3	0.2	0.1
e. Dental insurance premiums	0.3	0.4	0.4	0.2	0.2	0.3	0.6	0.5	0.1	0.4
f. Discounts on goods and services purchased from company by employees	0.1	0.1	0.1	0.1	0.1	0.1	**	0.1	0.1	**
g. Employee meals furnished by company	0.2	0.1	0.1	**	0.1	**	0.2	0.2	**	**

*Figure is considerably less than legal rate, because most reporting companies had only a small proportion of employees covered by tax.
**Less than 0.05%.

Source: Survey Research Center, U.S. Chamber of Commerce, *Employee Benefits 1980*, Washington, D.C., 1981. Used with permission.

ployee wishes help formulate the program, and if so, to what extent?

As we noted in Chapter 5, federal law, state law, and union bargaining contracts constrain the organization with respect to all three aspects of benefit policy. Competition for employees places further constraints on the organization; although benefits are not well publicized or much used as recruiting tools, many employees know enough about some specific benefits (day care, dental coverage) that these can make a difference in attraction and retention rates.

Although developing a benefits policy is a complex task, there appear to be general patterns that emerge for different kinds of organizations. Hay/Huggins Associates, for example, notes the level and characteristics of noncash components for different types of organizations.[2] Exhibit 9.3 shows the interaction of noncash and cash components of typical compensation programs for several kinds of organizations.

Components of the Benefit Package

There are three major components of the benefit package: security and health benefits, pay for time not worked, and services provided by the organization at reduced cost or no cost. In this section of the chapter, we will look at the major benefits that make up each of these components and provide some information on levels of benefits commonly provided and policy questions to be faced by the compensation specialist.

Security and Health Benefits

The component of employee benefits devoted to ensuring security and health is the most regulated. Some of the constraints placed on these benefits were noted in Chapter 5. The major benefits classified as security and health include OASDHI segments (especially social security, unemployment, and workers' compensation) insurance, severance pay, pensions, and other capital formation devices.

OASDHI/Old Age, Survivors, Disability, and Health Insurance.   The program that most employees know as Social Security includes more than just that. It includes retirement insurance, survivors' insurance, disability insurance, hospital and medical insurance for the disabled and aged

Exhibit 9.3 Organizational Style and Compensation Mix

Type of Organization	Working Climate	Reward Management Components				
		Cash		Noncash		
		Base Salary	Short-Term Incentives	Level	Characteristics	
Mature industrial	Balanced	Medium	Medium	Medium	Balanced	
Developing industrial	Growth, creativity	Medium	High	Low	Short-term-oriented	
Conservative financial	Security	Low	Low	High	Long-term-security-oriented	
Nonprofit	Societal impact, personal fulfillment	Low	None	Low-medium	Long-term-security-oriented	
Sales	Growth, freedom to act	Low	High	Low	Short-term-oriented	

Source: Reprinted, by permission of the publisher, from "Compensation Currents," *Compensation Review*, Second Quarter 1981. © 1981 by AMACOM, a division of the American Management Associations, p. 12. All rights reserved.

(medicare), black-lung benefits, and supplemental security income. OASDHI also includes provision for unemployment insurance, (to be discussed separately) and public assistance/welfare, such as aid to families with dependent children.

OASDHI benefits are financed equally by employer and employee through Federal Insurance Contributions Act (FICA) payments. FICA taxes are based on two factors: the tax rate and the size of the taxable base. Both of these factors have been increasing and are likely to continue doing so. Currently (1982) the tax rate is 6.70 percent; this includes both social security and Medicare funding. The base rate rose in 1982 from $29,700 to $32,400. Thus, an employee might pay as much as $2,170.80 in FICA taxes in 1982 (as compared to a maximum of $1,975.05 in 1981). The employer must match these payments.

The social security system is in disarray, but to herald its demise may be premature. If the system is to remain solvent, either FICA taxes must be raised or benefits must be lowered. In any case, individuals can not expect to maintain a preretirement life-style on social security benefit payments. Social security was never intended to provide more than a "minimum floor of protection" against risks.[3] It will never be more than that, even if it survives. Although it is a major expense for employers (equivalent to 5.8 percent of payroll in 1980)[4] and employees, it is not seen by most productive workers as a major "benefit."

Unemployment insurance. Mandated under OASDHI, the unemployment insurance programs are administered at the state level, and are supported through employer contributions. In 1980, employer taxes required to support unemployment payments amounted to about 1.4 percent of payroll. State laws vary, but basically the tax rate on employers is based on an "experience rate." Those employers who lay off more employees pay more; those with lower contributions to unemployment rates pay less.

Workers' compensation. Workers' compensation is a program administered by the states under varying state laws and paid for by the employer. Rules and regulations vary from state to state, as do employee contributions. In 1980, however, the costs of workers' compensation to employers were estimated to be about 1.6 percent of the payroll.[5] The function of workers' compensation programs is to provide support to those workers who are injured on the job or who sustain job-related medical problems (e.g., asbestosis, black lung, cancer associated with prolonged exposure to some chemicals). Payouts made under workers' compensation programs include payment of medical bills, support when the medical problem makes further work impossible (disability payments), burial expenses, and aid to widows and dependent children.

As with unemployment insurance, workers' compensation taxes are frequently experience-based: companies whose workers sustain most work-related injury/illness problems pay the most. Except in a few states such as Ohio, most workers' compensation insurance is underwritten by private insurance companies. Large organizations can also insure themselves. Thus, organizations can fit workers' compensation programs into the total benefit package with more flexibility than is allowed the treatment of other legally mandated programs.

Insurance.   Insurance is a large benefit expenditure for most organizations, equivalent to 6.2 percent of direct payroll costs in 1980.[6] Many different types of insurance are offered to employees, including life insurance, accidental death and dismemberment, health, dental and optical insurance, prescription drugs, psychiatric care, and auto insurance. All these types of insurance share some characteristics which make them good benefits from both the employer's and employee's point of view.

Employers may feel a responsibility for the health of an employee and his or her family. In any case, the employee beset by health problems *and* the worry about how to pay for them is not likely to be productive. In addition, the availability of paid care may induce employees to take care of problems they would otherwise live with; again, productivity may be improved. Employers may deduct expenditures on insurance premiums from taxable income; employees receive these benefits (within legislated limits) as nontaxable income. The insuring of a large group allows coverage at a rate lower than would be available to individuals. Also, employees are not required (generally) to submit to physical examinations or other qualifying tests, which makes insurance available to more employees and lower costs. Finally, group programs tend to have lessened administrative costs and record-keeping requirements, since these can be added into other personnel functions.

Health insurance is the most frequently provided insurance. Many programs are available. Some hospitalization programs guarantee certain services. Others provide dollar amounts for specific services according to a schedule. Surgical insurance is sometimes separated out from general medical/hospital care. Basic plans, such as Blue Cross, provide coverage for most health needs. Additional coverage can be provided through major medical insurance. If an organization is located near a health maintenance organization (these provide comprehensive prepaid medical coverage) the Health Maintenance Organization Act requires that HMO membership be a health insurance option for employees.

Newer forms of health-related insurance are becoming more common. Dental insurance now accounts for benefit payments equivalent to 0.3 percent of the payroll.[7] Nearly three-fifths of plans in one survey provided dental care.[8] Usually, bridgework and orthodontia are excluded from coverage, especially if the employer pays the full premium. Prescription drugs are increasingly paid for by employers' plans. In those organizations in which some behavioral problems (abuse of controlled substances, stress-related antisocial behavior) are recognized as symptoms of illness rather than as sins, treatment rather than punishment is the preferred solution. In these organizations, insurance is provided for outpatient psychiatric counseling. Insurance for routine eye care is now provided by many organizations (two-fifths of plans covered in one survey did so)[9]; fewer provide coverage for frames and lenses. A rarer form of insurance, hospice care for the terminally ill, is now offered by such companies as RCA and Westinghouse, and through insurers such as Blue Cross.[10] Although 500 hospice programs are available, geographic coverage is spotty and employee reaction is mixed so far.

Accidental death and dismemberment insurance is provided by many organizations. It can be a useful supplement to workers' compensation, and is particularly useful for employees who travel for the organization. Regular life insurance is also provided by most organizations. The type of insurance provided is usually group term life insurance (coverage is for the period of a specified term, and premiums do not build up assets) provided in some multiple of base annual salary. Most companies pay the premium for coverage between 1.5 and 2.5 times an employee's annual salary; many plans allow the employee to buy additional coverage at the group rates.

A final form of insurance that is beginning to be offered as a benefit is auto insurance. A few companies now offer such insurance, paying about 40 percent of the premium. Two problems preventing more widespread adoption are the federal tax code (which treats employer premium payments for auto insurance as taxable income to the employee) and the Taft-Hartley Act (which does not include group auto insurance as a legitimate benefit under collectively bargained trust funds jointly administered by labor and management).[11]

Severance pay. Because of unemployment compensation, many organizations give no severance pay; others still provide payment to employees when they leave, usually in lieu of notice.[12] Average severance pay for executives is about three months' pay; many organizations extend company insurance coverage for a month or two as well.[13] Other benefits provided for terminated employees include placement services such as resume banks, job-finding seminars, and the use of office space to operate from while job hunting.

Pensions

Pensions and their variants (profit-sharing plans, stock option programs) have two distinct purposes. The first is to ensure that employees will continue to have some income after they retire. The second is to defer income realization, and therefore defer income taxation, until after retirement and thus have the income taxed at a lower rate. For executives, a related purpose is capital formation by providing opportunities to realize capital gains and thus avoid high rates of taxation on standard income.

Under many pension programs, both employer and employee make contributions. The employee contribution is usually some percentage of base pay. The employer contribution is usually based on the amount required to provide expected payouts at retirement. Thus, these contributions depend on the employee's current age, years of service, current compensation, and expected retirement data. Benefits under most pension plans may be paid out only when the employee terminates, whether through normal retirement, early retirement, death, discharge, or quitting. The amount paid out in benefits varies with type of termination, and may be either a lump sum (in some cases of discharge or quitting), installment (in the case of retirement or early retirement; these are most frequent in all cases), or both (in the case of death, where a survivor may receive both a capital amount and installment payments). Some organizations (primarily government, but also Heinz, Xerox, and others) adjust benefit payments to account for inflation.[14]

As we have noted, standard pension contributions by employers are based on actuarial requirements or expected pension payouts. Employer obligations are unrelated to organizational success. For this reason, many employers use a variant of the pension: the profit-sharing plan.[15] The major features of a profit-sharing plan are implied by the title. Usually, employees make no contribution to the plan. The employer's contribution is a function of before-tax profit, and thus will vary from year to year.

The contribution is usually allocated among employees on the basis of annual salary, ignoring age and seniority. At termination of employment, whether through retirement, death, discharge, or quitting, the benefit in the employee's account is distributable, usually in a lump sum. In some cases, an employee can draw on the profit-sharing account before termination.

Another means of tax deferral or tax avoidance for employers and employees is the employee stock ownership plan (ESOP). Actually, there are three primary types of ESOPs. [16] The stock bonus plan is the first form of ESOP. A trust is established to benefit employees, and the company contributes its own stock (or money to be used to buy its own stock). A limit of 15 percent of salary is imposed. Vesting rules apply, and the employee gets stock only on retirement or other termination of employment. The organization can deduct the contribution; the employee is not liable for taxes until he or she actually receives stock from the trust.

A leveraged ESOP is similar to the stock bonus format, except that the trust can go into debt to purchase stock of the organization. The corporation guarantees the loan and contributes cash to service the loan. Created under the Tax Reduction Act of 1975, TRASOPs are the third form of ESOP. A TRASOP is an investment credit ESOP in which both employer and employee contribute to the trust fund on a matching basis. Vesting is 100 percent and immediate, but stock in an employee's account may not be distributed for seven years, except on termination of employment, death, or disability. Employers receive investment tax credit for TRASOP contributions.

There are a number of advantages to an employer in using an ESOP rather than regular pension or profit-sharing plans. [17] The advantages are that:

1. There is no reduction in working capital, because payments are made in corporate stock.

2. Retention and motivation goals may be served when employees have an "ownership stake" in the organization.

3. The ESOP trust may help the organization avoid takeover; however, the courts may not allow ESOP trust shares to be voted. [18]

4. ESOP contributions are not based on profit, so operating losses (and resultant tax benefits) can be credited; at the same time, contribution levels are not a function of payroll, so contributions can be lessened in adverse economic times.

5. Service of employees prior to ESOP establishment does not create employer liability, as could service prior to establishment of a pension program.

ESOP disadvantages include increased costs of administration and dilution of ownership. Employees are not always enthusiastic about ESOPs, and unions generally oppose them.[19] When companies are closely held, the value of stock contributed to the ESOP may be questioned.

Many employers are looking at stock options again as a tax-deferred income opportunity for executive employees. Under the Economic Recovery Tax Act of 1981, individuals may be granted incentive stock options (ISOs) of up to $100,000 each year. Gain on stock from option price to exercise price is not paid until the stock is sold; then any gains are taxed as capital gains rather than ordinary income. A change in the law is costly to grantors of options. Under earlier option programs, the company could take as a tax credit the difference between option and exercise price; it may not do so with ISOs.[20]

Regardless of the kind of pension program an organization decides to set up, the employer has several decisions to make:

1. What mix of pension, profit-sharing, ESOP, and option benefits will be offered?

2. How much will employees get?

3. How will differences in benefits be determined? Some possibilities are seniority, profits, salary level, age, or a mix.

4. How much will employees contribute to the plan?

5. Will benefits be subject to cost of living adjustments?

6. Will other employee income (such as social security) affect benefit levels?

7. When will benefits start? Can employees retire early for reduced benefit levels?

8. What happens to benefits if employment terminates for reasons other than retirement?

9. How are payouts to be made (lump sum, income flow, or combination)?

10. How is vesting to be handled?

11. Can the employee draw on benefit funds (e.g., borrow against them) while still working for the organization?

12. How is the fund to be administered?

13. To what extent will employees participate in fund administration?

14. How is the fund to be insured against economic adversity?

The answers to many of these questions are constrained by the IRC, ERISA (Employee Retirement Income Security Act), ADEA (Age Discrimination in Employment Act), and other federal laws. Still, employers have some choice with respect to all of them, and they should be prepared to make policy decisions.

Pay for Time Not Worked

Most employees do not work eight hours a day, five days a week, fifty-two weeks a year; yet almost all salaried employees are paid as if they did. In essence, most organizations pay employees for time they do not work as well as for time they do. The most widely recognized forms of pay for time not worked are vacation, holidays, and sick leave, but other types exist as well. Pay for time not worked is important to the compensation analyst, because an increase in paid time off is equivalent to an increase in wage rate. Total payment for time not worked amounted to nearly 10 percent of direct wages in 1980.[21]

Vacation pay.   The cost of vacations (or pay in lieu of vacations) was about 5 percent of direct payroll costs in 1980.[22] The vacation policies of interest to compensation specialists are summed up by answers to the following questions:

1. Who should get vacation time and how much? Usually vacation is a reward for service; employees who have worked a longer time for an organization receive more vacation time. The loose-leaf services provide information on current vacation practices. Typically, white-collar workers get more than blue-collar, executives get more than hourly workers, and part-time workers may get none at all. Current practices are shown in Exhibit 9.4.

2. What if a holiday, sickness, or other "time off with pay" event occurs during the vacation?

3. To what degree can vacation time not taken be saved and carried over to another pay period? Can vacation time be combined with authorized nonpaid absences?

4. Under what circumstances will employees get extra pay rather

than paid time off? Some organizations use accrued vacation time as a form of severance pay. If the organization wants the employee to forego vacation, will it pay double for that time period?

5. When is vacation pay to be given? When long-term employees have a month or more of vacation, their paid time off might cover two or three paydays. Most organizations give all vacation pay in advance; others observe regular paydays.

Holidays. Holidays cost employers the equivalent of 3.4 percent of total payroll costs in 1980.[23] In 1979, more than 60 percent of companies in one survey offered nine or more holidays; 19 percent offered eleven or more.[24] These holidays included (in order of popularity):

New Year's Day

Thanksgiving Day

Labor Day

Independence Day

Memorial Day

Christmas Eve

Good Friday

Day after Thanksgiving

New Year's Eve

Washington's Birthday

Employee's Birthday

Floating Holiday

Veteran's Day

Day after Christmas

Easter Monday

President's Day

Columbus Day

Easter Sunday

Election Day

Holiday policies affecting compensation include:

1. The holidays to be observed. For those holidays which fall on different weekdays each year, what happens when the paid holiday

Exhibit 9.4   Vacation Time in Companies Having Plant and Office
Employees

Length of Service	1 Week		6-9 Days		2 Weeks		11-14 Days	
	Office	*Plant*	*Office*	*Plant*	*Office*	*Plant*	*Office*	*Plant*
6 months	73.4%	66.6%	—	—	2.2%	2.6%	—	—
1 year	32.5	49.6	1.7%	2.5%	60.8	43.8	3.3%	2.5%
2 years	6.6	20.7	0.8	0.8	85.1	71.9	5.0	5.0
3 years	2.5	5.8	0.8	2.5	86.8	83.5	5.0	5.0
5 years	2.5	4.0	0.8	0.8	51.7	56.6	6.0	5.0
8 years	1.7	2.5	0.8	0.8	30.3	35.0	7.6	9.2
10 years	1.7	2.5	—	—	9.0	9.8	4.1	6.6
15 years	1.7	2.6	—	—	3.3	4.3	1.7	2.6
20 years	1.7	2.5	—	—	3.4	4.0	1.7	2.5
25 years	1.7	2.5	—	—	3.3	4.1	1.7	2.5

Source: "Prentice-Hall Survey: 1982 Vacation Policies," *P-H Personnel Management: Policies and Practices* Report #18, 2-16-82, Englewood Cliffs, N.J., p. 224.

falls on a Saturday or Sunday? On a Tuesday or Thursday? Will
Friday or Monday be granted in these cases?

2. Is everyone eligible for holiday pay? Eligibility questions involve
   hourly workers who miss the day before or after the paid holiday,
   as well as part-time workers, and workers who are laid off, on sick
   leave, or on vacation.

3. Pay rates. There are two issues here. The first involves the rate
   of pay for pieceworkers, commission workers, and workers getting
   a shift premium. The second involves the rate of pay for employees
   who are required to work on holidays.

4. Extra religious holidays. If all employees get Christmas off, should
   members of other religions get holy days off with pay too? (Many
   organizations solve this problem by granting one to three "individual" holidays with pay to all employees.)

3 Weeks		4 Weeks		5 Weeks		Other	
Office	*Plant*	*Office*	*Plant*	*Office*	*Plant*	*Office*	*Plant*
2.2%	2.6%	—	—	—	—	22.2%*	28.2%*
1.7	0.8	—	—	—	—	—	0.8*
2.5	0.8	—	—	—	—	—	0.8*
4.1	2.5	0.8%	—	—	—	—	0.8*
39.0	32.8	—	—	—	—	—	0.8*
59.6	51.7	—	—	—	—	—	0.8*
66.2	68.0	19.0	12.3%	—	—	—	0.8*
43.8	51.2	47.1	35.0	0.8%	1.7%	1.7**	2.6**
21.0	27.0	59.6	52.5	11.8	9.8	0.8**	1.7**
17.4	22.3	51.2	48.8	21.4	17.3	3.3**	2.5**

* Varies from 1 to 10 days.
** Varies from 17 to 30 days.

Sick leave. Sick leave pay equaled about 1.3 percent of total payroll costs in 1980.[25] As with other forms of pay for time not worked, the organization must develop policies that speak to compensation issues:

1. Who gets sick leave, and how much? Does this vary by type of employee?

2. Does sick leave build up or does it disappear at the end of the year? Can unused sick leave be traded for extra pay? What happens to accrued sick leave when an employee terminates?

3. What level of pay will be given for sick leave? This applies mainly to workers who get shift premiums or who are on some piecerate system.

Some employers have found sick leave to be one of the more abused benefits. Instead of differentiating vacation and sick leave, employees are simply given a set amount of time when they are not required to work but will still be paid. Such a policy encourages workers not to report in sick unless they are in fact sick; more important, it saves the employer the expense of an audit system for sick leave.

Miscellaneous pay for time not worked.   There are a number of miscellaneous paid times borne by organizations. Reservists generally are paid for the time they spend in summer camp, and some reservists get full or partial pay if they are called back to military service. Voting time is paid for by many employers; more than thirty states require workers to have time off to vote. Presidential election days are more likely to result in full paid days off; for local elections, an hour may be all that is granted. Jury duty, marriage leaves, bereavement leaves, and leaves associated with childbirth are all recognized policy issues in most organizations. The Ford Foundation, for example, gives eight weeks of full pay to male employees to care for a newborn or adopted child.[26] Other organizations, such as Xerox, grant "social service leaves" with full salaries and fringe benefits to employees who do such things as help small companies fight employees' drug and alcohol problems or help disabled persons make their homes barrier-free for wheelchairs.[27] Still other employers provide paid sabbaticals for employees, pay for jury duty time, or pay for time devoted to public service activities.

Employers also pay employees for internal nonwork time. Coffee breaks, rest breaks, and lunch breaks are commonly paid for. Employers frequently give workers time to clean up and time to prepare for work. Travel time is sometimes paid for as well. The issue for the compensation analyst is how much of the money spent on nonwork time has some return to the organization. Does it help in attracting, retaining, or motivating employees? How does that paid time interact with wage levels?

Services

Compensation analysts have not traditionally been as concerned with services to employees as with the other two categories of benefits. Yet, these services are frequently more visible to employees than health or security benefits, or pay for time not worked. This visibility makes the inclusion of paid services into the equity equation a high probability; thus compensation analysts should look at employee service benefits as an integral part of the compensation package. There are many kinds of services. Many of the services fill other human resource function needs, and so must be considered on broader grounds than compensation program requirements alone. A full study of services is beyond the scope of this book, but we will look at a few services that exemplify the total range. Services differ from other benefits in not being provided to all employees as a matter of course. Some services, such as executive perquisites, are limited to a class of employees. Others, such as relocation benefits, are provided on the basis of need. Finally, some services, although theoretically available to all employees, are in fact limited to those who are interested in the service (day care, gymnasium facilities), or who can afford to pay for it (charitable matching, credit unions).

Perquisites. A perquisite is a benefit tied to a specific job. The most widespread executive "perk" is a company car for private use. One study reported 56 percent of surveyed organizations providing this service at an average cost per care of $4,530 per year.[28] Other perks include country club membership, payment for spouses to accompany executives on trips, entertainment expenses, and physical examinations. Financial counseling, including tax preparation, legal advice, and investment advice for top executives, is frequently offered.

Many perquisites are considered by the IRS to be attempts to provide extra untaxed income to favored employees; often such perks are therefore declared taxable income. The necessity of the service for the employee to carry out his or her job is frequently the deciding factor.

Charitable matching. Many organizations give money to charitable groups as a public relations gesture. Frequently, employee input is sought. One means of doing this is to match gifts employees make to institutions. The National Center for Higher Education puts out a list of 824 corporations such as Weyerhaeuser, Shell Oil, Chase Manhattan Bank, and American Express, that will match employees' gifts to universities, secondary schools, and in some cases elementary schools. Nearly 50 percent of these organizations match on a greater than dollar-for-dollar basis.

Special facilities. Meal and coffee-break facilities are the most common special facilities. Subsidized meals are not infrequent, especially when commercial restaurants are not readily available to employees. In addition to meal facilities, many organizations provide health facilities and employee "country clubs."

Special occasion bonuses. Bonuses include service awards, Christmas checks, and turkeys at Thanksgiving. Generally, these bonuses are small in terms of individual costs, but collectively they can be quite expensive.

Savings plans, credit unions, and IRAs.   In an attempt to help employees build up capital, many organizations sponsor savings plans. Some employers match part of employees' savings as a motivation to save. Credit unions are similar programs, usually without employer matching of deposits. However, employers usually provide space and employees to run the credit union. Under the Economic Recovery Tax Act of 1981 individuals covered by corporate pension programs can in addition invest up to $2,000 per year in a tax-deferred Individual Retirement Account (IRA). Few organizations are managing IRAs for their employees, but many are making it easier for employees to set up IRAs by allowing insurance companies, brokers, and mutual funds to sell IRAs to employees on company time.[29] In addition, many organizations set up payroll deduction plans to make it easy for employees to participate in savings plans, credit unions, and IRAs.

Miscellaneous services.   Organizations provide hundreds of miscellaneous services to employees. Such services include partial payment of adoption fees (such benefits range from $500 to $2,200),[30] arrangement for discount buying services (one company has an arrangement with twelve local auto dealers to sell to its employees at $125 over cost),[31] or even company housing (Pepperdine University has sold condominiums to faculty in Malibu at about one-third of prices for comparable units in the area).[32]

   Why should a compensation specialist be concerned with such benefits? Many employees think of these fringes as essential parts of the compensation package. Consider the case of Pepper Rogers. When fired in 1979, his $42,300 contract had two years to go; and Georgia Institute of Technology, for whom he coached, continued to pay that amount. However, Mr. Rogers's fringe benefits ended, and by his estimation they were worth $496,980 for 1980 and 1981 combined.[33] This is an extreme case, but many employees see their fringes as an integral part of the job, and thus these benefits become important to the compensation package in attracting, retaining and, motivating employees.

Notes

1. U.S. Chamber of Commerce, *Employee Benefits 1980* (Washington, D.C., 1981).
2. Compensation Currents. *Compensation Review,* 2nd Quarter, 1981, p. 12.
3. R. J. Myers, *Social Security* (Homewood, Ill.: Richard D. Irwin, 1975), p. 22.
4. U.S. Chamber of Commerce, *Employee Benefits.*

5. Ibid.

6. Ibid.

7. Ibid.

8. D. R. Bell, "Dental and Vision Care Benefits in Health Insurance Plans," *Monthly Labor Review, 103* (June 1980), pp. 22–26.

9. Ibid.

10. *Wall Street Journal,* Tuesday, November 3, 1981, p. 1.

11. *Wall Street Journal,* Wednesday, January 7, 1981, p. 15.

12. C. S. Ives, "Benefits and Services—Private," in Dale Yoder and Herbert G. Heneman, Jr., eds., *ASPA Handbook of Personnel and Industrial Relations* (Washington, D.C.: Bureau of National Affairs, 1975), pp. 6-185–6-233.

13. *Wall Street Journal,* Tuesday, October 13, 1981, p. 1.

14. Deborah Rankin, "Tying Pensions to Prices," *New York Times,* Sunday, July 19, 1981, p. F13.

15. Prentice-Hall Editorial Staff, *Employee Benefits* (Englewood Cliffs, N.J.: Prentice-Hall, 1979), p. 25,054.

16. Randy G. Swad, "Stock Ownership Plans: A New Employee Benefit," *Personnel Journal, 60* (June 1981), pp. 453–55.

17. Ibid.

18. G. Christian Hill, "Retirement Issue: Employee Stock Plans: An Economic Cureall or a Dubious Benefit?" *Wall Street Journal,* Monday, December 8, 1980, p. 1.

19. Ibid.

20. "A New Life for Stock Options," *Business Week,* October 12, 1981, pp. 148–151.

21. U.S. Chamber of Commerce, *Employee Benefits.*

22. Ibid.

23. Ibid.

24. Prentice-Hall Editorial Staff, *Working Hours-Holidays-Vacation,* Prentice-Hall Personnel Policies (Englewood Cliffs, N.J.: Prentice-Hall, 1978), p. 7102.

25. U.S. Chamber of Commerce, *Employee Benefits.*

26. "Daddy Days," *Wall Street Journal,* Tuesday, April 21, 1981, p. 1.

27. Jeffrey A. Tannenbaum, "Paid Public-Service Leaves," Wall Stret Journal, Wednesday, May 6, 1981, p. 27.

28. *Wall Street Journal,* Thursday, July 9, 1981, p. 1.

29. "What the New IRA Rules Do For You," *Business Week,* September 14, 1981, pp. 122–26.

30. "When Companies Help Pay for Adoption," *Business Week,* November 2, 1981, p. 56.

31. *Wall Street Journal,* Tuesday, October 13, 1981, p. 1.

32. " 'Company Housing' on the Rise in California as Schools and Firms Try to Lure Employees," *Wall Street Journal,* Monday, October 26, 1981, p. 25.

33. "Sacked Football Coach Sues School for Cash in Lieu of Lost Perks," *Wall Street Journal,* Thursday, October 16, 1980, p. 16.

10

The Compensation Program

So far we have looked at building an internal wage structure through job evaluation, at collecting labor market data and integrating those data with the internal structure to price jobs, and at methods of determining individual pay within the structure. Options available in designing benefit packages and means of merging benefits with salaries to make up the compensation package were also discussed. In this chapter we will look at three areas important to implementation of the compensation package:

—issues in planning and administration

—audit, control, and budgeting the program

—communicating the program.

The best-constructed compensation program will founder if these implementation issues are not thoroughly and successfully addressed by the organization.

Planning and Administration

The key issue in planning and administering the compensation program is integrating the program with organizational goals. This is possible of course, only if the organization has set some explicit goals and carries on strategic planning activities. Many texts discuss strategic planning in detail. It is enough here to note that the compensation program, which involves a major expense to the organization and affects the performance and satisfaction of all employees of the organization, must be congruent with overall organizational goals if it is to help the organization achieve those goals. Lawler, for example, has shown how pay systems must be structured if the organization is to pursue organizational development strategies.[1] Regardless of the organizational goals the compensation system must support, there are several compensation policy issues that must be decided if the compensation program is to be congruent with any strategy.

Compensation Policy Issues

Policy issues in compensation speak to the design of the system. Each of these policy areas must be considered by the organization, and decisions must be considered in light of the rest of compensation policy decisions and the degree to which those decisions support organizational goals. Many policy issues, and factors influencing decisions on those issues, are related to equity.

Equity emphasis. It is impossible for the organization to meet external, internal, and individual equity goals completely. When there is a conflict between equity goals (the market values jobs differently than job contribution to the organization would indicate) the organization must choose which equity goal takes precedence or how much each equity goal will be compromised. A major concern of organizations in inflationary times is salary compression. Meeting external equity goals (the market value of new employees) without increasing compensation of all current employees in that job category violates individual equity goals.

External equity policies. External equity policies deal with the relationship of the compensation program to the external market. A major policy issue in this area is whether the organization wishes to undercut, meet, or exceed the market in terms of the salaries it pays. In general, the more competitive the organization chooses to be with respect to the market, the more quality it can demand of employees.

A closely related policy issue is whether the company chooses to lead or to lag behind the market in implementing survey data. Briefly, when survey data are obtained, they are usually out of date. Even estimates of current data, if used to price an organization's jobs, would result in a pay structure lagging behind the market, since the market may be expected to move upward while the organization's pay structure is in effect. Means of dealing with this problem will be discussed in the section on "Auditing, Adjusting, and Budgeting Salary Structures."

A third external equity issue that organizations must face is response not to the market, but to the value of the dollar. Cost-of-living adjustments, popular in the 1960s and 1970s, had largely gone out of favor by the beginning of the 1980s. Some organizations still attempt to respond to inflation by indexing salaries to the Consumer Price Index or by instituting other cost-of-living adjustments (COLAs).

Internal equity policies.   Organizations must deal with two major internal equity policies. The first is a decision as to the split in the compensation package between wages and benefits. This is primarily an internal equity issue, because many benefits are distributed equally across salary levels. The larger the proportion of total compensation that is devoted to benefits, the smaller the difference between jobs as reflected by the total compensation package. Benefits tend to lessen internal equity differentials. There are, in addition, some external equity issues with respect to which benefits an organization ought to offer to remain competitive with the market.

The more important internal equity issue has to do with the choice of job evaluation system. In choosing a job evaluation system, and the factors that will be used to evaluate jobs, the organization is making value judgments that will be reflected in final salary differentials. Many of the determinants of these policy decisions and the consequences of these decisions are discussed in Chapter 7. Additional information may be found in the National Academy of Sciences report on job evaluation as it affects wage differentials across the sexes.[2]

Individual equity policies.   Individual equity policies and their consequences were discussed in Chapter 8. Basically, the policy issues involved in individual equity decisions are (1) whether the organization will recognize individual contribution differentials in the pay system at all, and (2) if individual differentials are to be recognized, what mix of performance, seniority, or other contributions will be recognized.

Compensation Administation Issues

Aside from broad policy issues, the organization must also make decisions about several administrative issues. These issues can be divided into two broad areas. The first is responsibility for policy decisions and administration of the program. The second is the degree to which individual employees have knowledge of and participate in pay decisions.

Responsibility. Responsibility for the compensation progam is typically centered in the Human Resources Department. However, many decisions are made by other organizational members. Broad compensation policy in larger organizations is usually set by a compensation committee, which operates at the same level as the board of directors, with some participation by top management. Administrative issues are decided by a Salary Administration Committee, which usually includes personnel and upper-level management members. Finally, job evaluation committees composed of compensation specialists and lower management typically make job evaluation recommendations. The degree to which the compensation specialist serves as a resource person or a sole decision maker varies with the organization.

In large organizations with many divisions and locations, a decision must be made as to where compensation decisions will be made. Some organizations have a centralized system, with policy and administration located at corporate headquarters; others locate as much compensation administration as possible at the local level. The tradeoff is between control of the compensation program and the responsiveness of the program to local needs.

Participation. The second area of administration issues is the amount of employee participation in the compensation process. There are several issues in question. The first and most important is whether pay and the pay system should be secret or open. If compensation is to attract, motivate, and retain workers, and if the compensation system in an organization meets external, internal, and individual equity standards, then open information on the system may be beneficial. However, perceptions of inequity in the system will only be strengthened by openness if the system is in fact inequitable. Opening up the pay system is risky for most organizations, yet one of the largest organizations, the United States government, has an open pay system that seems to operate well in spite of external inequity (lack of competitiveness) at upper levels. It would be hard to argue, for example, that closing the government's system would make it easier to attract or retain upper-level civil servants.

A second participation issue is the degree to which employees help determine compensation packages. Few organizations go to the extremes of Romac Industries Inc., where an employee who wants a raise must post a request on a bulletin board and submit to a secret ballot of his or her coworkers. [3]

A more usual form of employee participation lies in the area of benefits. Not all employees find all benefits equally attractive. A single employee with no dependents may have little use for term life insurance, whereas for a single parent such coverage is crucial. Some organizations construct a flexible benefits program. In this "cafeteria" approach, the organization makes available a wide variety of benefits, and the employee chooses a set dollar amount that has maximum perceived utility. Such participation should maximize the effect of benefits on attracting, motivating, and retaining employees.

Very little research has been done on the effects of participation in compensation programs. One study indicated that employee participation in the design of a base pay plan resulted in increased job satisfaction, pay satisfaction, understanding of the pay plan, and trust in management. [4] Costs of employee participation were not measured.

The final participation issue is the availability of an appeals system for employees. If equity is to be preserved in the system, it is probably necessary to set up a formal system for employees to appeal system decisions.

Auditing, Adjusting, and Budgeting Salary Structures

The compensation planner's most important responsibility is cost control. In order to achieve cost control and forecast of compensation costs, the planner must take three sequential planning steps: (1) auditing the current structure for external, internal, and individual equity; (2) adjusting the structure to correspond to the organization's external market pricing philosophy as well as internal and individual equity objectives; and

(3) forecasting the budget that will be required to achieve such a structure. In each of the examples to follow in this section we will make the following assumptions:

1. You are the chief compensation planner for Fay/Wallace Corporation, a major manufacturing concern.

2. Fay/Wallace has adopted a lead/lag pricing policy with respect to the external market. That is, the company chooses to be leading the market at the beginning of a plan year, meet the market in the middle of the plan year, and lag behind the market by the end of the plan year.

3. You are at the end of a current plan year. It is now December 31.

4. You have salary survey data from the external market that is six months old, gathered last June.

5. The best estimate you have of salary increases in the external market for this past year is 8 percent.

6. Your best estimate is that salary increases in the external market next year will be 13 percent.

7. You are concerned with five salary grades (see Exhibit 10.1).

Many of the audit, adjustment, and budgeting techniques to be presented here were developed by Dr. John Davis, Principal in the consulting firm of Waters/Trego, Inc., Dallas, Texas and formerly Manager of Compensation for Sun Gas Co. of Dallas. Dr. Davis, in addition, has been instrumental in developing the quantitative courses as part of the professional certification program of the American Compensation Association (ACA) (see Chapter 11) and trains compensation planners in the use of these methods under ACA auspices.

Auditing the Current Structure

The first step in compensation planning is to audit one's current structure for external, internal, and individual equity. Exhibit 10.1 contains information from a survey of external market rates together with Fay/Wallace Corporation's current pay structure for pay grades 20 through 24. The low rate, midpoint, and high rate are displayed for both data sets.

External equity.   The first audit question is: How competitive is the company's structure with the market? We have used a compa-ratio to

Exhibit 10.1   Comparison of Fay/Wallace Corporation with Survey (Monthly Salaries)

Grade	No. of Co. / Incumbents		Average Low	Average Midpoints	Average High	Low	Midpoint	High
		Survey					*Fay/Wallace*	
24	25 /	225	990	1,195	1,400	931	1,123	1,316
23	36 /	230	880	1,040	1,200	827	978	1,128
22	36 /	182	800	923	1,045	752	868	982
21	32 /	228	740	843	945	696	792	888
20	34 /	235	700	790	880	658	743	827

assess competitiveness. A *compa-ratio* is defined as the ratio of the market midpoint rate (numerator) to the company's midpoint rate (denominator). Davis has labeled such a compa-ratio a *competitive compa-ratio* (CCR). The CCRs for our structure with respect to the market is 1.06 for each pay grade. That is, as of last June the market was 6 percent above our company's wage structure. We would have to compare this information to where we had *originally planned to be with respect to the market* this past year.

Internal equity.   In Chapter 7 we discussed the development of an internal wage structure and indicated that two operational criteria must be examined to assess the degree to which a current structure is achieving internal equity: (1) midpoint separations (the distance in percentage terms between the midpoint rates of adjacent pay grades), and (2) percentage overlap between adjacent pay grades. The midpoint separations in this structure range from 7 to 15 percent. These data indicate an accelerated wage progression as one moves from one pay grade to the next. The planner would have to compare this fact to the objective established on the basis of job-evaluation results.

External Equity	Internal Equity		Individual Equity		
Midpoint Competitive Compa-Ratio	Midpoint Separation Fay/Wallace	Grade Overlap	Grade Width	Average Rate	Compa-Ratio
1.06	1.15	.51	.41	1,286	1.15
1.06	1.13	.52	.36	844	.86
1.06	1.10	.59	.31	876	1.01
1.06	1.07	.68	.28	792	1.00
1.06			.26	796	1.07

The data in Exhibit 10.1 suggest substantial overlap between adjacent pay grades (51 to 68 percent). The planner would have to ask if such overlap is warranted or causing undue inequities when wage comparisons are made across pay grades.

Individual equity. Three operational criteria are employed by the planner in assessing individual equity. First is pay-grade width or spread: do we have sufficient range from the low rate to the high rate to leave room for all the individual pay distinctions we want to make for seniority and merit? In Exhibit 10.1 we have measured grade width as the range of rates from lowest to highest as a percentage of the minimum rate for each grade. The range widths in Exhibit 10.1 vary from 26 to 41 percent. The planner would have to examine the company's criteria for making individual wage adjustments and ask if these ranges are too wide or too narrow.

The second operational criterion for measuring individual equity in the structure is the actual distribution of individual wage rates. Exhibit 10.1 displays both acutal average wage rates being paid and the compa-ratio for each grade. The compa-ratio is the ratio of the actual average for the grade (numerator) to the midpoint for the grade (denominator).

The compa-ratio for pay grade 24, for example, is derived as follows: compa-ratio (CR) for grade 24 = \$1,286/\$1,123 = 1.15. The average person in pay grade 24, therefore, is 15 percent above the midpoint. The compa-ratio is a rough measure of the position of the actual distribution of wages in the structure. When salaries are compressed toward the top, we expect the compa-ratio to exceed 1.00. When they are compressed toward the bottom of the range, we expect the compa-ratio to be less than 1.00.

A third criterion provides an even more accurate picture of how well we are using our current structure and can be obtained by plotting actual frequency distributions of wage rates within each grade. This is presented for our current structure in Exhibit 10.2. In this case, we can see a great deal of wage rate compression in all grades except grade 22. In grades 20 and 24, individual wage rates are compressed toward the top. Part of this compression may be quite reasonable; that is, all the employees in this grade may be equivalent in terms of seniority and merit. The planner would have to check to see if this is, in fact, the case. On the other hand, the fact that we had fallen 6 percent behind the market by the middle of this year may mean that we are hiring in at rates higher than our minimum rate and compressing wage rates in a way that violates individual equity. The compression in grade 23 represents a different kind of problem, one in which all rates are clustered at the minimum rate. Again, this compression may make sense. All people may be new to this grade and of equivalent merit. You should note, in our discussion, that there is no correct or incorrect level of compression or compa-ratio. These are neutral indices that merely describe the current structure and distribution of actual wages. The planner bears the responsibility of diagnosing these indices according to the company's actual employees and individual equity objectives.

Structure Formation and Adjustment

Once the structure has been audited, the planner must consider whatever adjustments must be made to come closer to the employer's external, internal, and individual equity objectives. The most common adjustment, faced annually by compensation planners, is adjusting the current year's structure for anticipated movements in the external wage structure (the market) for the next plan year. In our example, the planner must now adjust the structure not only to the market in the current plan year, but to *the forecasted market* for the next plan year.

Exhibit 10.2 Fay/Wallace Corporation: Current Wage Structure

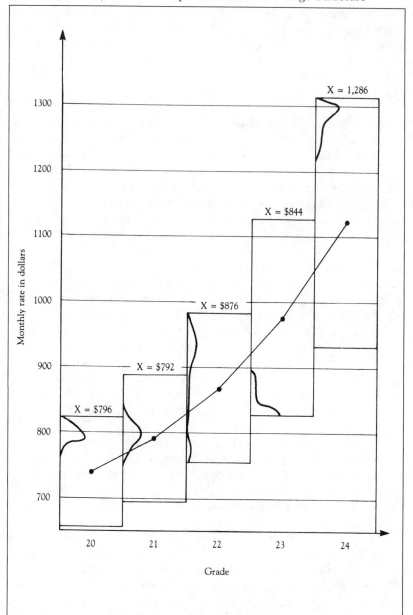

Exhibit 10.3 displays a graphical device designed by John Davis to help the planner make the structure adjustments just described. The bars in the graph represent the June salary survey data for this past year (see Exhibit 10.1). The unborken *I* lines in the graph represent our company's current internal wage structure. As seen in Exhibit 10.3, our current wage structure had fallen 6 percent behind the market by June of our current plan year.

Step 1: Adjusting the structure. The first step in adjusting the structure to the market can be done simply in Exhibit 10.3 by setting lows, mid-points, and highs for our internal structure to the lows, midpoints, and highs of the market as of this past June. This has been done in the graph by the broken *I* lines. The initial adjusted structure for the next plan year is displayed in Exhibit 10.4. It has been established simply be setting the current structure to the nearest dollar (or other measure) of the market-place for this past June of the current plan year.

Step 2: Adjusting for old data. There is a time problem at this stage, however, and that is that the data is six months old (last June). We have to adjust our initial structure to bring it six months forward to December 31 (the end of the current plan year). We have accomplished this by taking the fraction $6/12$ (representing June as half of the year) and multiplying it by the anticipated percentage increase in the market for the entire year (8 percent). Multiplying $6/12$ by 8 percent yields 4 percent, for an adjustment factor of 1.04. Thus, we will have to multiply the structure in Exhibit 10.4 by 1.04 to bring it up to the marketplace as of December 31, the end of our current plan year.

Step 3: Setting competitive policy for next plan year. The third step in adjusting the current structure is to establish the company's pricing policy for the next plan year. It is important for the compensation planner to note that he or she is *setting a single structure that will remain constant for one year* (or whatever planning horizon the company has set). The marketplace is not going to stay constant during that same period. In our current economy, we would expect the external market structure of rates to increase during the next plan year. Thus, the planner is confronted with the problem of setting a structure as of January 1, that will have to ride a moving market through next year. Compensation managers have developed three strategies for dealing with this problem: (1) a lead policy,

Exhibit 10.3 Fay/Wallace Corporation Salary Survey Comparison

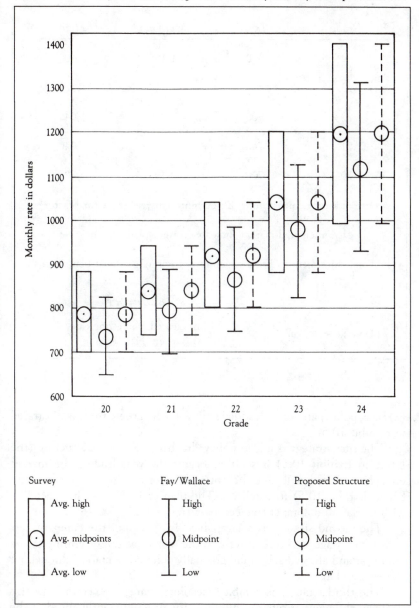

Exhibit 10.4   Initial Adjusted Structure, Next Plan Year

Grade	Low	Midpoint	High
24	990	1,195	1,400
23	880	1,040	1,200
22	800	920	1,040
21	740	840	940
20	700	790	880

Date of survey data = June 30, current plan year (6/12 time factor)

Anticipated market increase, current plan year: 8%

Total adjustment to bring structure to beginning of next plan year:

$$\frac{6}{12} \times 8\% = 1.04$$

(Time factor of survey)   (Anticipated market increase, current plan year)

(2) a lag policy, and (3) a lead/lag policy. Each of these three is illustrated in Exhibit 10.5.

The first strategy is a lead policy. In this case, a wage structure (the *l* line in Exhibit 10.5) is set that begins the year leading the market enough so that it will take the entire year for external wage rates (the bar in Exhibit 10.5) to catch up. The plan ends the year in exact line with market and competitive compa-ratios of 1.00.

The second strategy is a lag policy. In this case, the company sets its internal wage structure exactly to the market at the beginning of the plan year and allows itself to fall gradually behind the market throughout the entire plan year.

The third strategy is a mixed, lead/lag strategy. According to this strategy, the planner sets the internal structure sufficiently ahead of the

Auditing, Adjusting, and Budgeting Salary Structures

Exhibit 10.5   Lead, Lag, and Lead/Lag Policies

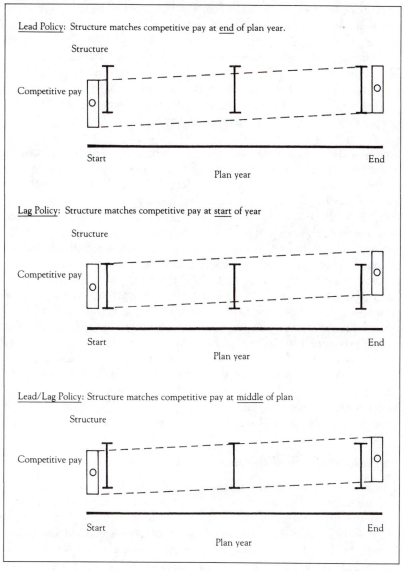

Source: John H. Davis, *Quantitative Analysis for Compensation Decision Making* (Scottsdale, Az.: American Compensation Association, 1980), pp. 4-8 to 4-9. Used by permission.

market at the beginning of the plan year to allow the market to catch up to the structure midway through the plan year. The company starts the year out by leading the market and finishes the year behind the market.

Actually, any policy between the extremes of lead and lag is possible. The choice of strategy depends entirely on the company's concerns with the extra expense of leading the market and its problems attracting employees from the market when lagging. We will assume that Fay/Wallace Corporation has opted for a lead/lag policy.

Step 4: Making final adjustments in the structure.   The fourth step in adjusting the current structure for the next plan year consists of four substeps illustrated in Exhibit 10.6. Step 1 is to adopt the company's policy regarding the market for the next plan year. We have just noted that Fay/Wallace has adopted a lead/lag policy. Step 2 is to forecast wage movements in the external market for the next plan year. In our example, let us assume that inflation has picked up and market analysts forecast an increase of 13 percent in wages during next year. We want to be meeting the market in June of next year and therefore, in step 3, we halve this estimate (to 6.5 percent) for adjustment purposes. Step 4 consists of developing the final index for arriving at the final adjusted structure for the next plan year. We do this by multiplying the adjustment to bring the structure up to December 31 of the current plan year (1.04) times the adjustment necessary to implement a lead/lag policy for next year (1.065). The product of these two adjustments is 1.11, the final adjustment to be made to our initial adjusted structure (Exhibit 10.4). Multiplying the initial adjusted structure by 1.11 yields the final adjusted structure the planner will recommend to management (Exhibit 10.6).

Forecasting Required Budgets

The final step in preparing a compensation plan for the next plan year is to forecast the budget, or total amount of money that will be required to finance the compensation program. Forecasting a budget should always begin with information about the current plan year's budget experience. Exhibit 10.7 organizes two kinds of information about the plan year we just ended: (1) what we had planned to do and (2) what actually occurred. At the beginning of the current plan year, we planned on having 200 employees. We planned no increases in personnel this year. We

Exhibit 10.6   Final Adjusted Structure, Next Plan Year

Step 1:   Adopt lead/lag policy.

Step 2:   Anticipate 13% increase in market during next plan year.

Step 3:   Adjust structure 6.5% (one-half of 13% increase) to achieve lead/
lag for next plan year.

Step 4:   1.04   (Total adjustment to bring current structure up to
market at end of current plan year.)

        × 1.065   (Total adjustment needed to achieve lead/lag in next
plan year.)

           1.11   (Total adjustment to structure)

Yields:

Final Adjusted Structure, Next Plan Year

Grade	Low	Midpoint	High
24	1,099	1,327	1,554
23	977	1,155	1,332
22	888	1,021	1,154
21	821	932	1,043
20	777	877	977

budgeted $4.8 million for salaries, allowing us to pay an average salary of $24,000. The average of all the midpoints at the beginning of last year was $24,742. We did not anticipate an increase in the midpoints this year. We began the year with the average compa-ratio within grades at 0.97. We wanted to allow for this compa-ratio to increase throughout the year as people came up for merit increases. We planned to have a compa-ratio of 1.07 by the end of the plan year. If everything had gone as planned, we would have forecast 1.07 × $4,948,400 (the total mid-

Exhibit 10.7 Fay/Wallace Corporation Current Plan Year Salary Budget

Planned	No.	Total Salary Budget	Average Salary	Total Midpoint	Average Midpoint	Compa-Ratio
Plan year start	200	4,800,000	24,000	4,948,400	24,742	0.97
Plan year end	200	5,294,800	26,474	4,948,400	24,742	1.07
Increase	0%	10.3%	10.3%	0%	0%	10.3%
Actual						
Plan year end	230	5,920,600	25,742	5,804,510	25,237	1.02
Increase	15%	23.4%	7.3%	17.3%	.2%	5.2%

point), or $5,294,800 necessary to budget our pay plan. This forecast called for a 10.3 percent increase in the salary budget. The year did not end as planned, however. In fact, three things threw our forecast off. First, there was a net increase of 15 percent in personnel this year, placing upward pressure on the total salary budget. The loss of senior people and the replacement with junior people, however, kept the compa-ratio much lower than we anticipated. In fact, it increased to only 1.02, placing some downward pressure on the salary budget. Finally, as people were promoted faster than we anticipated, the average midpoint increased slightly, placing upward pressure on the salary budget. The net effect of all these forces was to result in an actual total expenditure of $5,920,600, representing a 23.4 percent increase over the year before.

Our problem now is to incorporate the budget experience represented in Exhibit 10.7 into a budget plan for the next year. We will begin with the budget plan in Exhibit 10.8. We are starting the new year with a total of 230 employees. As we did last year, we anticipate no new employees this year. We have just ended a year in which our total expenditures on salaries (salary budget) were $5,920,600. Our current midpoints total $5,804,510. In our market adjustment planning (in the last section), we decided to move the entire structure up by 11 percent. Multiplying

Exhibit 10.8   Fay/Wallace Corporation: Initial Salary Budget Forecast for Next Plan Year

	No.	Total Salary	Total Midpoint	Compa- Ratio
Start of Plan Year	230	$5,920,600	$6,443,006[a]	.92
Desired End of Plan Year	230	6,443,006	6,443,006	1.00
Increase	0%	8.8%	0%	8.7%

[a] 6,443,006 = $5,804,510 × 1.11

where:

$5,804,510 = total midpoint at end of current plan year

1.11 = structure adjustment to market
(See Exhibit 10.6)

the current total midpoint by 1.11 gives us a new total midpoint for the next plan year of $6,443,006. We are beginnning the new plan year, therefore, with a compa-ratio of 0.92 ($5,920,600/$6,443,006).

The next step is to decide how much we want to move the compa-ratio by the end of the next plan year. In our case, we forecast that with promotions and new hiring, we would like the compa-ratio to reach 1.00 by the end of the year. This will require a total salary budget of $6,443,006 (1.00 × $6,443,006). That translates into an 8.8 percent budget increase for the next plan year.

A final step in the budgeting process involves adjusting the forecasts for the next year by an experience factor, representing how far off our forecasts were from actuality this current year. In effect, we are using knowledge of error in the past to build room for error in the future. Davis has developed an experience factor (F) to estimate such error. It is defined in Exhibit 10.9 as the ratio of the compa-ratio planned for the year end to the compa-ratio that acutally occurred at the end of the plan year.

In our case, Exhibit 10.7 shows that this ratio would be 1.07/ 1.02 = 1.05. The experience factor can be multiplied by the total salary budget forecasted to obtain a total salary budget that will take past fore-casting error into account. In this case, for example, Exhibit 10.8 suggests that we will require a total salary budget of $6,443,006 to accomplish a compa-ratio of 1.00 by the end of the next year. Our estimates were off

Exhibit 10.9   Calculating Experience Factor (F)

1. $F = \dfrac{\text{Compa-ratio planned at plan year end}}{\text{Compa-ratio actual at plan year end}}$

   $= \dfrac{1.07}{1.02}$

   $= 1.05$

2. Planned total salary needed to achieve desired compa-ratio =

F	×	Unadjusted total salary to get desired compa-ratio	=	Planned total salary
1.05	×	$6,443,006	=	$6,765,156

by 5 percent last year, however (the experience factor of 1.05). To cover ourselves, we multiply the anticipated total salary budget ($6,443,006) by the experience factor (1.05) and arrive at a planned total salary budget needed of $6,765,156 for the next plan year. Exhibit 10.10 completes the planner's presentation. To achieve a compa-ratio of 1.00 we will have to aim for a compa-ratio of 1.05. If we anticipate the midpoints to remain the same throughout the year, we will require a total salary budget of $6,765,156. This, finally, will require a 14.3 percent increase in our salary budget.

Communications

Knowledge of the compensation system and the process used to construct it will not guarantee acceptance of the system. Employees who do not know about the system and its construction, however, are not likely to place much trust in it. How much an organization chooses to disclose to employees about the pay system will vary; it is crucial that whatever the organization wants employees to know about the compensation system be communicated in an explicit, formal fashion.

It is important to remember that the behavioral function of the compensation system is to attract, motivate, and retain employees. As we noted in Chapter 4, compensation systems can be thought of as operating motivationally in terms of equity theory and expectancy theory. In either case, correct knowledge about outcomes for the individual is necessary.

What then, are some specific communications needs? Employees, of course, know their gross and net salary each pay period; paychecks provide that information. A large part of the compensation package, however, is not communicated to employees in many organizations: that is the benefits package. As benefits become a larger portion of the total compensation package, many employers have begun to report to employees the value of that package. An example of such a report is shown in Exhibit 10.11.

Employers need to integrate into a formal program whatever information about the compensation process they wish employees to know. The report of the American Compensation Association/American Society for Personnel Administration joint task force dealing with pay programs suggests these six subjects for inclusion in any communication of a pay

(Text is continued on p. 244.)

Exhibit 10.10 Fay/Wallace Corporation: Final Salary Budget Forecast for Next Plan Year

	No.	Total Salary	Total Midpoint	Compa-Ratio
Start of Plan Year	83	$5,920,600	6,443,006	0.92
Desired End of Plan Year	83	6,443,006	6,443,006	1.00
Increase	0%	8.8%	0%	8.7%
Planned End of Plan Year	83	6,765,156	6,443,006	1.05
Increase	0%	14.3%	0%	14%

Your salary increase budget: 14.3%

Exhibit 10.11   Personal Benefits Statement—IBM

Dear IBMer,

This marks the twenty-fifth consecutive year that we have provided personal benefits statements to all employees. Since that first statement, seven new benefit plans have been established and more than ninety improvements have been made. Our objective now, as it was then, is to provide a comprehensive and balanced program that will continue to serve your needs effectively.

I trust you find this statement a convenient source of information showing how the plans apply to you and that it will be useful in your personal planning.

Sincerely,

In 1981 IBM paid

$30.2 million for Survivors

$292.2 million for Medical/Dental

$551.9 million for Retirement

$347.4 million for Social Security

in addition to payments for other plans such as holidays, vacation, sickness and accident and disability

---

Service

As you look over your *Benefits Statement* there's one number to keep in mind. It's your length of service with IBM. As of December 31, 1981, it was

•

This number is important when figuring several of your benefits, for example, Retirement, Life Insurance, and Vacation.

Time Off

To allow you personal time away from work, IBM provides vacations and holidays. There are 11 holidays each year. In 1982 your vacation will be

•

And if you've deferred any vacation from previous years, those days are additional.

Exhibit 10.11   *(continued)*

Your Protection Today

Survivors Benefits
(As of 12/31/81)
To help protect your survivors,
the IBM benefit program provides
several coverages.

Group Life Insurance
The beneficiary you named will
receive

-

Periodically review your beneficiary
designation to be sure it is current.

Survivors Income
Your spouse, eligible children or
dependent parents can receive
monthly payments up to a total of

-

This is in addition to your Group
Life Insurance Coverage.

Travel Accident Insurance
If you die accidentally while travel-
ing on company business, the beneficiary you have named will receive

-

This is in addition to your Group
Life Insurance and Survivors
Income Coverage.

**Medical and Disability Income
Benefits** (As of 12/31/81)
When a serious illness or injury
occurs, the combination of medical
expenses and regular living costs
can put a strain on your budget.
The IBM benefit program provides
substantial assistance to help meet
both needs.

Sickness and Accident Income
If you're unable to work due to
sickness or accident, you'll still
continue to receive your regular
salary for up to 52 weeks in a
period of 24 consecutive months.

Exhibit 10.11   (*continued*)

Your Protection Today

**Total and Permanent
Disability Income**
Once you've been with IBM for five years, if you become totally and permanently disabled, you'll receive monthly, for 18 months, following Sickness and Accident payments.

•

After that, you will receive payments as long as your disability lasts, up to age 65, in the monthly amount of

•

At age 65 you would receive an income from the IBM Retirement Plan. You may also qualify for Social Security Disability Benefits during your disability.

If you have less than 5 years service, you will receive benefits for up to 18 months based on your length of service.

Payments in 1981
During 1981, benefit payments were made on your behalf as indicated:

Sickness and Accident Income Plan

•

Dental Plan

•

Hospitalization Plan

•

Major Medical Plan

•

Surgical Plan

•

Exhibit 10.11   *(continued)*

Your Retirement Security

The IBM Retirement Plan provides an income, with various options, to help you provide for your financial security.

Your Retirement
If you retire at age
your estimated annual lifetime income will be

•

(assuming your benefits are paid as a single life annuity without adjustment for a Pre-Retirement Spouse Option)

That means payments would begin on

•

Your estimated annual income (on the same basis) at selected earlier retirement ages would be

This amount	Starting At Age
•	

Joint & Survivor Income
At retirement you can choose a joint & survivor income, which means your designated survivor will receive a lifetime income after your death.

If you're married, your retirement payment automatically will be in a 50% joint & survivor form unless you choose otherwise. Here are some estimated amounts at the 50% rate (assuming you and your survivor are the same age and there has been no adjustment for a Pre-Retirement Spouse Option).

If You Retire At This Age	You'd Get This Annual Income	At Your Death, Your Survivor Would Receive
•		

Pre-Retirement Spouse Option (PRSO)
Unless declined, this coverage is automatic at the 50% level with a reduction in your retirement income, if you're married and eligible to retire but remain an active IBM employee. The coverage provides a lifetime income for your surviving spouse if you die before you actually retire.

•

Exhibit 10.11   *(continued)*

Your Retirement Security

**Group Life Insurance
at Retirement**
If you retire before age 65, you'll
have 50% of your Group Life Insurance coverage until you're 65.
Group Life Insurance for retired employees 65 and over will be $5,000.

Vested Rights
If you leave IBM before retirement
with at least 10 years of service,
you have vested rights to a
retirement income. As of

-

Your estimated annual vested
rights income, payable at age 65
on a single life basis, is

-

If you have 15 years of service,
reduced benefits are available as
early as age 55. With 10-14 years
of service reduced benefits are
available at age 62.

Social Security
Social Security can pay benefits
during retirement, if you're disabled, or at your death. For every
dollar you pay to Social Security,
IBM contributes an equal amount.

Let's consider one of the benefits.
Your estimated annual Social
Security retirement benefit (based
on your 1981 compensation and
current Social Security benefit
computations) will be.

This Amount   Starting At Age

-

IBM
®

Source: Courtesy IBM.

program's objectives: (1) the methods used in job analysis and job evaluation; (2) organizational policy with respect to matching the market on pay levels; (3) the role of performance and performance appraisal in determining individual pay; (4) pay increase policy and administration; (5) the effect of governmental and economic constraints on the amount of money available for compensation purposes; and (6) pay policies and regulations used in compensation administration on a day-to-day basis.[5] A variety of communications techniques, both formal and informal, are suggested.

Notes

1. E. E. Lawler, III, *Pay and Organization Development* (Reading, Mass.: Addison-Wesley, 1981).

2. D. J. Treiman, *Job Evaluation: An Analytic Review* (Washington, D.C.: National Academy of Sciences, 1981).

3. D. O. Stuhaug, "Want a Raise? At Romac You Do a Little Politicking with Your Peers," *Daily Journal of Commerce and Northwest Construction Record*, Seattle, Washington, February 5, 1979, p. 1.

4. G. D. Jenkins, Jr., and E. E. Lawler, "Impact of Employee Participation in Pay Plan Development," *Organizational Behavior and Human Performance* 28 (1981):111–28.

5. *Elements of Sound Base Pay Administration* (Scottsdale, Ariz.: American Compensation Association/American Society for Personnel Administration, 1981).

11

Compensation as a Profession

$\mathbf{N}$ow that you have had an opportunity to consider compensation theory and practice, you probably have questions about our field as a profession. Where do compensation specialists fit into contemporary organizations? What kind of income do compensation professionals make? What kind of career progression do most compensation professionals follow? Is postgraduate training necessary for a career in compensation? What professional organizations do compensation professionals belong to? What information resources do compensation professionals rely on in planning compensation objectives, goals, strategies, policies, and practices?

The purpose of this concluding chapter of *Compensation Theory and Practice* is to answer such questions by describing the major dimensions of our profession. In developing materials for this chapter we have relied heavily on three major sources: (1) a survey of the personnel and industrial relations profession carried out by the American Society for Personnel Administration, (2) information provided by the leading United States association of compensation professionals, the American Compensation Association, and (3) the views of a major professional in our field, Dr.

N. Fredric Crandall, National Director of Salary Administration Consulting for Coopers and Lybrand in Dallas, Texas.

Position and Income of Compensation Professionals

Compensation is a specialty within the broader profession of personnel and industrial relations. In 1980, the American Society for Personnel Administration (ASPA), the major professional organization in the human resources field, commissioned the A. S. Hansen Company to survey the major dimensions of the profession.[1] The results of this study provide insight into the functions of personnel and industrial relations within large and small organizations together with the role of the compensation. The survey clearly identifies compensation as one of the key areas of personnel and industrial relations within organizations. Companies faced with increasing labor costs, and labor costs increasing as a percentage of operating budgets, with major productivity problems, and with international competition are increasingly turning to compensation policymakers as the key players in strategies to control costs and regain a competitive edge in domestic and international markets.

What types of salaries do compensation professionals make? Exhibit 11.1 shows the range as well as the average salaries for personnel (and compensation executives) in two major groups. The first group consists of personnel executives in companies whose personnel units have fifteen or more positions. The second group includes personnel positions in smaller organizations.

The data in Exhibit 11.1 show a wide variation in salaries by specialty within the personnel/IR field. Average salaries in areas related to compensation range from $16,694 (for benefits administrators) to $24,582 (for compensation and benefits administrators); the latter is second only to labor relations specialists and top plant personnel/IR officers. In 1980, compensation and benefits administrators earned up to $46,750; their salaries were equivalent to those of other executives in such functional areas as finance, marketing, production, and accounting.

Compensation Career Paths

What educational and career preparation is needed to become a compensation professional? Most people have come into the compensation area by moving laterally from line management into a staff compensation

Exhibit 11.1   Range of Compensation and Average Compensation (Salary Plus Bonus) for Personnel/IR Positions, 1980, by Size of Personnel Unit

Position	Range, 10th to 90th Percentile	Average
Personnel units with 15 or more positions		
Top personnel and industrial relations executive	$54,500–137,000	$79,178
Top divisional, subsidiary, or regional PA/IR executive	29,300–64,838	41,824
Top corporate personnel executive	33,000–83,300	54,882
Top community/public relations executive	40,298–77,000	56,197
Top international personnel/IR executive	46,300–86,700	56,130
Personnel units with 14 or fewer positions		
Top personnel/IR position	$26,000–60,300	$36,583
Manager of personnel	19,218–40,500	26,500
Employment and recruiting supervisor	15,600–33,580	21,530
Interviewer	11,922–20,780	15,574
Equal employment opportunity specialist	12,343–29,900	20,443
Labor relations supervisor/specialist	25,800–42,000	29,515
Labor relations representative	20,679–28,713	22,856
Wage and salary analyst	13,550–21,500	17,727
Compensation and benefits administrator	17,300–46,750	24,582
Benefits administrator	11,717–25,615	16,694
Security/safety specialist	14,680–30,780	23,020
Training supervisor/specialist	14,973–36,849	23,120
Personnel assistant	10,665–18,500	13,699
Plant personnel/IR manager	15,852–37,453	24,640

Source: ASPA/Hansen *Salary Survey on Personnel and Industrial Relations (PAIR) Positions.* Berea, Ohio: American Society for Personnel Administration, 1980. Reprinted by permission of the American Society for Personnel Administration.

ition. That path is still the main route. Much of their expertise has n gained from actual experience and continuing executive development. Increasingly, however, students are obtaining specialized training in ipensation at the undergraduate and graduate levels. Many schools of ness, for example, offer undergraduate majors in human resource inistration. Within these majors, many programs include elective sework in principles of compensation. At the graduate level, many \ programs include majors in personnel and industrial relations with alized coursework in compensation. In addition, several major institutions in the United States, including the universities of Minnesota, Wisconsin, and Illinois, Michigan State University, Cornell University, and Loyola University of Chicago offer specialized master's degree programs in personnel and industrial relations. Students can gain advanced training in compensation in these programs.

Many students contemplating graduate work in business face a tradeoff between the MBA degree and a Master's in Industrial Relations, a tradeoff of breadth versus depth. The MBA degree will force the student to become familiar with and competent in all areas of business administration, including finance, accounting, marketing, production, and the legal environment in addition to personnel and industrial relations. The MBA keeps all career options of business administration open to the student. The problem is that such programs will not offer as much depth in specific compensation topics as a Master's in Industrial Relations will. the latter program, however, closes off career opportunities in other functional business administration areas without additional training or experience. For the student choosing to specialize in the personnel and industrial relations area, we strongly recommend course familiarity with at least accounting, budgeting, and finance. Compensation professionals must be able to tie compensation planning effectively into the broader financial objectives and considerations of the organization.

Professional Associations

The hallmark of any profession is a professional society that identifies the work and profession of its members. A professional asociation serves several crucial functions for its membership: (1) the development, maintenance, and dissemination of a common body of knowledge regarding theory and practice, (2) opportunities for professional development and renewal of professional skills, (3) a forum for expressing and sharing ideas and knowledge with other professionals. The leading association in our field is the American Compensation Association (ACA) based in Scottsdale, Arizona.[2] The ACA consists of over 7,000 active members who work as professionals in compensation administration and carry out research. It is a nonprofit organization whose objective is to improve practice in the design, implementation, and management of employee compensation and benefit programs. Since its beginning in 1955, the ACA has sponsored a wide range of programs of development and improvement that have left their mark on professional practice.

Perhaps the most visible of the ACA's activities is its certification program for compensation professionals. The designation of Certified Compensation Professional (CCP) is earned through the satisfactory completion of a series of certification examinations in each of these areas:

Certification I: Objectives, principles, terminology, and regulation of employee compensation.

Certification II: Job analysis, job descriptions, and job decision making.

Certification III: Quantitative analysis for compensation decision making.

Certification IV: Designing and administration of wage and salary programs.

Certification V: The compensation of salespersons.

Certification VI: The compensation of executives.

Certification VII: Designing and administration of employee benefits programs.

Certification VIII: Improving employee effectiveness with pay.

Certification IX: International compensation.

In addition to the certification program, the ACA sponsors national and regional conferences on a variety of compensation issues. It also sponsors specialized symposia on such issues as executive compensation, comparable worth, the designing of compensation programs for banks, and the design and administration of compensation programs in health care institutions.

There are two other organizations that provide services to the compensation professional: the American Society for Personnel Administration (ASPA),[3] and the Human Resources Division of the Academy of Management.

The ASPA, based in Washington, D.C. (after 1983) is a broadly based association of professionals in all fields of personnel and industrial relations, including compensation. The ASPA and ACA have had a long history of cooperative projects in disseminating information to compensation practitioners. Their most recent efforts in this regard resulted in *Elements of Sound Base Pay Administration,* which advised members on such issues as how to protect compensation structures against legal liability, including the comparable worth problem.[4]

Members of the Human Resource Division of the Academy of Management are primarily university professors who teach in the personnel/ IR area and carry out programs of research dealing with problems in their field. Several of the researchers in this division have specific teaching and research interests in compensation, and their work provides basic theory and information that will shape compensation practice in the future.

Information Sources

No one can practice compensation very long without requiring information. Such needs can range from very simple answers and routine administrative questions (what percentage should be withheld for Social Security?) to very complex policy and theory questions (can an incentive system be set up that will have a demonstrated impact on performance in our organization?). The information sources (beyond texts such as this one) include: (a) journals, (b) abstracts and indices, (c) government statistical series, and (d) commercial loose-leaf services.

The major journals directly involved in compensation practice are *Compensation Review*, published by the American Management Association, the *Employee Benefit Plan Journal*, and the *Journal of Pension Planning and Compliance*. Each of these journals focus very narrowly and directly on practical matters of policy and strategy in the design and implementation of compensation and benefit plans.

Several research-oriented journals focus on more basic areas of theory and research in compensation (as well as on other areas of the personnel field and the field of organizational behavior). These include the *Academy of Management Journal*, the *Academy of Management Review*, *Industrial Relations*, *Industrial and Labor Relations Review*, *Personnel Psychology*, *Journal of Applied Psychology*, and the *Monthly Labor Review*.

In addition to journals, professionals in our field should become familiar with the major indices and statistical abstracts commonly used. Although a complete review of such sources is beyond the scope of this book, these sources include the *Business Periodicals Index*, *Human Resource Abstracts*, *Personnel Literature*, *Personnel Management Abstracts*, and *Psychological Abstracts*. The United States government, in addition, publishes a variety of monthly, weekly, and annual data on wages and salaries, benefits, employment, and unemployment, of direct interest to the planner designing and budgeting wage and salary structures.[5]

Finally, compensation professionals find loose-leaf services available from Prentice-Hall, Commerce Clearing House, and the Bureau of National Affairs to be extremely useful in keeping current with changes and trends in our field. The services are organized around matters of practice in all areas of personnel and industrial relations, and are updated with loose-leaf replacements on a weekly basis. Prentice-Hall and the Bureau of National Affairs have services devoted entirely to compensation.

The View of a Professional: An Interview with N. Fredric Crandall

The most valuable source of information for the student who contemplates a career in compensation are the practitioners in our field who deal with policy and strategy with actual employers on a daily basis. We asked one such person to share his views with us about the major concerns and directions our profession is taking in the 1980s.

N. Fredric Crandall is Senior Consultant with the Acturial Benefits and Compensation Group of Coopers & Lybrand in Dallas, Texas. He is responsible for executive compensation and salary consulting services in the Dallas office and is National Director of Salary Administration consulting for Coopers & Lybrand. He is an active member of the personnel and human resources professional community both in Dallas and nationally. He presently is President of the A.S.P.A. Foundation and serves on A.S.P.A.'s Research Committee. He provides education and training in the field of compensation through the executive development programs of many universities around the country and through the American Compensation Association. He is a course developer for the ACA and serves as an advisor to the ACA's program for Certification of Compensation Professionals (CCP). Dr. Crandall holds the B.B.A. degree from the University of California at Berkeley, the Master's Degree from the Graduate School of Management at U.C.L.A., and the Ph.D. in Industrial Relations from the University of Minnesota.

Compensation Theory and Practice (CTP): Who makes the compensation decision today in most organizations? What kind of people do you see making compensation decisions?

Crandall: In order to answer that question, you have to ask youself what types of compensation decisions there are. There are policy decisions that are made relative to compensation strategy and planning; these would be made at a group or corporate level. In addition, there are operating compensation decisions that relate to individual rates of pay of employees. These decisions are generally made by managers, supervisors, or line operating people, and are quite important because they relate directly to people and can have a direct effect on individual performance. However, if there is not a competent structure based on the considerations of internal and external equity that a planning and policy staff develops, then you don't have the superstructure by which operating managers can make compensation decisions relative to each individual employee.

CTP: If a young person in college came to you who was interested in a career in the compensation profession, what would you advise him or her to do?

Crandall: The general career path has traditionally been one familiar in the personnel administration field. An entry-level position is often a job-analyst position, in which an individual is responsible for writing job descriptions. He or she then moves up into positions of increasing responsibility in related compensation positions.

The compensation professional must coordinate carefully with line managers, because many important compensation decisions are made by line managers. To be a competent compensation administrator, one has to have a good understanding of the operating characteristics of the organization and especially the financial characteristics. Compensation is a financial type of reward and is a financial activity, and if one wants to be an effective administrator in compensation, one has to get a good understanding of financial analysis as well as personnel administration and human resource administration. The most effective compensation administrators I have observed are compensation administrators who are familiar with the financial or accounting function of the organization. A top compensation executive generally has a good grounding in both the financial and the human-resource side of the business.

CTP: Given that, where do most people in compensation today come from? What part of the organization do you find most compensation analysts and managers coming from?

Crandall: Well, I'd say they come from two places: one is from the controllers department and the other is from the personnel department.

CTP: What do you see as the major compensation issues today?

Crandall: Major compensation issues today fall under the umbrella of *performance.* That is a very broad statement, but let's go back a few years to before the Economic Recovery Tax Act of 1981 was passed. A major issue in executive and managerial compensation was protecting employee pay from the dual problems of the increasing level and rate of inflation and higher tax brackets. Organizations were being placed under increasing pressure to effectively provide compensation which provided tax advantages to individuals. The Economic Recovery Tax Act of 1981 really changed quite a bit of that due to specific provisions that provided advantages for executive and managerial compensation and changes in the taxation of employees. As I stated before, the biggest issue that most companies are currently facing is tying individuals' pay to their achieved performance in order to provide cost-effective compensation, and compensation that is related to what people actually achieve in their work.

CTP: What's the toughest problem facing today's compensation administrator?

Crandall: The toughest specific problem to face the compensation administrator today is communicating compensation objectives—finding an effective way for individuals in an organization to communicate with each other relative to directives of management in terms of employee performance, and the desires of employees in terms of the nature and level of rewards for work performance. Finding a way to communicate to individuals why they are being paid, what they are being paid for, and what to expect in the future continues to be an important issue.

CTP: Is there an easy problem facing compensation managers: one they could solve if they just did the right thing?

Crandall: The easiest problem to resolve relates to inconsistencies in compensation practices. Over a period of time, we often forget written policies and procedures and veer from them in one way or another. We seem to forget the implied promises we make to individuals in an organization, and we change compensation programs that make implied promises to people. We become more flexible than we should in administering compensation programs that have highly structured designs.

CTP: What do you tell your clients when the results of a job evaluation disagree very strongly with market data on both the up side and the down side? That is, what do you say when your job evaluation indicates the job is worth a lot more than you actually have to pay for it or vice versa?

Crandall: The client has to decide which constraints on the compensation program are most important: what the market is telling them that a job is worth or an internal evaluation. Frequently, clients ask that a market study be completed and they have expectations as a result of this study. They hope to confirm internal judgments of job worth. They find out that they are either so far behind in the market that they cannot hope to catch up in a short period of time (because of cost considerations), or they are far above the market already. In either case, there is disappointment, because a client has asked the consultant either implicitly or explicitly to solve a problem using the framework of the market for validating decisions that it wishes to make internally. And what happens in that case is that the consultant, but more importantly the client, loses direction because its expectations cannot be met. For example, a recent client of mine went to great time and expense to do a market study and found out that his organization paid approximately 25 to 30 percent above the market. He lost the rationale for making adjustments in pay that had initiated the study. What he found out was that he was effective in relating to the market, and consequently he was faced with making a decision to increase salaries, which could not be justified by the market.

When these presumed criteria for making pay decisions cannot be validated by empirical data, the organization has to rely directly on its *strategy and philosophy* in dealing with people. Of course, management could have begun at this point. In essence, it is the hardest issue for an organization to face in compensation, finding its own way in the world without relying on clear empirical signposts.

CTP: What do you recommend an employer do about pay compression?

Crandall: Compression is a problem in which a number of individuals are receiving about the same pay, even though there are a number of individual and organizational differences that are presumably important to the organization. There is only one way for an employer to solve pay compression, and that is to differentiate pay among individuals on clear and important criteria. In the short term, it is necessary to increase the pay of some, have the pay of others remain the same, and, of course, decrease the pay of still others. Decreasing the pay of individuals when you are undergoing a compensation study is generally not a well-received solution, so therefore increasing the pay—increasing your compensation budget—is about the only way in the short term to solve compression problems. In the long term, there are a number of ways to solve a compression problem. For example, it is possible to differentiate your markets externally to minimize the conflict between external and internal criteria, or to redesign jobs and job families to bring the evaluation of jobs in line with external market factors.

CTP: Does that make pay compression an easy problem then?

Crandall: The "problem" is not easily solved, and it may unexpectedly creep up on you. Pay compression is a problem that is symptomatic of the fact that the three major criteria for an effective pay program— external, internal, and individual equity—are not necessarily reconcilable.

CTP: A number of job analysis techniques, specifically the PAQ [Position Analysis Questionnaire], have been extended to be used as job evaluation techniques. Do you have any comments?

Crandall: I think that job evaluation techniques are becoming increasingly more sophisticated and there are a number of new techniques that are being experimented with currently. They are based conceptually and empirically more in the psychometric framework than traditional job evaluation techniques. The field of quantitative job analysis is going to become increasingly more important to compensation practice, and I predict that organizations are going to rely more heavily on quantitative techniques in order to provide job-evaluation hierarchies.

CTP: If you were a practicing compensation manager and you were forced to choose between advice from an industrial/organizational psychologist and an economist, what would you do?

Crandall: I don't think that the advice of one is more important than that of the other. Most strategies for designing compensation programs in organizations are based on an integration of psychological measurement techniques and economic cost considerations. In addition, management science will be employed in data-processing computer applications and quantitative approaches to compensation planning.

CTP: Do you see that organizations can use inflation as a compensation tool to allow some people to fall back without actually changing their gross salary? Do you think inflation is a useful tool of a useful occurrence for the compensation manager in terms of management?

Crandall: Inflation has been and will be perhaps the biggest bane to a compensation administrator's existence for one simple reason: most of the tools that we have for administering compensation are what I would call static tools. They are based on measurement of individual behavior and measurement of job differences in two or three dimensions at a single point in time. Inflation is an acceleration of rates of pay that causes everything either to be stepped up or to be thrown out of kilter. When you have increasing rates of pay due to inflation, which doesn't relate to the compensation program, then pay increases are based on criteria that were not taken into account in the design of the program. The rationale for compensating individuals is lost. For example, let's take an individual, Joe Doakes, who is placed in a salary grade that has a minimum of $4 an hour and a maximum of $7 an hour. It is expected that increases in pay are based on the acceleration of rates of pay in the marketplace. Consequently, Joe Doakes moves through a structure on an "unidentified" criterion. The only way to solve that effectively is to change everyone's rate of pay as inflation goes up. People begin to get the understanding, and sometimes rightfully so, that the reason for the increase in their pay is the fact that prices are going up. The organization loses its control over managing the pay of people.

CTP: Would you comment on using incentive bonuses versus an adjustment to the base rate for purposes of merit pay or seniority?

Crandall: Bonus compensation has traditionally been a tool for providing lump-sum payments to individuals for a variety of reasons. For a number of years, incentive bonus compensation has been an effective tool for providing incentives for management and executive-level individuals. Incentive bonuses provide payments to managers and executives for reaching specific business goals on a timely basis. In the case of other personnel, however, bonuses have not been incentive-oriented. They have traditionally been after-the-fact types of payments, for example, Christmas bonuses and Thanksgiving bonuses. As a consequence, people begin to expect bonuses because they alway recur; they are not based on individual performance; and there is no differentiation as to level of payment or timing of payment.

Organizations are becoming increasingly aware of the elegance of incentive and bonus compensation when used together. They have found that a bonus can provide a lump-sum payment that is very often more meaningful than a salary increase because it is a one-time payment and it can be tied directly to performance. Such bonuses have more immediate utility to an employee than a salary increase, because they can be spent on a down payment or some sort of investment. In short, a bonus has a stronger power of motivation if based on individual performance. Most important is the fact that the bonus can be provided to people on a nonrecurring basis: it does not become part of the base salary and it is not a recurring item for any organization. I think to the extent that inflation continues to be a problem for high demand and skilled occupations, incentive bonuses will become a very effective tool.

CTP: What directions do you see for benefits in the next five to ten years?

Crandall: I think that in some sectors of the economy benefit compensation will become a larger percentage of base salary. This will occur in parts of the economy where labor is in high demand. I think that in other parts of the economy, where demand for labor will either slow down or decrease, benefits will taper off and perhaps decrease.

CTP: Do you see any sexy new benefits on the horizon?

Crandall: Yes, there are a number of benefits that are of increasing interest to employers and to employees. One is the automobile, or the automobile allowance (which has traditionally been the province of executive management). In the last fifty years, we have seen the emergence of benefits that provide more security for individuals. In the future, I think we are going to see benefits that provide for a higher quality of life and more effective use of family resources.

CTP: What do you see as the role of the American Compensation Association today?

Crandall: The American Compensation Association has grown dramatically in the last twenty-five years to an increasingly high stature, and it has perhaps taken a turn in the last five years from an organization in which information was exchanged and information was presented to its members to now being one of the most important business education organizations in the United States. It provides an excellent education program for learning the different compensation specialties and providing a basis for systematizing information in the profession. I think that its major strength is as an educational organization, and this mission will probably be felt more and more as we begin to define our field more systematically and our administrators begin to speak in one voice and one language.

CTP: What are the major problems in compensation that you think researchers, whether academic or otherwise, should concentrate on?

Crandall: That is probably the most important issue that we face. Research. Compensation needs an awful lot of research at the present time, in areas that perhaps have been neglected for too long. It may seem funny or even heretical to say this, but the most neglected area in compensation is the area of linking human behavior to pay. We still have a number of contradictory theories as to what makes people work and what the relationship is between rewards and performance. There needs to be more research of a nature that will provide both practitioners and academicians information about how to design programs that really do provide for effective human performance and effective organizational performance. There needs to be more research aimed at the area of rewards—total rewards—as they relate to pay and as they relate to the quality of life that people expect when they decide to work in an organization.

CTP: What are the key components in controlling compensation costs? What are the major areas organizations need to concentrate on?

Crandall: Perhaps the most difficult problem in controlling compensation costs is being able adequately to predict the size of a pay budget that will provide for organizational goals. The reason I say that is that often a compensation planning staff or an organizational staff unit that plans compensation will base plans on broad budgetary parameters, but those budgetary parameters are not taken into account in making individual compensation decisions. The circle is not closed as we move from the setting of the budget for the department and the allocation of pay to individuals. Very often, a line administrator in a department that is allocating compensation dollars to individuals will not use the same criteria that were used to set the budget at a corporate or a personnel department level.

CTP: What are the relative roles of line and staff then in cost control?

Crandall: The role of staff is to plan and to advise and to provide feedback on variants from the plan, and to assist in ensuring that plans for compensation budgets are meaningful and realistic. The role of the line is to ensure that dollars are spent in a most effective way to provide for high productivity and high performance. The staff's function is to meet the organization's goals relative to the planning function; and the line's function is to meet organizational goals relative to individuals who are actually doing the work.

CTP: Given some of the motivation theories that we sometimes read about—people needing to self-actualize or Herzberg's two-factor theory— do you think pay really motivates people?

Crandall: External reinforcers such as compensation can have an effect only to the extent that people understand them and that they are cues that create meaningful behavioral responses. What I am trying to say is that pay can motivate individual performance to the extent that individuals find the reward contingencies related to pay meaningful.

CTP: What are your feelings about pay secrecy as opposed to open-pay plans?

Crandall: There are two ways of looking at open-pay plans. Perhaps the most liberal approach to an open-pay plan is one in which each individual's rate of pay is open for all people. In public organizations where it is a matter of public record, that's generally the norm. However, in private organizations, an individual's pay has traditionally been considered to be his or her personal privilege of knowledge. On the other hand, a more realistic way of looking at open-pay programs is publication of the salary structure. That is a very useful tool in motivating people and providing for retention in your organization, in that individuals become aware of what their opportunities are for increased pay. To the extent that increased pay is motivating or the opportunity for increased pay increases retention, it's a very useful tool. However, if the story is not a very appealing one, an organization probably will not want to open up its pay policy and pay program. If it is paying poorly relative to the community, it perhaps doesn't want to announce that. Many organizations, on the other hand, feel that their pay strategy is proprietary and would prefer and, as a matter fo fact, require that it be secret in order to be effective relative to is competition in the labor market. All these things need to be considered by the employer in determining whether or not it wishes to publish its pay program. From a strictly behavioral science sense, to the extent that pay is motivating and increased pay is more motivating, it makes all the sense in the world to open up pay progressions so people understand them. Alternatively, if it is bad news, the organization probably doesn't want to open that up, because it is probably demotivating.

CTP: What do you think about pay as an organizational development tool, as a change agent?

Crandall: I think that, without question, an organization that undergoes a change in its pay program is undergoing a dramatic organization change. The major issue the organization faces is how it wants to handle that change. If it wishes to use the pay program as a leading edge for making changes in the social structure of an organization, it is a very effective tool because it gets people's attention.

CTP: Let's talk a minute about wage surveys. What's the survey worth to you? What are those data worth? When do you decide it costs too much to get it?

Crandall: An organization that has a mature compensation program develops a source of salary information and wage information over a period of time through trial and error. The sources are both organized survey sources and contacts in the community, usually on an informal basis. The cost of survey data is generally low relative to the total budget for administering compensation. That is to say, survey data are generally not expensive after you develop your initial contacts. That is a very broad statement, but it generally would be true. So the key issue is not the cost of any single survey in the given year, it's the relative cost, the cost of that survey over a stream of years relative to the reliability of information.

CTP: A related question: Survey data are generally static data. How do you track the market to know what it's doing on a monthly or semi-annual basis? What do you advise companies?

Crandall: Published survey data, whether you make or buy your survey data, generally come out once a year. There are a few data-based services that are beginning to provide what are called rolling surveys. That is, a commercially available survey, for example, will provide one-twelfth of its survey analysis each month and continue a rolling data base so that it is continually updating. In some industries, where compensation changes take place on a relatively routine basis throughout the year, that makes a lot of sense. Other industries and other labor markets go through changes at a particular time in the year. For example, in many industries, end-of-the-year increases come either in the latter two months of the year or in the first three months of the year. All of the survey work has to be done in the fall. In other industries, it is the summertime when compensation structures are changing.

CTP: What should compensation administators do to get their share of organizational resources? How should compensation people build a power base?

Crandall: The best way for compensation administrators to build credibility and strength of their function is to put themselves in the position of the chief executive officer of the organization, who is on the line for profit or loss in the decisions that they make, and to reflect on the conduct of the activities of the department in terms of a profit center rather than in terms of an expense center. Compensation people are responsible for spending an awful lot of money. The question is, how to do that effectively by having the biggest effect on the bottom line, instead of spending.

CTP: Should a typical organization have one pay system or several pay systems?

Crandall: That is an issue that has been debated for a number of years, and there is no simple answer to that question. For example, should there be one system for paying all individuals in the organization when we go beyond the issue of salary? Let's take a look at all forms of payment. Does it make sense, for example, to offer stock options to hourly employees? The answer to that question is probably no, to the extent that hourly employees don't have a direct effect on the long-term growth of the organization's performance in the stock market or in equity markets. Does it make sense to pay executives by the hour? Probably not, because the work results of the executive cannot be measured on an hourly basis.

CTP: What are the biggest problems your clients bring to you today?

Crandall: The biggest problems involve assisting an organization to define its philosophy and strategy for managing human performance. How does it go about creating effective rewards that will attract, motivate, and retain people? How does it go about doing this at the least cost? And how does it go about doing it while providing a quality of life for people that truly helps to raise the standard of living in our country?

CTP: What's the bottom line on compensation?

Crandall: There are two bottom lines on compensation. One is that the end of all compensation trials is a path lined with green. The other is that human beings' continual greed will always require effective compensation programs.

Notes

1. American Society for Personnel Administration, A. S. *Hansen Survey of Personnel and Industrial Relations Positions*, 1980.

2. American Compensation Association, P.O. Box 1176, Scottsdale, AZ 85252.

3. American Society for Personnel Administration, 30 Park Drive, Berea, Ohio.

4. ASPA and ACA, *Elements of Sound Base Pay Administration* (Berea, Ohio: American Society for Personnel Administration, 1981).

5. See Marc J. Wallace, Jr., N. Fredric Crandall, and Charles H. Fay, *Administering Human Resources* (New York: Random House, 1982), Chap. 15 for a discussion of information sources available to the compensation professional.

Glossary of Key Terms

across-the-board increase   A raise in base salary rate, expressed as either a percentage or a lump sum, given to all employees covered by a wage structure.

American Compensation Association (ACA)   The leading U.S. association of compensation professionals whose objective is to improve the design, implementation, and management of employee compensation and benefit programs. ACA also has a program allowing compensation professionals to become certified.

American Society for Personnel Administration (ASPA)   The major general professional organization for human resource managers. The ASPA Foundation sponsors research in personnel areas, including compensation, and offers certification programs.

area wage surveys   Wage surveys conducted by the Bureau of Labor Statistics in local labor markets. These are the basic surveys used by most compensation specialists.

Balkanized market   *See* segmented market

base wage   Wage earned by employee before such add-ons as shift differentials, performance bonuses, and overtime.

benchmark job   *See* key job

benefits   Compensation consisting of rewards to employees other than base salary. The three major benefit types are security and health benefits, pay for time not worked, and free or reduced cost services.

bonus   Any direct additional lump sum payment made on top of a base salary for either individual or group performance.

cafeteria bonus program   A program in which employees have a choice as to the benefits they receive, within a dollar limit. Usually a common core benefits package is offered (insurance, pension, profit sharing), plus a group of elective programs from which the employee may select a set dollar amount.

Certified Compensation Professional   A compensation or benefits professional who has successfully completed the certification program of the American Compensation Association.

classification method of job evaluation   A whole job, job-to-standard evaluation technique. Generalized classifications are defined in terms of several compensable factors, and a job is placed in whichever classification best describes it.

COLA   *See* cost-of-living adjustment

commission   A direct performance payment, usually for sales personnel, set as a percentage of gross or net sales. Group commissions for sales teams are allocated among team members on the basis of salary.

compa-ratio   The ratio of the actual average salary for a wage grade (numerator) to the mid point for the grade (denominator). The compa-ratio indicates the match between the distribution of actual salaries being paid in a class and the ideal. Generally a compa-ratio of about 1 is considered appropriate.

comparable worth   The idea that jobs have an inherent value, or worth, which can be compared across jobs of very different types (such as nursing versus parking meter maintenance). Jobs of greater inherent value should be paid more, according to adherents of the comparable worth doctrine.

compensable factor   Any factor used to provide a basis for judging job value in a job evaluation scheme. The most commonly employed compensable factors are responsibility, skill requirements, effort requirements, and working conditions.

compensation The provision of monetary and non-monetary rewards in return for employment.

compensation planning A forward oriented process that begins with the establishment of a mission for the compensation program. Compensation practices such as job evaluation, performance appraisal, job pricing, and merit formulae are considered on their merits as strategies to achieve the program's mission. Then policies are established and carried out in the service of these strategies. Finally, the entire process is audited for mission achievement.

competitive compa-ratio The ratio of the market mid-point rate (numerator) to a company's mid-point rate (denominator). The competitive compa-ratio helps the compensation specialist compare an organization's pay structure to the market.

cost-of-living adjustment (COLA) An adjustment in individual wages based on changes in the consumer price index. COLAs are no longer prevalent; they became popular due to union pressure and the misguided notion that organizations had an obligation to keep all wages and salaries growing faster than living costs. Salaries based solely on employee needs are unlikely to meet organizational needs.

cost reduction programs Performance bonus plans in which the emphasis is on increasing profits by reducing labor-related costs such as waste, scrap rates, and machine downtime due to human error.

The Davis-Bacon Act of 1931 A law requiring most federal contractors of construction or related contracts to pay wage rates and fringe benefits prevailing in the area.

Denver Nurses Case *Lemons* v. *Denver* is a major comparable worth case. Nurses employed by the city and county of Denver, Colorado, argued that even though parking meter repairers and other craft workers were paid more than nurses in external labor markets, it was still unfair for the city to pay nurses less than the crafts workers because the work performed by nurses was at least of comparable worth to the city as the work performed by the craft employees. The Court found against the nurses and upheld the criterion of the external market in setting wage rates.

derived demand A term refering to the fact that an employer's demand for labor is in part derived from the demand for the employer's product or service.

distributive justice An idea, attributed to George C. Homans, which provides the basis for equity theory. According to the principle of distributive justice, people in an exchange relationship are happiest when the ratios defining outcomes/inputs are equal for everyone in the exchange.

earnings   Total wages due an employee, including base pay, shift differentials, and bonuses.

employee benefits   *See* benefits

Employee Retirement Income Security Act of 1974   An act regulating employer pension programs.

employee stock ownership plan (ESOP)   An employee benefit in which the organization contributes its stock to an employee trust, usually as a form of profit sharing. Variants are the stock bonuses plan, a leveraged stock bonus plan (the trust can borrow money to buy more stock), and a TRASOP (in which employees match company contributions). ESOPs are useful as tax defferal devices for employees and as tax deductions for employers.

Equal Employment Opportunity Commission   A commission of the Federal government charged with enforcing the provisions of the Civil Rights Act of 1964. In addition, the commission is charged with enforcing the provisions of the Equal Pay Act of 1963 as it pertains to sex discrimination in pay.

Equal Pay Act of 1963   An amendment to the Fair Labor Standards Act prohibiting wage differentials based on sex between men and women employed in the same establishment when they have jobs which require equal skill, effort, and responsibility, and which are performed under similar working conditions.

equity   Anything of value earned through the provision or investment of something of value. In the case of compensation, an employee earns equity interest through the provision of labor on a job.

equity theory   A theory, most frequently associated with the ideas of J.S. Stacy Adams, proposing that in an exchange relationship (such as employment) the equality of outcome/input ratios between a person and a comparison other will determine fairness or equity. If the ratios diverge from each other, the person will experience reactions of unfairness and inequity (*see* distributive justice).

ESOP   *See* Employee Stock Ownership Plan

EVALUCOMP   The American Management Associations' job evaluation plan for office personnel, technicians, professional and scientific personnel, and management.

exchange rate Economically defined as the intersect of the labor demand and the labor supply functions in an external market. It constitutes the wage rate both employers are willing to pay and labor is willing to accept. From an economic viewpoint, the exchange clears the market. From a compensation viewpoint, the exchange rate defines the criterion of external equity.

exempt job A job not subject to the provisions of the Fair Labor Standards Act with respect to minimum wage and overtime. Exempt employees include most professionals, administrators, and executives.

external equity A fairness criterion that directs an employer to pay a wage that corresponds to rates prevailing in external markets for the employee's occupation.

external wage structure The distributions of wage rates across external labor markets. The external wage rate defines the variety of different wage rates an employer faces across different occupations and different labor markets.

ERISA *See* Employee Retirement Income Security Act of 1974

factor comparison method of job evaluation A specific factors (as opposed to whole-job) job-to-job comparison method of job evaluation. It is a complex system and not much used now.

The Fair Labor Standards Act of 1938 A federal law governing minimum wage, overtime pay, equal pay for men and women in the same type of job, child labor, and recordkeeping requirements.

Federal Insurance Contributions Act (FICA) The source of social security contributions withholding requirements, known commonly as FICA deduction. The current (1982) FICA tax is 6.70% on the first $32,400 earned. This rate is paid by both employee and employer.

felt fair pay Rate of pay that is fair for a job, determined by shared group norms on the basis of time span of discretion associated with the job.

FICA *See* Federal Insurance Contributions Act

flexible benefits program *See* cafeteria bonus program

fringe benefits *See* benefits

garnishment A court order requiring the employer of a debtor to deduct a portion of the debtor's pay and to deliver it to the creditor.

general training In human capital theory, any training that contributes marginal revenue product in all employment settings, thereby increasing the value of the trainee to all employers. Learning to weld is an example of general training.

green-circle   When a job is re-evaluated and an incumbent is making less than the bottom of the wage range assigned to that job, his salary is green-circled to assure that a speeded-up adjustment is made to bring him up to range.

Gunther v. County of Washington   A landmark case in pay discrimination based on sex. The U.S. Supreme Court ruled that plaintiffs are not prohibited from bringing pay discrimination suits under Title VII of the Civil Rights Act of 1964 by the Equal Pay Act of 1963. It is felt by many that this ruling opens up the courts to increased comparable worth litigation.

Harvard Business Review Syndrome   The adoption of management ideas read about in the prestigious journal with little or no thought to their applicability in a specific or current setting.

Hay System   A point factor job evaluation system which evaluates jobs with respect to "know-how," "problem-solving," and "accountability." It is probably the most widely used proprietary job evaluation system.

holidays   Specific days when employees do not work but are paid as if they did. Most companies in the U.S. give about 10 paid holidays per year.

human capital theory   A branch of labor economic thought proposing that the investment one is willing to make to enter an occupation is related to the returns one will earn over time in the form of compensation. We have used the theory in this book as one way of looking at the value a person brings to the job.

individual equity   A fairness criterion that directs employers to set wage rates for individual employees (workers on the same job, in the simplest case) accoring to individual variation in merit.

industry wage surveys   Wage surveys conducted by the Bureau of Labor Statistics in some 70 industries.

internal equity   A fairness criterion that directs an employer to set wage rates that correspond to the relative value of each job to the organization.

I.U.E. v. Westinghouse   A pay discrimination suit in which Westinghouse was found guilty of sex discrimination in pay. Westinghouse was found to have segregated women's jobs from men's jobs and established different pay rates for these groups, thereby discriminating against women.

job analysis A systematic study of the tasks making up a job, employee skills required to do the job, time factors, situation-specific factors such as technology used, physical aspects, information flows, interpersonal and group interactions, and historical traditions associated with the job. Job analysis provides the information needed to do job evaluations.

job evaluation A formal process by which management assigns wage rates or wage grades to jobs according to some preestablished method for judging internal job value to the organization.

job family A series of jobs clustered for job evaluation and wage and salary administration on the basis of common skills, occupational qualifications, technology, licensing, working conditions, union jurisdictions, work place, career paths, and organizational tradition.

just price doctrine A medieval theory of job value which posited a "just," or equitable wage for any occupation based on that occupation's place or station in the larger social hierarchy.

Kaiser Plan A cost reduction program in which specific cost savings due to employee effort are shared with employees.

key jobs Samples of jobs used in wage surveys and job evaluation. Key jobs should vary in terms of job requirements, should exist in many organizations, should represent all salary levels in the organization, and should be technologically stable. Also known as benchmark jobs.

labor demand The highest wage an employer or employers are willing to pay for a given level of employment or number of employees. Economists most often consider labor demand to be a function or line of points defining this wage for a series of employment levels.

labor market In labor economic theory, a place where labor is exchanged for wages. In practice, labor markets are identified and defined by some complex combination of the following factors: (1) geography, (2) education and/or technical background required, (3) experience required by the job, (4) licensing or certification requirements, and (5) occupational membership.

labor supply The minimum wage necessary to attract a given number of employees or level of employment. Economists most often consider labor supply as a function or line of points defining this wage for a series of employment levels.

lead or lag policy In annually adjusting wage structures to meet the market, the organization must decide when it will match (or follow or exceed) the market. If it chooses to match the market at the start of the year, it has adopted a lag policy; that is, it will lag behind the market the rest of the year as the market increases. If it chooses to project the market to the end of the year and match that, it has adopted a lead policy; that is, its wages will exceed the market rates during the year.

Lemons v. Denver   *See* Denver Nurses Case

leveraged ESOP   *See* employee stock ownership plan

The McNamara-O'Hara Service Contract Act of 1965   A law that requires certain federal contractors providing services to the federal government to pay area prevailing wage rates.

marginal revenue product (MRP)   Technically defined as the product of additional physical product (marginal physical product) generated by the addition of another unit of labor and the price at which the employer can sell the additional physical product. According to economists the marginal revenue product of labor defines the maximum wage an employer would be willing to pay for additional labor and is used to define an employer's demand for labor.

maturity curve   Survey data reporting wage or income trends for professionals (for example, engineers, accountants) as a function of time in the profession. Some organizations use maturity curves for pricing jobs rather than relying on job evaluation techniques.

merit increase   An adjustment to individual salary based on seniority, performance, or some other individual equity basis.

minimum wage   A minimum wage level for the majority of Americans, set by Congress under the Fair Labor Standards Act. Currently (1982) the minimum wage is $3.35.

monopsony   An economic condition in which one large purchaser dominates a market characterized by many small sellers. Monopsinists often find that because of their size relative to the sellers, they must pay increasingly higher prices to attract additional supply. This idea is used to explain why huge employers who dominate a single labor market often face upward sloping supply functions.

Multiemployer Pension Plan Amendments Act of 1980   Some unionized employers participate in pension programs with other employers. The program is usually administered by the union. The MPPAA requires an employee, once in such a plan, to assume liabilities for the fund, even on withdrawal from the plan.

National Position Evaluation Plan   A point factor job evaluation system which can be used to evaluate all jobs in an organization. It was developed from the old NEMA system.

NEMA   *See* National Position Evaluation Plan

non-exempt job   A job subject to the minimum wage and over-time provisions of the Fair Labor Standrds Act (*see* exempt job).

Old Age, Survivors, Disability, and Health Insurance Program (OASDHI)   An omnibus federal social bill including retirement, survivors and disability insurance (Social Security), hospital and medical insurance for the aged and disabled (Medicare/Medicaid), black lung benefits for miners, supplemental security income, unemployment insurance, and public assistance and welfare services.

open pay system   A compensation system in which information about wage ranges—at the extreme, even individual wage levels—is made public.

organizational development (OD)   Refers to attempts at improving organizational and individual behavior and performance through training and development efforts. Specific techniques may include group exercises, management by objectives (MBO), sensitivity training, and group discussion. Recently, proponents of organizational development have rediscovered an early principle of scientific management—that pay can be used as a powerful incentive for employees and groups to change their behavior.

overtime   Under the Fair Labor Standards Act non-exempt employees must be paid one and one-half times their normal wage rate for all hours worked in excess of 40 in any work week.

PAQ   *See* Position Analysis Questionnaire

pay compression   A wage distribution problem that exists when a number of individuals receive about the same pay even though there are a number of individual and organizational differences that the organization purports to recognize by wage differentials. The worst pay compression problem exists when subordinates make about the same as their boss.

Pension Benefit Guarantee Corporaton (PBGC)   A federal corporation set up in the Labor Department, similar to the Federal Deposit Insurance Corporation (FDIC) which guarantees vested pension rights. Insurance premiums are paid by employers with covered pension programs.

performance appraisal   Any system of determining how well an individual employee has worked during a period of time, frequently as a basis of a merit increase.

perquisite   A benefit tied to a specific job, (e.g., a company car for personal use, free meals for kitchen workers). Most perks are reserved for executives: country club memberships, first class travel rather than coach, and expense account entertainment.

piece rate   Direct performance payment based on production by a worker who receives a set amount for each piece produced.

point factor comparison method of job evaluation   The most prevalent form of job evaluation, the point factor method is a specific factors (as opposed to whole job), job-to-standards method.

Position Analysis Questionnaire   A job analysis technique which has been adapted to job evaluation by regressing PAQ results against wage survey data to get values of various job attributes.

prevailing wage   The wage in an area for a job said to be standard by the Department of Labor. This is usually the union rate.

profit sharing   A program in which some portion of profits is given to employees as a reward for performance.

Project 777   A market-based job evaluation system.

range   *See* wage range

range overlap   The degree to which two adjacent pay ranges coincide, important because overlap allows a job evaluated as higher than another (on internal equity grounds) to be paid less (on individual equity grounds).

ranking method of job evaluation   The simplest form of job evaluation, a whole job, job-to-job comparison.

red-circle   When a job is reevaluated and an incumbent is making more than the top of the wage range assigned to that job, the incumbent's salary is not lowered, but frozen, or red-circled, until adjustments to the structure bring that salary in line with the structure.

Rucker Share of Production Plan   A cost reduction program in which specific cost savings due to employee effort are shared with employees.

Scanlon Plan   A cost reduction program in which specific cost savings due to employee effort are shared with employees. The Scanlon Plan involves much employee participation, predating quality circles with most of the same techniques but without the hype. Mr. Scanlon was an

American union official. Scanlon plans appear to work best in medium size organizations.

segmented market A phrase referring to the fact that external labor markets are discontinuous. The market for physicians is different from the market for engineers, and movement from one to the other is restricted. Of most significance in the concept is the fact that labor demand and supply conditions vary across markets and explain much of the external wage variation observed across occupations. Segmented markets are sometimes called balkanized markets.

seniority Length of time an employee has worked in a specific position. Many organizations provide differentials for seniority, rewarding organizational loyalty.

shift differentials Extra wages given to employees who work during periods other than Monday through Friday from nine to five.

sick leave Paid time for not working due to illness or injury.

Social Security A federal insurance program designed to provide a base income to the retired and disabled. It was not designed as a complete retirement pension: its creators were successful beyond their expectations in achieving this.

specific training In Human Capital Theory, any training that contributes marginal revenue product only to the employer providing the training and not to other employers. Specific training adds nothing to the marketability of the trainee. Learning to fire a howitzer in the Army is (hopefully) an example of specific training.

stock bonus plan *See* employee stock ownership plan

take home pay Earnings less taxes, social security, and other deductions both voluntary and involuntary; the bottom line on the paycheck.

time span of discretion The maximum period of time during which the use of discretion is authorized and expected without review of that discretion by a superior. Time span of discretion has been used as a noneconomic definition of job value by Elliott Jacques.

TRASOP *See* employee stock ownership plan

unemployment insurance A state-administered, federally authorized, employer supported program designed to provide partial income replacement for a limited period when a worker loses his job through no fault of his own.

union shop agreement   A union security agreement whereby management agrees to require employees to join a union representing its employees as a condition of employment. Usually the provision calls for a new employee to join the union within some period of time (for example one month) after initial employment.

vacation pay   Extended period of time not worked but for which pay is received.

vesting   The ownership of accrued pension rights. Vesting is required for ERISA qualified pension programs. Basically, after 10 years of service, an employee "owns" all contributions made by the employer to the employee's pension plan. Vesting rules also apply to ERISA qualified ESOPs and TRASOPs.

wage and price controls   A federal program in which wages and prices are occasionally stabilized by government fiat. Most observers note that historically wages are easier to control than prices.

wage contour   A way of considering an external wage structure, developed by labor economist John Dunlop. He defines a wage contour as a stable group of wage determining units (bargaining units, plants, or firms) which are so linked together by (a) similarity of product markets, (b) resort to similar sources for labor, or (c) common market organization (custom) that they have common wage making characteristics. As a practical matter, compensation planners must be accurate in correctly defining the contours in which they are hiring and competing.

wage curve   A graph showing interconnected mid points of wage rates. Dollars are shown on the vertical axis, wage ranges are shown on the horizontal axis.

wage differential   Any difference in the wage two individuals get. Wage differentials may be due to occupation, industry, geography, company, performance, seniority, sex, race, age, or luck.

wage preference path   A concept employed to explain a union's effect on the supply of labor faced by an employer. Indifference analysis is used to derive a union leadership's preferences for various combinations of wage levels and employment levels. The line connecting these preferences for various levels of labor demand is called the wage preference path and defines the wage level the union will seek in bargaining for various levels of employment.

wage range   One segment of a wage structure. The range consists of a minimum wage level, a mid point, and a maximum. Jobs are assigned to wage ranges through the job evaluation process.

wage structure   The wage program of an organization composed of several pay grades and classifications. The organization must decide range width, overlap, and mid point differences.

The Walsh-Healy Public Contracts Act of 1936   A federal law requiring certain employers holding federal contracts for the manufacture or provision of materials, supplies, and equipment to pay industry-prevailing wage rates.

Workers' Compensation   State insurance programs designed to provide immediate money for medical care and support to workers who are injured on the job, and to provide support to dependents if the worker is killed. Employers support these programs through specially assessed taxes.

U.S. National War Labor Board (NWLB)   A government agency active in World War II. The Board had as its goals the settlement of disputes between management and labor unions. The NWLB was the first Federal agency to address wage discrimination between the sexes. It enforced the wage controls that gave the original impetus to the growth of benefits.

Name Index

Subject Index